# गोपथ-ब्राह्मणं।

# THE GOPATHA BRAHMANA OF THE ATHARVA VEDA

BIBLIOTHECA INDICA
A
COLLECTION OF ORIENTAL WORKS
PUBLISHED BY THE
ASIATIC SOCIETY OF BENGAL.

New Series, Nos. 215 AND 252.

# गोपथ-ब्राह्मणं।

# THE GOPATHA BRAHMANA OF THE ATHARVA VEDA.

IN THE ORIGINAL SANSKRIT.

EDITED BY

RAJENDRALALA MITRA
AND
HARACHANDRA VIDYABHUSHANA

GYAN

*Published by*

Gyan Publishing House
5, Ansari Road
Daryaganj, New Delhi-110002
Phone: 011-47034999, 9811692060
E-mail: books@gyanbooks.com

*Distribution Network*
gyanbooks.com
India, USA, Canada, UK, Australia, France



ISBN : 978-81-212-2592-2 (HB)
First Published, 1872

2nd Impression 2021

*Printed at:* Gyan Press, Delhi.



**गोपथ-ब्राह्मणं।**
**The Gopatha Brahmana**
**of the Atharva Veda**
Edited by: Rajendralala Mitra and Harachandra Vidyabhushana

# BIBLIOTHECA INDICA:

A

COLLECTION OF ORIENTAL WORKS

PUBLISHED BY THE

ASIATIC SOCIETY OF BENGAL.

New Series, Nos. 215 and 252.

# गोपथ-ब्राह्मणं।

# THE GOPATHA BRA'HMANA

OF THE ATHARVA VEDA.

IN THE ORIGINAL SANSKRIT.

EDITED BY

RA'JENDRALA'LA MITRA

AND

HARACHANDRA VIDYA'BHUSHANA.

CALCUTTA.

# LIST OF PROPER NAMES

*N. B.*—No references have been attached to such names as Indra &c. which occur very frequently.

## CHAPTER. III.

## CHAPTER. VI.

# CONTENTS

OF THE

# GOPATHA BRA'HMAṆA.

## FIRST BOOK.

### CHAPTER I.

## Chapter II.

---

## CHAPTER III.

## CHAPTER IV.

## Chapter V.

---

## SECOND BOOK.

### Chapter I.

---

## Chapter II.

# *ERRATA.*

| | | | | | |
|---|---|---|---|---|---|
| Page | 3 | line | 11 | *for* | constitute *read* constituted. |
| ,, | ,, | ,, | 33 | ,, | Upanisbad *read* Upanishad. |
| ,, | 7 | ,, | 10 | ,, | to; refers *read* to refers. |
| ,, | ,, | ,, | 12 | ,, | Professor *read* Professors. |
| ,, | 9 | ,, | 16 | ,, | Nárâyanna *read* Nárâyaṇa. |
| ,, | 10 | ,, | 24 | ,, | Isvarákrishṇa *read* I'ṣvarakrishṇa. |
| ,, | 11 | ,, | 11 | ,, | devinities *read* divinities. |
| ,, | 12 | ,, | 12 | ,, | Fragmentory *read* fragmentary. |
| ,, | 13 | ,, | 13 | ,, | devided *read* divided. |
| ,, | ,, | ,, | 28 | ,, | he *read* it. |
| ,, | ,, | ,, | 31 | ,, | pronoune *read* pronoun. |
| ,, | 15 | ,, | 29 | ,, | Añgarasa *read* añgarasáh. |
| ,, | 23 | ,, | 5 | ,, | austirity; by austirity *read* austerity; by austerity. |
| ,, | 28 | ,, | 5 | ,, | devided *read* divided. |
| ,, | 29 | ,, | 2 | ,, | fragementary *read* fragmentary. |
| ,, | 35 | ,, | 31 | ,, | Egyptins *read* Egyptians. |
| ,, | 37 | ,, | 4 | ,, | dicussion *read* discussion. |
| ,, | ,, | ,, | 29 | ,, | the *read* this. |

# INTRODUCTION.

Alike in interest and in extent, the Atharva is the least important of the four Vedas. It has none of the halo of that remote antiquity which recommends the Rig Veda to the earnest attention of the scholar, the historian, and the philosopher; and its subjects are of a character which cannot but place it in subordination to the other works of the class to which it belongs. The Rig deals in matters which are original, and stamped with the seal of the most primitive simplicity; the Atharva follows it almost as an expounder. In extent, the Sañhitás of the Rig, the Yajush, and the Sáma are considerably more elaborate, comprising, according to the Váyu Puráṇa, 8,600, 12,000, and 8,014 verses respectively; whereas that of the latter has only 5910 verses.* The *Charaṇavyúha* gives a greater number of richás (10,000) to the first; while the MSS. available make the last even smaller.

Again, the former have more than one Bráhmaṇa, some of considerable size, each, while the latter has an only Brámaṇa, and that of a limited extent. The number of Sákhás, Charaṇas and Pariśishṭas of the last are, likewise, limited, and of the few which are extant the authenticity is extremely doubtful.

Even the claim of the Atharva to be reckoned an integral part of the Hindu scriptures has been questioned, and more than one mediæval Indian writer has thought its necessary to discuss the subject at some length. The adverse opinion is

* Apud Wilson's Vishṇu Puráṇa p. 280. I have not been able to verify this in my MS. of the Váyu.

mainly, though not exclusively, founded on the repeated mention of the Vedas in ancient Sanskrit literature under the name of *Trayi-vidyá* or "the threefold knowledge," or simply *trayi'* "the three," (*iti vedáṣ strayas trayí.* Amarakosha.) including the Rig, the Sáma, and the Yajush, but omitting the Atharva. This, argue the impugners, is as plain an acknowledgement as could be, of the non-existence of the Atharva at an early period. and of its want of authority as a Veda; and, in support of this opinion, quote, among others, two passages from the Shaḍviñṣa Bráhmaṇa of the Sáma Veda, (1 p. v. kh.) in which it is said that "Prajápati created the (the first) three Vedas,*" and that "he produced the Rig Veda from the earth, the Yajur Veda from space, and the Sáma Veda from the heaven," (Lit. from this),† and also a ṣloka from Manu, which says, "Prajápati milked from the three gods Agni, Váyu, and Ravi, the three Vedas, Rig, Yajush, and Sáma for the accomplishment of sacrifices."‡

The defendants admit the premiss, but deny the conclusion. They assert that the term *Trayi'-vidyá*, is a common name for those parts of the Vedic literature which refer only to sacrifices, and as the hymns of the Atharva are not used in such sacrifices, they are very properly excluded, without in any way impugning their authenticity or authority as scriptures. There was, they add, only one Veda at first, and when the hymns comprised in it were classified, those which did not refer to sacrifices were put together, and these constitute a seperate class. Thus, "the Veda," says Madhusúdana Sarasvatí, "is divided into Rich, Yajush, and Sáma for the purpose of carrying out the sacrifice under its three different forms. The duties of the Hotri priests are performed with the Rig-

---

* प्रजापतिर्वा इमांस्त्रीन् वेदानसृजत ।

† ऋग्वेदः पृथिव्या यजुर्वेदोऽन्तरिक्षात्सामवेदोऽमुष्मात् ।

‡ अग्निवायुरविभ्यस्तु त्रयं ब्रह्म सनातनं । दुदोह यज्ञसिद्ध्यर्थमृग्यजुःसामलक्षणं

veda, those of the Adhvaryu priests with the Yajur-veda, those of the Udgátri priests with the Sáma-veda. The duties of the Bráhmaṇ and the sacrificer are contained in all the three. The Atharva Veda, on the contrary, is totally different. It is not used for the sacrifice, but only teaches how to appease, to bless, to curse" &c.,* This argument may, at first sight, appear more ingenious than convincing,; but, notwithstanding the broad and remarkable facts that the Hindus themselves have raised doubts regarding the authenticity of the Atharva, and that it did not contribute to those ceremonies and sacrifices which constitute the essence of Vedic Hinduism, the circumstances of its embracing a great number of hymns which occur likewise in the Rik Sañhitá, and of its being frequently named in the Bráhmaṇas of the other Vedas, leave little room for doubt that it was compiled, or put together, at about the same age when the other collections were completed. It is of course of a comparatively later date than the Rig Sañhitá, for it includes a portion of that Veda, and its position is doubless lower;† but that it belongs to the same age which resulted in the compilation of the Yajush and the Sáma, is what will scarcely be questioned. Dr. Max Muller, after a careful consideration of the whole question has come to this conclusion. He says, "Trayi vidyá" the threefold knowledge, is constantly used in the Bráhmaṇas with reference to their sacred literature. This however, proves by no means that at the time when the Bráhmaṇas were composed the songs of the Atharváñgírasa did not yet exist. It only shows that originally they formed no part of the sacred

* Apud Max Muller's Ancient Sanskrit Literature 445.

† "Its proper position, with reference to the other Vedas," says Professor Max Muller, "is well marked in a passage of the Taittiríya A'raṇyaka (V, 113) where the Yajush is called the head, the Rich the right side, the Sáman the other side, the Adeṣa (the Upanishad) the vital breath, and the Atharváñgiras' the tail." Ancient Sanskrit Literature, 447.

literature of the Bráhmaṇas. In some of the Brahmaṇas, the Artharváñgiras' are mentioned. The passage translated before shows that at the time when the S'atapatha Bráhmaṇa was composed the songs of the Atharváñgiras' were not only known, but had been collected, and had accually obtained the title of Veda. Their original title was the Atharváñgiras' or the Brigváñgiras, or the Atharvans; and these very titles show that songs which could be quoted in such a manner must have been of ancient date, and must have had a long life in the oral tradition of India."*

According to Puráṇic account the name of the Atharva Veda is due to a mythological personage, Atharvan, the eldest son of Brahmá, to whom, it is alleged, it was first imparted. From Atharvan it decended through a succession of pupils to Añgiras, from whose name the Veda is called A'ñgirasa, or Atharváñigirasa. It is, likewise sometimes, called Bhárgváñgirasa, and Brahma Vedá. The last name is accounted for on the assumption that it belongs to the Brahmá, or the chief priest, in the same way as the other three belong to the Hotá, the Adhvaryu, and the Udgátá. Inasmuch, however, as it contains nothing which a Brahmá can make use of at a sacrifice, the ascription is probably due to a desire to raise the Veda to a rank which it did not originally possess. The Gopatha Bráhmaṇa recognises all these several names, but the details it gives (as quoted below) are totally different from those of the Puráṇas.

Allegorically the Atharva is represented as a lean, blackman, sharp and irascible, amorous and fond of little things, possessing power to assume any shape it likes. It is describ-ed to belong to the family or clan (gotra) of Vaitána, and to have Indra for its special divinity, and the anustubh for its peculiar metre. Its upaveda or subsidiary branch is said to be the science of warfare, *s'astravidyá.*

* Ancient Sanskrit Literature, 446.

After its classification and arrangement by Vyása, according to the Vishṇu Purá a, "the illustrious Muṇi Sumantu taught this Veda to his pupil Kabandha, who made it twofold, and communicated the two portions to Devaderśa and to Pathya. The disciples of Devaderśa were Maudga, Brahmabali, Ṣaulkáyaní, and Pippaláda. Pathya had three pupils, Jájali, Kumudádi, and Ṣaunaka; and by all these were seperate branches instituted. Ṣaunaka, having divided his Sañhitá into two, gave one to Babhru, and the other to Saindhaváyana; and from them sprang two schools, the Saindhavas and Munjakeśas. The principal subjects of difference in the Sañhitás of the Atharva-Veda are the five kalpas or ceremonials: the Nakshatra Kalpa, or rules for worshiping the planets; the Vaitána Kalpa, rules for oblations, according to the Vedas generally; the Sañhitá Kalpa, or rules for sacrifices, according to different schools; the A'ñgirasa Kalpa, incantations and prayers for the destruction of foes and the like; and the Ṣánti Kalpa, or prayers for averting evil."*

The account given in the Bhágavata Puráṇa is similar to the above, but not without some peculiarities of its own. According to it, Vyása, after classifying the four Vedas, taught the Atharvan to Sumantu, "Sumantu, the learned in the Atharvan, imparted his Sañhitá to his pupil (whose name according to the commentator Ṣrídhara Ṣvámí was Kabandha). He (Kabandha) divided it in to two parts, and expounded them to Pathya and Vedadarśa. Ṣaulkàyani, Brahmavani, Modosha, and Pippaláyaní were the pupils of Vedadarśa (who learnt it from him). Now, Bráhmaṇ, hear of the pupils of Pathya. They were Kumuda, Ṣunaka, and Jájali, the knowers of the Atharva. The pupils of Vabhru were Añgiras (Sunaka) and Saindhaváyana, who learnt two Sañhitás, (from their tutor). Sávarṇa and others (pupils of Saindhaváyana) followed. The Nakshatra Kalpa, the Ṣánti Kalpa, Kasyapa, A'ñgirasa &c. (other parts of the

* Wilsons Vishṇu Puráṇa, p. 285.

Vedas, (whose teacher's name says the commentator, are not given). These are the teachers of the Atharvana."*

The *Charaṇavyúha*, which is believed by some to be an older and more reliable authority, does not, however, support these subdivisions. According to it, there were, originally, only nine different recensions of the hymns of the Atharvans. But neither the sákhás of the Váyu, nor those of the Charanavyúha, with one exception, are now available, and even of the nine schools of the latter the names are in many cases doubtful. According to Dr. Max Muller's conjectural emendations, the names are: 1. Paippaládas, 2. Ṣaunakas, 3. Dámodas, 4. Tottáyanas, 5. Jayálas, 6. Bráhmapaláśas, 7. Kaunakhins, 8. Devadarsanins, 9. Cháraṇavidyas.

These, however, are not all borne out by the six MSS. which I have consulted. They give—

| MS. with me. | MS. with a pundit. | No. 1477 Sanskrit College. | No. 1482 Do. | No. 1479 Text. Do. | No. 1479 Do. comment. |
|---|---|---|---|---|---|
| 1 Pippalás. | Staittas. | Pippalás. | Pippalás. | Pippalas. | Paippalás. |
| 2 Datás. | Damodas. | Dántás. | Dántás. | Damodas. | Dántás. |
| 3 Pradápalas. | Snátas. | Pradántas. | Pradantás. | Ttotas. | Pradantás. |
| 4 Taitá. | Autás. | Autas. | Taitas. | Kunattas. | Auptàs. |
| 5 Brahmadápalas. | Brahmapalas. | Brahmapalasás. | Brahmadápasa. | Brahmadápasa. | Brahmadás. |
| 6 Jábálás. | Jáyalàs. | Jábàlis. | Autás. | Jábálás. | Rásàs. |
| 7 Saunaki. | Sakunakhi.. | Saunakás. | Saunakás. | Saunakas. | Saunaki. |
| 8 Devadarsi. | Devadarsi. | Devadarsàs. | Vedarsi. | Devadarsi. | Vedadarsi. |
| 9 Cháranavidyás. | Charanavidyas. | Charanavidyás. | Charanavidyás. | Charanavidyás. | Charanavidyás. |

* अथर्ववित् सुमन्तुश्च शिष्यमध्यापयत् स्वकाम् ।
संहितां सोपि पथ्याय वेददर्शाय चोक्तवान् ॥ १ ॥
शौल्कायनिर्ब्रह्मबलिर्मोदोषः पिप्पलायनिः ।
वेददर्शस्य शिष्यास्ते पथ्यशिष्यानथो शृणु ॥ २ ॥
कुमुदः शुनको ब्रह्मन् जाजलिश्चाप्यथर्ववित् ।
बभ्रुः शिष्योथाङ्गिरसः सैन्धवायन एव च ॥ ३ ॥
अधीयेतां संहिते द्वे सावर्णाद्यास्तथापरे ।

Professor Max Muller puts all the names in the plural; but in my manuscripts some of the names are in the singular, and the Commentator observes that where the names are in the plural, there many original teachers are implied; where they are in the singular only one original teacher is understood: *yatra vahuvachanam tatra vahavah: yatraika vachanam so eka eva.* Looking to these discrepancies, it may be fairly concluded that the names had become already obsolete when the Charaṇavyúha was complied.

The exception above alluded to, refers to the text which is now current under the name of the Atharva Veda Sañhitá, of which an excellent edition has been published by Professor Roth and Whitney. To which of the nine recensions it belongs I know not. Some pandits take it to be the text of the Ṣaunakas, but on no reliable authority that I am aware of. It comprises twenty chapters (Káṇḍas) of which the last two are said to be supplementary. The following is Professor Whitney's summary of its nature and contents: " The Atharva is, like the Rik, a historical and not a liturgical collection. Its first eighteen books, of which alone it was originally composed, are arranged upon a like system throughout, the length of the hymns, and not either their subject or their alleged authorship, being the guiding principle; those of about the same number of verses are combined together into books, and the books made up of the shorter hymns, stand first in order. A sixth of the mass, however, is not metrical, but consists of longer or shorter prose pieces, nearly akin in point of language and style with passages of the Bráhmaṇas. Of the remainder, or metrical portion, about one sixth is also found among the hymns of the Rik, and mostly in the tenth book of the latter; the rest is peculiar to the Atharva. Respecting their authorship the tradi-

---

नक्षत्रकल्पः शान्तिश्च काश्यपाङ्गिरसादयः ॥ ४ ॥
एते चाथर्वणाचार्य्याः

tion has no information of value to give: they are with few exceptions attributed to mythical personages. The greater portion of them are plainly shown, both by their language and internal character, to be of much later date than the general contents of the other historic Veda, and even than its tenth book with which they yet stand nearly connected in import and in origin. The condition of the text also in those passages found likewise in the Rik, points as distinctly to a more recent period as that of the other collection. This, however, would not necessarily imply that the main body of the Atharva hymns, were not already in existence when the compilation of the Rik took place. Their character would be ground enough for their rejection and exclusion from the canon, until other and less scrupulous hands were found to undertake their seperate gathering into an independent collection. The nineteenth book is a kind of supplement to the preceding ones, and is made up of matter of a like nature which had either been left out when they were compiled, or had been since produced. The twentieth and last book is a liturgical selection of passages from the hymns of the Rik, and it is not easy to see how it should have become appended to the Atharva as a portion of its text."*

No record has any where been met with of the number of Bráhmaṇas which the Atharva Veda originally included. At present the Gopatha is the only one which is accessible.

If the Atharva is thus poor in its hymnological and liturgical portions, it is particularly rich in Upanishads. The Rig Veda is represented by only two Upanishads, the Aitareya and the Kauśitakí; the Sáma by two, the Chhándogya and the Talavakára; the White Yajush also by two, the Vrihadáraṇyaka and the Vájasaneyí; the Black Yajush, by four, the Taittiríya, the Maitráyaní, the Yájñika, and the Setáśvatara; whereas the Atharva has no less than fifty-two affiliat-

* Journal, American Oriental Society, IV, 256.

ed to it, besides a number of others of more or less doubtful authenticity. The three codices of the so-called A'tharvaṇa Upanishads which I have seen are all imperfect. Each of them has a seperate order of arrangement. One of them includes the Talavakára of the Sáma Veda; another the Taittiríya, of the Black Yajush; and the third, which is the most modern, the Gopála-tápaní, the Gopíchandana and other works which are excluded from the other two. The fifty two, besides, are made up by counting the different chapters of the Svetásvatara and other treatises as distinct works. After a careful comparison of the three I have compiled the following conjectural list; viz:

1. Garbha.
2. Prasna.
3. Brahma.
4. Kshurika.
5. Chulika.
6. A'ruṇeya.
7. Práṇágnihotra.
8. Muṇḍaka.
9. Máṇḍukya.
10. Vaitathya.
11. Alátaṣánti.
12. Nílarudra.
13. Nádavindu.
14. Brahmavindu.
15. Amritavindu,
16. Dhyánavindu.
17. Tejovindu.
18. Yogaṣikhá.
19. Yogatattva.
20. Sannyása.
21. Kaṇṭhaṣruti.
22. A'tman.
23 *to* 27. Mahá.
28 to 33. Kaṭhavallí.
34. Náráyanṇa.
35. Vrihannáráyaṇa(?)
36. Mahánáráyaṇa.
37. Sarva.
38. Hañsa.
39. Paramahañsa.
40. Kálágnirudra.
41-42. Ráma-tápaní.
43. Kaivalya.
44. Jábála.
45. A'ṣrama.
46. Piṇḍa.
47. Siras.
48. Ṣikhá.
49-50. Nrisiñha-tápaní.
51. *Svetáṣvatara.*
52. Garuḍa.

The commentary of Náráyaṇa omits Nos. 10, 11, 20, 28 to

33, 35, 36, 45, and 51, and supplies their places by Brahmavidyá, Sámányа, Shaṭchakra, Gopála-tápaní, Vásudeva, Gopichandana, A'tmabodha, Gaṇapati, Krishṇa, Atharvaveda, and a second Mahá, following in this respect the modern MS of the text.

It should be noticed, however, that, strictly speaking, the Upanishads cannot be called integral parts of the Vedas, for they have generally been placed in opposition to those works. Thus Jaimini, in the Púrva Mimáñsá, defines the Vedas to be "works intended to promote ceremonial observances; those which do not promote them are not Vedas."* Prabhákara, in the same way, says, "there is no part of the Vedas which is purely descriptive, and which does not induce, restrain, enjoin, or prohibit actions."† In the Muṇḍaka Upanishad the Vedas are condemned as teaching "secondary knowledge" (Apará vidyá), which is to be rejected in favor of the teaching of the Upanishads."‡ Nárada, in the Chhándogya Upanibsad, appears before Sanatkumára, and says that he has studied the Rig, the Yajush, the Sáma and the Atharva Vedas, and other subjects, but that they have not sufficed to give him true knowledge, and he accordingly seeks instruction in the Upanishads.‖ Kapila holds the Vedic or revealed means of attaining salvation to be as ineffectual as the temporal one ; and Iṣvarákrishṇa, working in this light, condemns the Vedas as worthless, because the rewards attainable by them are transient.§ The Gopatha Bráhamaṇa, likewise, makes the Upanishads stand apart from the Vedas (I,21). Seeing, further, that the so-called A'tharva-

* आम्नायस्य क्रियार्थत्वादानर्थक्यमतदर्थानाम् १।२।१।

† प्रवृत्तिनिवृत्तिविधितच्छेषव्यतिरेकेण केवलवस्तुवादी वेदभागो नास्ति।

‡ अपरा ऋग्वेदो यजुर्वेदः सामवेदः अथर्ववेदः इत्यादि।

‖ Chhándogya U. p. 116.

¶ अविशेषश्चोभयोः।

§ दृष्टवदानुश्रविकः सह्यविशुद्धिक्षयातिशययुक्तः।

ṇa Upanishads do not occur as parts of any extant Bráhmaṇa or A'raṇyaka of the Atharva-veda, they may very reasonably be taken to be altogether independant of that Veda. It should, nevertheless, be borne in mind that some of the works of this class have existed from a very early period, and Manu, Vyása and other high authorities have recognised their right to be thought as parts of the Ṣruti, and the whole of the Vedánta depends for its authority on their authenticity as scriptures. Most of these tracts are theological in their character, with a special leaning, in some cases, to particular devinities of the Hindu pantheon. But altogether they are of so miscellaneous a character,—so inconsistent with each other,—so dissimilar in language, style, and subject, that they cannot be taken to be the productions of one age, much less of one author. For brief accounts of the contents of these, I must refer the reader to my "Notices of Sanskrit MSS." Vol. I, and to the learned dissertation of Professor Weber in the first two volumes of the *Indische studien.* Unreliable translations of these are to be met with in Duperron's *Oupanikhat.*

The Gopatha Bráhmaṇa is divided into two parts; the first (*Purvárdha*) comprising five chapters; and the second (*Uttarárddha*) six chapters. The chapters are of unequal length, and comprise from 39 to 15 paragraphs or Kaṇḍikás each, the longest being the first two (39 and 34); and the shortest the last two (15 and 16); the others ranging from 19 to 26 Kaṇḍikás.

The language of the Gopatha is similar to that of the other Brahmáṇas, having all their archaisms, grammatical irregularities, and elliptical and involved style; but it is at the same time somewhat simpler. It has no pretension to rhetorical ornament, and rarely rises to any thing like elegance of diction. Metaphors and allegories occur in the work frequently, but they constitute its subject, and not the ornament of its language. With the exception of a few quotations from the hymns of the Rig Veda, and several anustubh ṣlokas, the work is throughout in prose, resembling in this respect the Aitareya more closely than the Bráhmaṇas of the Yajush and the Sáma. This resemblance is also observable in its subject. Nothing is treated of in it in full or in all its detail. The reader is presumed to be familiar with the rituals of the Vedas, and has only particular topics brought to his notice which serve to ellucidate some obscure point, or is worthy of being known as important; and even these are discussed in such a disjointed, fragmentory, abrupt way, that they entirely fail to be, to us at least, in any way interesting. Myths, legends and parables constitute the staple of the work; but they are short, inconsequential and pointless. They are intended to explain the origin, nature and fruits of particular ceremonies; but, being most inartistically set forth, fail to attract attention. The case may have been different before, but certain it is that they have ceased to interest the people of this country since the last two thousand years.

The work opens with the creation of the world, to which the bulk of the first chapter is devoted. As the subject has been treated in it with greater detail than in any other Veda, and is of some interest, I shall attempt to give a paraphrase of it here with the omission only of such eulogistic and explanatory passages as break the thread of the narrative.

"Om! Verily, Brahma alone by itself only existed at first. It willed. 'I alone exist as the highly adorable.* Ho! I must create from myself a second Deva like unto me.' It worked, upon, it well warmed, it fully heated its self. On the forehead of this working, well-warmed and fully heated (being) perspiration broke forth. 'Well pleased thereby, it said, " I, the highly adorable, know well all that should be known."

* महद्वै यक्षं The rendering above given is doubtful.

"He* worked again, he warmed himself well again, he fully heated his self; thereupon seperate streams of perspiration flowed from all the pores of the body of that working, well-warmed and fully heated being. They pleased him. He said, 'by these I shall support all and every thing whatever; by these I shall create all and every thing whatever; by these I shall attain all and every thing whatever.'

"Having thus created water † he looked down, and in the water beheld his own shadow. The seed of the beholder, of its own accord, oozed out, and dropped into the water. He thereupon worked and well warmed and fully heated the water. The belaboured well-warmed and fully heated water, along with the seed, devided into two. Thereof that which was gross, common, very saline, unpotable, unpalatable, and unsteady, along with the seed in it, became the ocean; the other which was potable, palatable and quiet, was worked upon and well warmed and fully heated, and thereby whatever seed was in it dried up, and because it dried up (*abhrijyata*), therefore it became Bhrigu.

"Having created Bhrigu he disappeared. Bhrigu, having thus been created, looked towards the east. Speech resounded, "Váyu, Váyu" (wind). He turned; he looked towards the south. Speech resounded, "Mátariṣvan, Mátariṣvan," (wind). He turned; he looked towards the west. Speech resounded, "Pavamána, Pavamána," (wind). He turned; he looked towards the north. Speech resounded, "Váta, Váta," (wind). He replied: "I know it not." "No," (said the other) "Look below into the water;" and because he said "look below into the water" (*Atharván*) therefore Atharvaṇ proceeded from it; and hence

---

* In the first para. Brahma (neuter) is 'followed by the neuter pronoune *tad* (it,) but in the second the masculine *sa* (he) is substitued without any change in the antecedent.

† The word is in the plural number in the text.

Atharvaṇ is called by that name. Verily, of that venerable sage (rishi) Atharvaṇ, the whole body with its members down to the smallest hair and the vital airs, was like that of Brahma. To him, Atharvaṇ, said Brahma; "Having created the beings of Prajápati protect them." And because he said, *Prajápateh prajá srishṭvá pálayasva,* therefore Prajápati came into being, and became the lord of creation. Atharvaṇ verily is that Prajápati.

"He (Brahma) worked upon, and well warmed, and fully heated that sage Atharváṇ. Out of that wrought, well-warmed and fully heated Atharvaṇ he formed ten Atharvaṇa sages; one of one richá, one of two richás, one of three, one of four, one of five, one of six, one of seven, one of eight, one of nine, and one of ten richás. Those Atharvaṇa rishis, he worked upon, and well warmed and fully heated, and therefrom ten A'tharvaṇa rishis proceeded, the eleventh, twelveth, thirteenth, fourteenth, fifteenth, sixteenth, seventeenth, eighteenth, nineteenth, and twentieth.

"He worked upon, well warmed, and fully heated those A'tharvaṇa as well as the Atharvaṇa rishis, and whatever *mantras* he beheld in those wrought, well-warmed and fully heated rishis, the same became the A'tharvaṇa Veda. He worked upon, and well warmed, and fully heated the A'tharvaṇa Veda, and from it issued forth the mind-like syllable Om.

"He again worked upon, well warmed and fully heated his self. From his self he created the three regions earth, ether and heaven. He verily produced the earth from his feet, the ether from his belly, and the heaven from his head. He worked upon, well warmed and fully heated the three regions, and therefrom created the three gods Agni, (fire,) Váyu, (air,) and A'ditya (sun). He verily made Agni out of the earth, Váyu out of the ether, and A'ditya out of heaven. He worked upon, well warmed and fully heated the three gods, and therefrom produced the three Vedas, Rig, Yajush and Sáma; the

Rig Veda from Agni, the Yajur Veda from Váyu, and the Sama Veda from A'ditya. He worked upon, and well warmed and fully heated the three Vedas, and therefrom produced the three great Vyáhritis *bhuh*, *bhuvah* and *svah*; the first from the Rig Veda, the second from the Yajur Veda, and the third from the Sáma Veda.

"The water which encircling the seed (formed) the ocean, flowed towards the east and the south, the west and the north, and because it flowed (*samavadravanta*,) therefore is it called *samudra*, ocean. It was frightened, and said, "Lord, we install thee as our king." And because encircling (*vritvá*) it remained, therefore was Varaṇa produced from it, and since Varaṇa was formed of it, therefore is it indirectly called Varuṇa, for verily the gods are fond of indirect, and inimical to direct, allusions.

He, Varuṇa, seperated (*amuchyata*) from the ocean; he became Muchya, and because Muchya was born of him therefore is he called indirectly Mrityu, for verily the gods are fond of indirect, and inimical to direct, allusions. He (Brahma) worked upon, well warmed and fully heated that Varuṇa alias Mrityu, and from all the members of the body of that wrought, well-warmed and fully heated Mrityu fluids (rasa) exuded; these formed the fluids of his body (aṅgarasa), and those fluids of his body are indirectly called Aṅgiras, for verily the gods are fond of indirect, and averse to direct, allusions.

"He (Brahma) worked upon, well warmed and fully heated that Aṅgiras, the sage, and therefrom proceeded the Viṅṣina Aṅgirasa rishis. He worked upon well warmed and fully heated the Viṅṣina Aṅgirasa sages, and therewith formed the ten A'ṅgirasa A'rsheyas (sons of sages) having sixteen, eighteen, twelve, one, three, four, five, six, two, and seven richás. He worked upon, well warmed and fully heated the Aṅgirasa sages and the A'ṅgirasa A'rsheyas, and whatever mantras he perceived in them therewith he formed the A'ṅgirasa Veda. He worked upon and well warmed and fully heated that A'ṅgirasa Veda, and therefrom proceeded the two syllables *Janat*.

"It, the A'ñgirasaVeda, remained above, leaving these regions, therefore the reader of the A'ñgirasa remains above.

"He (Brahma), looked towards the sides, the east, the south, the west, the north, above and below, and worked upon and well warmed and fully heated them; and therefrom prepared the five Vedas, Sarpa Veda, Piśácha Veda, Aśura Veda, Itihása Vedá, and Puráṇa Veda. From the east side he formed the Sarpa Veda, or the science of serpents; from the south the Piśácha Veda, on the science of hobgoblins; from the west the Aśura Veda, or the science of giants; from the north the Itihása Veda, or the science of history; and from above and below the Puráṇa Veda, or the science of ancient legends. He worked upon, and well warmed and fully heated the five Vedas, and therefrom formed the five great Vyáhritis, *Vridhat, Karat, Guhan, Mahat* and *Tat*; Vridhat from the Sarpa Veda, Karat from the Piśácha Veda, Guhan from the Aśura Veda, Mahat from the Itihása Veda, and Tat from the Purána Veda.

"He looked forwards and backwards, and worked upon and well warmed and fully heated them, and formed therefrom the preeminent syllable Sam.

"He again worked upon, and well warmed and fully heated himself, and from his mind produced the moon, from his nails the stars, from the hairs of his body herbs and trees, and from his minor vital airs the other numerous objects.*

"He again worked upon, and well warmed and fully heated himself; he beheld the threefold seven-stringed and twenty-one-membered sacrifice (Yajna). Thereof this Rig Veda verse may be quoted: "Agni formed the threefold and seven-stringed sa-

* The word used is "deván" gods, but seeing that in the Rig Veda even pestles and mortars and leather strainers are named devas, the word, it may be presumed, is here used in the sense merely of created objects, and not of devine beings especially. The use of the word *anyán* "others" as opposed to herbs and trees can suggest no other meaning.

crifice." On that subject this supplementary sloka may also be quoted: 'The seven sacrifices of cooked rice, are seven-stringed.'

"He collected it; he performed a sacrifice with it. In that sacrifice Agni officiated as Hotá, Váyu as Adhvaryu, Surya as Udgátá, Chandramas as Brahmá, Paryyaṇya as Sadasya, herbs and trees as oblation spoons; the Adhvaryu Viśvedevas as Hotrakas, and the Atharváṅgirasas as Goptáras.

"These learned officiating priests, having completed the sacrifice, thus addressed it, 'may this resulting oblatory butter make not the immortal creation heedless.' Verily these guardians are called the leaders of sacrifice *sadah-prasarpakán*. To these, says Prajápati, plentiful fees should be awarded; for inefficient priests who have not observed Brahmacharya and are wanting in earnestness, are verily enemies of the sacrifice; the enemies of the sacrifice injure the institutor thereof; the enemies of the institutor injure the Ritvijas; the enemies of the Ritvijas injure the fees; the enemies of fees injure the institutor with his children and cattle; the enemies of his children and cattle injure the institutor in this world and in heaven; the enemies of heaven and earth injure half the resources of the institutor's life: they only accomplish half a sacrifice."

Having thus described the origin of creation the work proceeds, after two short paragraphs on certain expiations for flaws in the performance of sacrifices, to describe the creation of the universe from the syllable Om. It says, "Brahma verily created Brahmá on a lotus leaf. Of a truth he Brahmá, thus created, was engaged in the reflection, 'by what single syllable can I perceive all desirable objects, all regions, all Devas, all Vedas, all sacrifices, all words, all fruition, all creation, whether fixed or moving.' He performed a Brahmacharya; he beheld the syllable Om, of two letters, four instants, all pervading, preeminent, unchangeable, the Brahma, the Bráhmí, the Vyáhriti, the godly Brahma. From it was produced all desirable objects, all regions, all Devas, all Vedas, all sacrifices, all words, all fruition, the whole creation fixed and moving.

"From its first letter was produced heaven; and from its second letter vigor and the luminaries.

"From its first vocalic instant were produced the earth, fire, herbs, trees, the Rig Veda, the mystic syllable (*Vyáhriti*) *bhu*, the Gáyatrí metre, the threefold stoma, the eastern side; the spring season, the instrument of speech—tongue, and the power of taste.

"From its second vocalic instant were produced ether, air, the Yajur Veda, the mystic syllable *bhuva*, the traistubha metre, the fifteen-fold stoma, the western side, the summer season, the organs of breath—the nostrils, and the power of smelling.

"From its third vocalic instant were produced the heaven, the sun, the Sáma Veda. the mystic syllable *svah*, the jagati metre, the seventeen-fold stoma, the northern side, the rainy season, the seats of light,—eyes, and the power of vision.

"From its consonantal instant b were produced the waters, the moon, the Atharva Veda, the stars, the circumflex Om its life, *janat*, the Añgirasas, the anustubh metre, the twenty-one-fold stoma, the southern side, the autumn season, the seat of knowledge—mind, and the power of knowing.

"From its consonantal instant m were produced the Itihása Purána, speech, metrical language, *nárasañsi*, the Upanishads, the commanding syllables *Vridhat, Karat, Guhan, Mahat, Tat*, and *Sam*, the great Vyáhriti Om, harmony of many corded instruments, voice, dancing, singing, music, the Chaitraratha Devas, lightning, light, the vrihatí metre, the thirty-three-fold stoma, the upper and lower sides, the cold and dewy seasons, the organs of hearing—ears, and the power of audition."*

*Though the syllable is said to comprehend four instants, yet three vocalic and two consonantal instants are here recounted; probably the last two are counted as one.

A legend now follows in which the Devas are said to have overcome the Asuras by starting to the attack led by Om, to which they promised every preeminence. The subsequent kaṇḍikás of the first chapter are devoted to the praise of Om, its origin, derivation and uses, its different positions in the different Vedas, and its place in the Gáyatrí, the meaning of which is explained at length.

The account given of the Gáyatrí is the fullest I have met with in the Vedas, and will perhaps be interesting to many as containing the oldest ideas of the Bráhmaṇas on the subject. The account is given in the form of a narrative, and is as follows :—

"Gláva of the race of Mitra (Maitreya) repaired to Maudgalya, who was well versed in the (science of) eleven syllables, and, seeing him engaged in the duties of Brahmacharya, said: 'How is this? Whatever exists in this Brahmacharya, and whatever Maudgalya is performing are all perishable.'

"A desciple of Maudgalya, hearing this, repaired to his tutor, and said, 'the man who has this day become our guest speaks ill of your learning.'

"'What does he know, fair youth?' enquired the teacher.

"'He reads the three Vedas, sir,' replied the pupil.

"'Invite near me, fair youth, the most forward pupil of the man who has come to question my learning.

"The pupil of Maudgalya called a pupil of Gláva, and said to his tutor, 'Here he is, sir."

"(Of him enquired Maudgalya) 'What, fair youth, does your tutor profess?.'

'He reads the three Vedas, sir', replied the youth.

"(Gláva said), 'How do you, fair youth, speak thus of your tutor to us who have got all the three Vedas in our mouth? How do good people so speak of good people? He does not wish to reply to the question I have asked him, nor does he know it.'

"Maudgalya, thereupon, said to his own pupil, 'Repair, fair

youth, to Gláva of the race of Mitra, and address him, saying, 'instruct me, sir, and explain to me the Sávitrí, (*i. e.* the Gáyatri,) of twenty-four syllables and twelve couples, of which Bhrigváñgirasas are the eyes, and in which all this creation subsists.' Should that Brahmachári tutor, fair youth, happen not to know it, and to ask a Bramachári pupil (like you) to explain the Sávitrí, to him, then tell him, 'as you said to Maudgalya, so are you ill-instructed, since questioned by me you have given no answer. You shall have to submit to privations for a year.'

"The pupil repaired to where the other (Gláva) was, and asked the question (which his tutor had suggested to him).

"He (Gláva) gave him no reply. Thereupon the pupil said, 'as you said to Maudgulya, so are you ill-instructed, since questioned by me you have given no answer. You shall have to submit to privations for a year.'

"He, Maitreya, to his own pupils, said; 'forsaking me, repair as you list, to your homes. I said of Maudgalya that he was ill-instructed, and yet have failed to answer the question put to me by him; I shall therefore go and pacify him.'

"On the fallowing morning Maitreya, taking a handful of sacrificial wood (in token of submission) went to Maudgalya and said, 'Sir, I am Maitreya.'

'Wherefore are you come?' (enquired Maudgalya.)

'I have (said Maitreya) called you ill-instructed, and yet have failed to answer the question put by you, I have therefore come to pacify you.'

"He (Maudgalya) said; 'it is said that you have committed every sin by coming here in a conveyance. I give you this auspicious car of mine (instruction); go away in it.'

"The other said, 'what you say is neither ungenerous nor unkind, and for it have I come to you.' Then approaching him (nearer) enquired, 'Sir, to whom do wise men allude by (the phrase) "the adorable glory of the god Savitá"? and advise me as to what they mean by *dhiya* (intellect); and, should you know it, tell me the courses through which the sun moves on (*pra-chodayát*)." *

"To him said the other thus; 'wise men say the Vedas and the chhandas (metres) are the preeminent parts (*vareṇya*) of the sun; and the glory (*bharga*) of that god is aliment, (*anna*). I tell you also that *dhiya* means duties, (*karmáṇi*) and the courses, those by which the sun moves on."

"Having understood this, Gláva requested him, saying, 'teach me, sir, who is Savitá (sun) and what is the Sávitri?'

"(Maudgalya replied)," the mind (*manas*) is the sun, Savitá, and speech the Sávitrí. Wherever there is mind, verily there also is speech, and wherever there is speech, there also is mind; thus there are two sources and one couple. The fire, Agni, is Savitá, and the earth, the Sávitri; wherever there is earth there always is Agni, and wherever there is Agni there always is earth; thus there are two sources and one couple. Váyu of a truth is Savitá, and ether, the Sávitrí; wherever there is Váyu there is ether (*antariksha*), and wherever there is ether there is Váyu; thus there are two sources and one couple. The sun, A'ditya, is Savitá, and sky (*dyau*), the Sávitrí; wherever there is A'ditya there always is sky, and where there is sky, there also is A'ditya; thus there are two sources and one couple. Chandramas, the moon, verily is Savitá, and the stars, the Sávitrí; wherever there is moon there also are stars, and wherever there are stars there is the the moon; thus there are two sources and one couple. The day (*ahan*) is Savitá, and the night (*rátri*), the Sávitrí; wherever there is day there is night, and wherever there is night there also is day; thus there are two sources and one couple. Heat (*ushṇa*) is Savitá, and cold (*síta*), the Sávitrí; wherever there is heat, there also is cold, and where there is cold, there also is heat; thus there are two sources and one couple. The cloud

* These questions include all the leading words of the sacre[d] Gáyatrí.

(*abbhra*) is Savitá, and rain (*varsha*) the Sávitrí; wherever there is cloud there is rain, and where there is rain, there is cloud; thus there are two sources and one couple. The lightning (*vidyut*) is Savitá, and the thunder (*stanayitnu*), the Sávitrí; wherever there is lightning there is thunder, and where there is thunder there also is lightning; thus there are two sources and one couple. Life (*práṇa*) is Savitá, and food (*anna*), the Sávitrí; wherever there is life there is food, and where there is food there also is life; thus there are two sources and one couple. The Vedas are Savitá, and the metres (*chhandas*), the Sávítrí; wherever there are Vedas, there are metres, and where there are metres, there also are the Vedas; thus there are two sources and one couple. Sacrifice (*Yajña*) is Savitá, and fee (*dakshiṇá*), the Sávitrí; wherever there is sacrifice there is fee, and where there is fee there also is sacrifice; thus there are two sources and one couple. These verily are the twelve couples.'

"Verily Brahma beheld this recepacle, the adorable prosperity, (the Sávitrí alias Gáyatri). Meditate on it. If it be religiously held, (*vrate*), it abides* in truth. He, Savitá, having created Bráhmaṇas from the Sávitrí, held it within him, hence the first foot of the Sávitrí is *savitur vareṇyam* the preeminient portion of Savitá, (a play upon the word *vrata*, religiously held and thence *váreṇyam* the preeminent.) By the earth is upheld the Rig hymns; by the Rig hymns, Agni; by Agni, prosperity (çrí, here intended for Sávitrí); by prosperity, woman; by woman, a couple; by a couple, man; by man, work; by work, religious austerity; by religious austerity, truth; by truth, Brahma, by Brahma, Bráhmaṇa; by Bráhmaṇa, devotion; by devotion are Bráhmaṇas bepraised, made voidless, and unbroken. His thread (lineage) remains unbroken, and the abode of his life remains undisturbed who knows this the first foot of the Sávítri, or knowing explains it.

* प्रत्यतिष्ठात् The verb is in the past tense.

"'We comtemplate the glory of the god,' (*bhargo devasya dhímahi*) is the second foot of the Sávitrí. By ether is the Yajush upheld; by the Yajush, Váyu; by the Váyu, cloud; by the cloud, rain; by the rain, herbs and trees; by herbs and trees, animals; by animals, work; by work, austirity; by austirity, truth; by truth, Brahma; by Brahma, Bráhmaṇa; by Bráhmaṇa, devotion; by devotion iṣ Bráhmaṇá bepraised, made voidless, and unbroken. His thread (lineage) remains unbroken, and the abode of his life remains undisturbed, who knows this the second foot of the Sávitrì, or knowing explains it.

"'He who irradiates our understanding,' (*dhiyo yo nah prachodayát*,) is the third foot of the Sávitrí. By the sky is the Sáma upheld; by the Sáma, A'ditya; by A'ditya, light; by the light, rain; by the rain, hérbs and trees; by the herbs and trees, animals; by the animals, work; by work, austerity; by austerity, truth; by truth, Brahma; by Brahma, Bráhmaṇa; by the Bráhmaṇa devotion; by devotion is the Bráhmana bepraised, made voidless, and unbroken. His lineage remains unbroken, and the abode of his life remains undisturbed, who knows this the third foot of the Sávitrí, or knowing explains it.

"By the Bráhmaṇa who thus knows this, is, of a truth, Brahma acquired, digested and well understood. By Brahma is the ether acquired, digested and well understood. By the ether is Váyu acquired, digested and well understood. By Váyu is the light acquired, digested and well understood. By light is water acquired, digested and well understood. By water is earth acquired, digested and well understood. By earth is food acquired, digested and well understood. By food is life acquired, digested and well understood. By life is mind acquired, digested and well understood. By mind is speech acquired, digested and well understood. By speech are the Vedas acquired, digested and well understood. By the Vedas is sacrifice acquired, digested and well understood. Verily these twelve great elements are situated in this order, and thereof is sacrifice the highest.

"Those who know the above think that they know it (rightly); but in reality they know it not. Sacrifice is established on the Vedas; the Vedas are established on speech; speech is established on the mind; the mind is established on life; life is established on food; food is established on the earth; the earth is established on water; water is established on light; light is established on wind; the wind is established on ether; the ether is established on Brahma; Brahma is established on Bráhmaṇas acquainted with Brahma. Verily he is conscient of Brahma who knows this. He achieves meritorious acts, and sweet odours,—he destroys all sins, and enjoys endless grace,—who knows this; as also he, who knowing this, adores the Upanishad which has the Sávitrí, the mother of the Vedas, for its subject."

This interpretation differs from what is generally received by later authors, inasmuch as it seperates the epithet *vareṇya* from *bharga*, and makes the two distinct. This, however, is more apparent than real, for it is merely allegorical, and does not alter the sense. Otherwise it is on all fours with the belief of the Hindus that the object adored is Brahma or the universal soul, and therefore also of the sun, and not the sun itself as represented by its rays. As the interpretation is the oldest we possess, and was given within a short time after the Gáyatrí had been composed, this fact is worthy of note, particularly as it is at variance with the version given by some European orientalists, notably by the late Professor Wilson, which makes the sun itself to be the object of worship. It is of course impossible to say what the author of the Gáyatrí himself had in view, but his Indian commentators, both ancient and modern, are at one in believing that he rose from nature up to nature's God, and adored that sublime luminary which is visible only to the eye of reason, and not the planet we daily see in its course.

The Chapter closes with a kaṇḍiká on the importance of *A'chamana*, or washing of the face before commencing a ceremony.

The second chapter devotes its first nine kaṇḍikás to the duties appropriate to Brahmachâris, or religious students, inculcating dispassion, mendicity, chastity, devotion to the tutor, and other virtues, and fixing the time to be devoted to such a course of life from twelve to twenty-four years. The rules are very much the same as those given in the Grihya Sútras, and call for no remark. A legend follows in which a sage of the name of Kábandhi, son of Kabandha, an A'tharvaṇa Rishi, is described as an intelligent disputant, a knower of the Mimáñsá (*mimáñsaka*), and self-sufficient to a degree. He discourses with the priests of the great king Yauvanásya Mándhátá, and questions them about the duties of priests and the particular knowledge necessary for them. The replies are brief and inconsequential. Several other legends follow, which describe the various requirements of sacrifices. Of these brief accounts will be found in the table of contents. They are, as usual with Bráhmaṇic legends, inane, and designed mostly to establish the preeminence of the Atharva over the other Vedas.

The third chapter opens with an injunction that the four priests at a sacrifice should know the four Vedas, and that a sacrifice with three priests versed in the Rig, Yajush, and Sáma, is, like an animal with a less number of feet than four, or a man with one foot, or a car with one wheel, incapable of moving on satisfactorily. Certain expiations are then recommended for the offence of speaking on the part of the priests when engaged at a sacrifice. A curious legend then follows in which questions are propounded as to why the hair grows first on the head and then on the other parts of the body? why men have mustache and women have it not? why the teeth first cut out of the lower jaw? why they shed and grow again? and why and how other organs of the body perform their functions? and they are explained by references to various parts of the Darṣapaurṇamása sacrifice; as also regarding certain accidents to the sacrificial fire and their expiations. Passing over two other short legends of little importance, we come to a set of rules regarding the distribution of the sacrificed cow among the different persons engaged in the sacrifice. According to them the Prastátá is to receive the two jaws along with the tongue; the Pratihartá, the neck and the hump; the Udgátá, the eagle-like wings or briskets; the Adhvaryu, the right side chine with the shoulder; the Upagátá, the left chine; the Pratiprasthátá, the left side shoulder; the Brahmá and the wife of the Rathyá,* the right rump; the Brahmaṇachchhañsi, the right hip lower down the round; the Potá, the thigh (leg†); the Hotá, the left rump; the Maitrávaruṇa, the left round; the Achchhávka, the left leg; the Neshṭá, the right arm, (clod); the Sadasya, the left clod; the master of the house, the sirloin and some part of the abdomen (flank? *sada* and *anúka*); his wife, the loin, or the pelvic region, which she is to bestow on a Bráhmaṇ; the Agnidhra, the stomach (*vanishṭu*), the heart, the kidneys, and the right fore-leg (váhu); the A'treya, the left leg; the householder who ordains the sacrifice,‡ the two right feet; the wife of the householder who ordains the sacrifice, the two left feet; and both of them in common the upper lip; the Grávastut, three bones of the neck, (vertebræ,) and the manirjáh (whatever

---

* दक्षिणा श्रोणिरथ्यास्त्रीब्राह्मणः । The passage is evidently corrupt, and I am doubtful of its import. The meaning above given is a mere guess.

† I cannot make out the distinction between the *avarasaktha* "hip lower down" and the *uru* "thigh." I suspect the last to mean the leg.

‡ पत्रपतेर्हतप्रदस्यः । I do not know the difference between this person and the householder who gets the sirloin.

that be); the man who leads the cow, three other vertebræ and a half of the perinæum; the Chamasárdhvaryu, the bladder; the Subrahmaṇya, the head; the man who invites people to a Soma sacrifice, the hide. These altogether make a total of thirty-six parts. Dire imprecations are hurled against those who venture to depart from this order of division. The chapter is brought to a close with some subsidiary rules regarding *díkshá* or initiation *i. e.* the formal engagement of priests at a sacrifice.

The fourth chapter continues the subject of initiation, giving directions as to the order in which the different priests are to be initiated, and the several assistants who are to officiate under the chief priests. Some of the principal ceremonies and the gods who preside over them are then named, and the rewards due for the performance of those ceremonies are given in detail. The latter half of the chapter is devoted to a description of the mystic connection of the year with ceremonies.

The first six kaṇḍikás of the fifth chapter continue the subject of relation of ceremonies to the year, and sum it up with an allegory in which the year is represented as a human being, and its different members are formed by the different ceremonies noticed in the preceding kaṇḍikás. The seventh gives the order which the ceremonies should successively follow; the first is Agnyádhána, then Purváhuti, then Agnihotra, then Darśa and Paurṇamása, then Agrayana, then Cháturmásya, then Pashubandha, then Agnishṭoma, then Rájasúya, then Vájapeya, then Aṣvamedha, then Purushamedha, then Sarvamedha, then Dakshiṇávánta, then Dakshiṇá, then Adakshiṇá, the last three forming parts of the Sahasradakshiṇá.* A legend follows in which Prajápati is represented to have performed all the other ceremonies, and, attaining thereby only perishable rewards, subsequently to have secured eternal

* This passage in the original text is evidently incorrect, and my version is conjectural.

fruition by the ceremony of Sahasradakshiṇá (one involving a fee of a thousand heads of cattle). Passing over some unimportant paragraphs we come to the twenty-third, which gives some details about the classification and particular times of sacrifices. All ceremonies are devided into three classes; 1st including all those in which the cooking of rice or frumenty is the most important element, hence called *Pákayajna**;—2nd those in which the offering of clarified butter is the most important—*Haviryajṇa*,; and 3rd those in which the Soma beverage holds the most prominent place,—*Somya* or *Somayajna*. Each of them includes 7 different kinds of sacrifices. Thus—

*Class*, I. *Pákayajna*, comprising, 1, Sáyam homa; 2, Prátar homa; 3, nine kinds of Sthálipáka; 4, Bali; 5, Pitriyajṉa; 6, Ishṭakáh; 7, Paṣu.

*Class*, II. *Haviryajna*, comprising, 1, Agnyádheya, 2, Agnihotra; 3, Paurṇamási; 4, A'mávásyá or Darṣa; 5, the nine Ishṭis; 6, the four Cháturmásyas; 7, Pasubandha.

*Class*. III. *Somayajṇa*, comprising, 1, Agnishṭoma; 2, Atyagnishṭoma; 3, Ukthya; 4, Shodasimán; 5, Vájapeya; 6, Atirátra; 7, A'ptoryáṃa.

The last two kaṇḍikás of the chapter are devoted to the creation and requirements of ceremonies, and the uses of the different Vedas in the performance thereof.

* Although the cooking of rice is a *sine qua non* in these ceremonies, yet some authors are of opinion that *páka* here does not mean cooking. "It signifies, according to Indian authorities," says Max Muller; "either *small* or *good*. That *páka* is used in the first sense appears from such expressions as yo mat pákatarah, "he who is smaller than we." But the more likely meaning is *good* or *excellent* or *perfect*; because, as the commentators remark, these ceremonies impart to every man that peculear fitness without which he would be excluded from the sacrifices, and from all the benefits of his religion." *Ancient Sanskrit Literature*, 203.

The contents of the Second Book are even more desultory, inconsequential and fragementary than those of the first. No subject is taken up *ab initio,* or described otherwise than casually, and with reference to some particular point of doubt only. The author of the work starts with the assumption that the reader is familiar with the subject, and needs elucidation only with reference to some abstruse point or other. The Book opens with a direction to throw out a wisp of hay from the seat of the Brahmá, and on the necessity of the Brahmá's remaining silent when filling the sacrificial vessel called *praṇitá,* and of the alter being surrounded by a strip of cloth named *paridhi.* Then follows a legend intended for the praise of Brahmá as the most important member of the clerical staff. It is said that Prajápati once performed a sacrifice without awarding to Rudra his share of offerings. Rudra wished that since he had been cut out of the ceremony it should not yield the desired return, and accordingly, seizing and piercing it, cut off a portion from it. The resulting fragment is the *Prásitra* food. It was given to Bhaga; but no sooner that divinity beheld it than his eyes dropped out, for which he is called "the Blind Bhaga." He took it not. It was next offered to Savitá, who took it, but his hands thereupon were immediately cut off, and he had to put on golden hands, whence he is praised as the "golden-handed." The oblation was next offered to Pushan, who tasted it, but that broke his teeth, therefore he is called the "toothless eater of cakes." It was then offered to Idhmáñgirasa, who likewise tasted it, and thereby lost his head: the oblation returned to the Yajṇa. Thereupon it was offered to Varhi A'ñgirasa, who, partaking of it, had his body disjointed. The food reverted to its place. It was offered next to Vrihaspati A'ñgirasa, who was frightened by the idea of an impending danger, and repeated a mantra, which ultimately resulted in the glorification of the Brahmá as the head of the sacrifice. The legend, though pointless and uninteresting, is of importance as containing the germ on which the Pauránic tale of Daksha's great sacrifice has been elaborated. According to the popular version, which is founded on that of the Bhagavata Puraṇa, once on a time Daksha, the mind-born son of Brahmá, happened to be present at a Viṣvasrig sacrifice celebrated by his father, and, on the arrival of Ṣiva there, was wanting in courtesy to him. A quarrel thereupon broke out between the two, and culminated in a curse from Daksha, who ordained that thenceforward Ṣiva should not be allowed a share at a sacrifice. Subsequently Daksha himself celebrated a grand sacrifice such as creation had never before beheld, resplendant with all that unlimited wealth and divine command could bring together. To it assembled all the gods, with their wives, all the Rishis, and nymphs, and Pitris and Gandharvas from the farthest parts of the world, and the only persons designedly excluded were Umá and her lord Ṣiva. Umá, seated in her blissful mansion on the crest of the Kailása mountain, beheld the crowds that were moving towards her father's house, and soon heard of the rejoicings that were going on to which she had been purposely excluded.

"Wroth of heart was Umá;
"To her lord she spake:—
"'Why dost thou, the mighty,
"'Of no rite partake?
"'Straight I speed to Daksha
"Such a sight to see:
"If he be my father,
"He must welcome thee."

But her lord could not be prevailed upon to go to a feast to which he had not been invited, and so she started alone. Mounting her favorite bull, and followed by a wild band of her lord's spritely attendants, she hurried through space, and in a twinkling alighted amidst the godly company when feasting and joy and merriment were at their height in the mansion of her father.

"Greeting, gods and sages,
Greeting, father mine!
Work hath wondrous virtue,
Where such aids combine.

"Guest-hall never gathered
Goodlier company:
Seemeth all are welcome,—
All the gods but me."

Spake the Muni Daksha,
Stern and cold his tone;—
"'Welcome thou, too, daughter,
Since thou com'st alone.

"But thy frenzied husband
Suits another shrine;
He is no partaker
Of this feast of mine.

"He who walks in darkness
Loves no deeds of light;
He who herds with demons
Shuns each kindly sprite.

"Let him wander naked,—
Wizard weapons wield,—
Dance his frantic measure
Round the funeral field.

"Art thou yet delighted
With the reeking hide,

Body smeared with ashes,
Skulls in necklace tied?

"Thou to love this monster;
Thou to plead his part!
Know the moon and Gangá
Share that faithless heart

"Vainly art thou vying
With thy rivals' charms
Are not coils of serpents
Softer than thine arms?"*

These would be bitter words to any faithful wife to hear said of her lord; to Umá, who was the pattern of her sex, and the most devoted of wives, enjoying on that account the proud title of Satí *par excellence*, they proved the most poignant, touching her to the very core of her heart. In a mighty cry of angnish she upbraided her father, and, dilating on the merits of her husband and the injustice that had been done him, ended by declaring that she would no longer retain a body which she owed to so wicked a father. Anon she became speechless with overwhelming wrath, took her seat at the northern side of the altar which by law belonged to her lord, and, covering herself with the hem of her cloth, gave up her life in a fit of profound meditation. Awe-struck and dumb the company beheld the tragedy, without being able to make any attempt for her rescue. Her attendants now rushed forwards; but Bhrigu, the chief priest, in an instant poured an oblation on the fire, and brought forth from the flames a mighty host of frightful Ribhus who soon compelled them

* Waterfield's *Indian Ballads and Poems*. The Bhágavata makes Daksha utter these reproaches when he meets Śiva at the festal hall of his father, but the popular version brings them to this place.

to run away. When Ṣiva heard the news there was no limit to his wrath; terrific flames burst forth from every pore of his body, and, as in an agony of violent grief he plucked a lock of hair from his head, it assumed the form of a most stupendous giant with a thousand arms. This apparition at once went forth to the place of Daksha, accompanied by a numerous retinue of fiends, and dealt destruction on every side. The gods fled in terror, and the festal hall was heaped with carnage. Bhaga had his eyes plucked out; Bhrigu's beard was torn; and Pushan's teeth suffered complete demolition; while most of the Devas were tied hand and foot and trampled upon. But the foremost among the victims was Daksha himself, whose head was lopped off, and thrown into the burning altar, where it was soon reduced to ashes. The gods now met in solemn conclave to devise means for putting a stop to the rapidly increasing havoc, and besought Vishṇu and Brahmá to come to the rescue. Then they all went to Ṣiva and most earnestly supplicated his mercy, and so far prevailed on him as to bring him to the scene of devastation. But when that divinity beheld there the corpse of his dearly beloved wife, his grief and wrath revived again. He stuck the corpse on the point of his trident, and began a wild maddened dance which threatened immediate destruction to the universe. Vishṇu, at this juncture, felt himself unequal to the task of pacifying the fury of Ṣiva; but, knowing that as long as the dead body of Umá would be in sight so long the surging grief would not subside, he cut it off bit by bit with his discus, and threw it wide about the earth.* This expedient

* Fifty-one such bits were thrown about, and the spot where each of them fell formed a sacred *pítha,* which is held in the highest veneration to this day. The Tantra-chudámaṇi gives the following account of the different parts into which the body was divided, and the places where they fell: viz. 1, the crown of the head at Hingulá (Hinglaj); 2, the three eyes at Sarkarára; 3,

proved efficacious, and Ṣiva was at last induced to restore the killed and wounded to life and health. But Daksha's head having been burnt, it had to be replaced by that of a goat,* which was lying handy by the altar.

The Káliká Puráṇa differs from the Bhágavata in

the nose at Sugandhá; 4, the top of the neck at Káṣmira; 5, the tongue at Jválámukhi; 6, the right breast at Jálandhara; 7, the heart at Vaidyanátha; 8, the knees at Nepála; 9, the right hand at Mánasa; 10, the navel in Utkala; 11, the right cheek at Gaṇḍakí; 12, the left arm at Vahulá; 13, the elbow at Ujjayaní; 14, the right arm at Cháttála, Chandraṣekhara; 15, the right foot at Tripurá; 16, the left foot at Triṣrotá; 17, the pudendum at Kámagiri (Kámákhyá); 18, the right great-toe at Yugádyá; 19, other right toes at Kálipíṭha, (Kálighát); 20, the fingers at Prayága; 21, the thighs at Jayanti; 22, the earings at Váránaṣi; 23, the back of the trunk at Kanyáṣrama; 24, the right ankle at Kurukshetra; 25, the wrists at Manivedaka; 26, the back of the neck at Ṣrísaila; 27, the backbone at Kánchi; 28, one hip at Kálamádhava; 29, the other hip at Narmadá; 30, the left breast at Rámagiri; 31, the hairs of the head at Vrindávana; 32, the upper row of teeth at Ṣúchi; 33, the lower row of teeth at Panchaságara; 34, the left talpa (shoulder blade?) at Karatoyá; 35, the right do. at Ṣríparvata; 36, the left ankle, at Vibhásha; 37, the belly at Prabhásha; 38, the upper lip at Bhairavaparvata; 39, the chin at Jalasthala; 40, the left cheek at Godávari; 41, the right shoulder at Ratnávalí; 42, the left shoulder at Mithilá; 43, the leg bone at Nalápáti; 44, the ears at Karnáṭa; 45, the mind at Vakreṣvara; 46, the palm at Jasora; 47, the lower lip at Aṭṭahása; 48, the necklace at Nandipura; 49, the anklets at Lanká; 50, the toes of the left foot at Viráṭa; 51, the right leg at Magadha. How the mind and the ornaments formed parts of the body, are Tántric mysteries which I cannot unravel. The Bhágavata has nothing to say about this division, as, according to it, the body was consumed by a fire which was evolved from the Devi's profound meditation.

* Ram according to Wilson; the Sanskrit word in the Bhágavata Puráṇa is *aja*, which means both a goat and a sheep.

many important particulars, and the Váyu differs the most. But they all agree in making Daksha's refusal to recognise the greatness of Rudra *alias* Şiva, and Umá's suicide as the original causes of Daksha's disgrace. The Vedic legend has nothing to say about the substitution of a goat or ram's head for that of Daksha, but the myth on the subject must be of considerable antiquity, seeing that we have a ram-headed divinity among the most ancient sculptures of Egypt, representing one of the eight great gods of the country. His name was variously spelt Kneph, Neph, Nef, Cnouphis, Chnoubis, Noub, and, perhaps also, Nou.† Like Daksha, he appears in sculptures as "a man with the head of a ram," and if not the progenitor, Prajápati, "at least the leader, of the gods."‡ Elswhere he is described as the "spirit of the god, which moved upon the face of the waters." § Daksha, however, had many wives, while Neph had only two; and Satí, the daughter of Daksha, became, among the Egyptians, Saté (Juno) one of the wives of their Jove. Anyhow there is a remarkable analogy between the two gods, and the idea suggests itself that perhaps they owe their origin to a common source, or one of them is derived from the other. The Pauráṇic story of the sacrifice and its consequences is, however, an allegorical representation of a quarrel between the Vaishṇavites and the Sivites, which terminated by the admission of Şiva into the Hindu pantheon, and has no connexion with Egypt.

The second chapter begins with some detailed instructions on the offering of flesh meat on the A'hitágni. That fire always wishes the Yajamána to offer it such delectable food, and the Yajamána who offers animals fit for Indrágni to it once

---

* Wilson's Vishṇu Puráṇa p. 61.

† Wilkinson's Ancient Egyptians, N. S. I. p. 241.

‡ *Ibid*, I, 238.

§ *Ibid*, I 236.

every six months, accomplishes the offering of his own-self to Indra and Agni. The same offering should be made by those who desire long life, or numerous descendants, or crowded herds. For a prayer to Yama for long life, the offering meet is a green parrot; and for numerous progeny the offering to Tvashṭrá should be a mare. Then follows a legend in which the Devas issue forth under five generals to conquer the Asuras. Agni leads the Vashus, Soma the Rudras, Indra the Maruts, Varuṇa the A'dityas, and Vrihaspati the Viṣvedeváh; but they are defeated, and at last are obliged to regain their lost ground by a Yajṇa. The 13th kaṇḍiká gives an account of how Vasishṭha, through having seen Indra in person, obtained certain stomas for himself. These stomas are subsequently recited, and the advantage of knowing them is explained. We next come to a number of details about the appointment of the Agnidhra, the offering of Pravitáhuti, and salutations to Prajápati, Sadasya and other priests. The twenty-third kaṇḍiká insists upon the necessity of truthfulness on the part of the priestly staff, giving as a reason that none can like a liar.

The first half of the third chapter is devoted to the mystic syllables Vashaṭ and Hiñ, the advantages of repeating them during a sacrifice, the best way in which, and the proper times when, they should be repeated, and the various metres appropriate at the morning, the noon, and the evening ceremonies.

The most important legend in the third chapter refers to the relation which the Rig Veda bears to the Sáma. According to it "at first there existed only the Rik and the Sáma. Sá was the name of the Rik, and Ama that of the Sáma. The Rik (feminine) said to Sáma (masculine), 'let us unite for the multiplication of animated beings.' 'Not so;' replied Sáma; 'my greatness is higher than yours.' The Rik divided herself into two, and addressed the other; but got no reply. She divided herself into three, and again addressed him. Thus she became three-fold, and because she became three fold, therefore is he (the Sáma) praised by three Riks, sung with three Riks, and completed with three Riks. Hence it is that one man has many wives, but never one woman many rival husbands. Because, of a truth, the dicussion was between Sá and Ama, therefore was Sáma produced, and hence the Sáma got the character of Sáma, and by it is pacification (sáma) produced, and superiority attained. Whatever is born, it is pacified, (Sáma); that which is Sámaless or unappeased is condemend. Each of the two, Sáma and Rik, became five-fold; these five parts are A'háva, Hiñkára, and Prastáva, first; Udgítha, the middle; and Nidhana and Vashaṭ the last."

The last three chapters of the Gopatha Bráhmaṇa treat principally of peculiarities and details regarding the morning, noon, and evening rites in connexion with the Ekáha, the Uktha, the Ekáshṭaká and other minor sacrifices; but they are not of sufficient importance to require fuller descriptions than what occur in the table of contents.

In the whole range of the Gopatha there is not a single circumstance mentioned which is calculated to throw any light on the political condition of India at the time when the work was composed. The only kings named are Yauvanáṣva Mándhata, Janamejaya, and Parikshit. Of other persons, we have Angirá, Bhrigu, Vasishṭha and other well known Vedic sages alluded to, but under circumstances which afford no information regarding their lives. The places mentioned are Kuru, Páñchála, Káṣí, Magadha and other northern provinces; but none beyond the Vindhiyan range.

In presenting the the first edition of the Gopatha Bráhmaṇa to the public I have to express my regret that it appears under two very serious disadvantages; 1st, that it has no commentary attached to it; and 2nd that different portions of it have been edited by two individuals at different times, without consulting each other.

When the work was first undertaken it was expected that a commentary would somewhere turn up, and that it would be printed along with the text; but careful enquiry at Benares, and in the Madras and the Bombay precidencies showed that none was extant, and a complete edition could not be accomplished. As however several excellent and correct manuscripts of the text came to hand in course of the search, it was thought preferable to print the text alone, rather than drop the undertaking altogether, particularly as it was supposed that the ripe scholarship and varied knowledge of the late Paṇḍit Harachandra Vidyábhushaṇa, who had volunteered to edit the text and supply a gloss, would stand in good stead of a commentary. The Paṇḍit, however, died soon after the publication of the first fasciculus, and the MS. of his gloss was not accessible after his death; the idea of printing a gloss had, therefore, to be abandoned, and the writer of this note confined his labours to the preparation of an eclectic text, with all the *varæ lectiones* of his codices added in foot notes, and a free sprinkling of punctuation to make the reading easy, the MSS. consulted having none.

The following are the MSS. which have been made use of in preparing the text for the press—

1st. क—From the Bombay Government; comprising 78 folia, each 9×5¼ inches, and having 9 lines on each page. The writing is clear, but not neat. There are marks of its having been revised. It contains only the first half of the work (*Purvárdha*).

2nd. ख—From the Benares College Library; 162 folia, each 13×5; 5 lines on a page; dated, Samvat 1878. A carelessly written and unrevised MS. Like the preceding, it comprises only the first part of the work. A fragment of the first two adhyáyas of the second half without pagination accompanies this. It has 9 lines on each page, and bears marks of having been revised.

3rd ग—From the Library of the Asiatic Society of Bengal;

a bound volume, 11 × 7 inches, No. 274. It includes the two parts of the Bráhmaṇa, and also the Pratyaṅgirá Kalpa, It is carelessly written, and not revised Dated, Samvat 1878.

4th घ—From the writer of this note; lost by the late editor.

5th च—From Ráo Bahádur Gopála Hari-deṣamukha of Bombay; 92 folia; each 9 × 4½, bearing 10 lines on each page. Not dated, but apparently old. Badly but correctly written, and carefully revised. It contains only the second half of the work.

6th छ—From the Bombay Government; 38 folia, foolscap; written in the oblong puthi form, and having 13 lines on each page. It has been newly copied, but not revised. It contains the Uttarárdha complete.

7th. ज—From the Bombay Government; a carefully written old MS. patched in several places, and containing the Purvárdha. It comprises 75 folia, each measuring 9 × 3 inches, and having 8 lines on each page. It bears a date of four figures of which the first two are 1 and 5, and the fourth 2; the third is illegible.

8th झ—From the Bombay Government; 59 folia, measuring 9 × 4½ each, and having 9 lines on each page. It is carefully written and correct. and bears date, Samvat 1795 = Ṣaka 1660.

9th ट—From the Library of the Asiatic Society of Bengal, No. 760; 64 folia, each measuring 11 × 4½ inches, and having 12 lines on a page. It is well and correctly written, and contains both parts of the work. It bears date, Samvat 1746, and has the epigraphs written in red ink.

These codices differ but slightly, and their differences. such as they are, are due mainly to unintelligent or negligent copyists. The Bombay texts, for which I am indebted to the kind aid of Dr. George Buhler, are almost alike; and appear to be the most trustworthy. It is to be regretted that No. 7, was received after the first 96 pages had been printed, and its variants, therefore, could not be embodied in this edition.

# ओं नमो ब्रह्मणे।

## ओं नमोऽथर्ववेदाय।

—:ऽ०००ऽ:—

## गोपथब्राह्मणपूर्व्वभागे

### प्रथमः प्रपाठकः।

ओं ब्रह्म ह वा इदमग्र आसीत्, स्वयन्त्वेकमेव (१) तदैक्षत, (२) महद्वै यक्षं, तदेकमेवास्मि, हन्ताहं मदेव मन्मात्रं द्वितीयं देवं निर्मम इति, तदभ्यश्राम्यदभ्यतपत् समतपत्, तस्य श्रान्तस्य तप्तस्य सन्तप्तस्य ललाटे स्नेहो यदार्द्र्यमाजायत (३) तेनानन्दत्तमब्रवीत् (४) महद्वै यक्षं सुवेदमविदामह इति। तद्यदब्रवीत् महद्वै यक्षं सुवेदमविदामह इति, तस्मात् सुवेदोऽभवत्तं वा एतं सुवेदं सन्तं स्वेद इत्याचक्षते। परोक्षेण परोक्षप्रिया इव हि देवा(५) भवन्ति प्रत्यक्षद्विषः॥१॥

स भूयोऽश्राम्यद्भूयोऽतप्यत् भूय आत्मानं समतपत्तस्य श्रान्तस्य तप्तस्य सन्तप्तस्य सर्वेभ्यो रोमगर्त्तेभ्यः पृथक् स्वेदधाराः प्रास्यन्दन्त। (६) ताभिरनन्दत्, तदब्रवीदाभिर्वा अहमिदं सर्वं धारयि-

---

१ स्वयम्भ्वेकमेवेति क, ख, ग,।

२ तदैक्षीत इति ख, ग,। तदीक्षत इति क, घ,।

३ यदार्द्द्र्यमाजायत इति ख, घ,।

४ तदब्रवीदिति ख, घ,।

५ देवता इति ख, ग,।

६ प्राक् स्यन्दन्त इति क, ख, ग।

ष्यामि यदिदं किञ्चाभिर्वा अहमिदं सर्वं जनयिष्यामि यदिदं किञ्चाभिर्वा अहमिदं सर्वमाप्स्यामि यदिदं किञ्चेति। तद्यदब्रवीदाभिर्वा अहमिदं सर्वं धारयिष्यामि यदिदं किञ्चेति, तस्मात् धारा अभवं(१)स्तद्धाराणां धारात्वं यच्चासु ध्रियते। तद्यदब्रवीदाभिर्वा अहमिदं सर्वं जनयिष्यामि यदिदं किञ्चेति, तस्माज्जाया अभवंस्तज्जायानां जायात्वं यच्चासु पुरुषो जायते, यच्च पुत्त्रः पुन्नामनरकमनेकशततारं तस्मात् त्राति पुत्त्रस्तत् पुत्त्रस्य पुत्त्रत्वं। तद्यदब्रवीदाभिर्वा अहमिदं सर्वमाप्स्यामि यदिदं किञ्चेति, तस्मादापो अभवंस्तदपामप्त्वमाप्नोति वै स सर्वान् कामान् यान् कामयते ॥ २ ॥

ता अपः सृष्ट्वाऽन्वैक्षत, तासु स्वां छायामपश्यत्(२)तामस्येक्षमाणस्य स्वयं रेतोऽस्कन्दत्तदप्सु प्रत्यतिष्ठत् तास्तत्रैवाभ्यश्राम्यदभ्यतपत्, समतपत्, ताः श्रान्तास्तप्ताः सन्तप्ताः सार्द्धमेव रेतसा द्वैधमभवं(३) स्तासामन्या अन्यतरा अतिलवणा अपेया अस्वाद्वस्ता अशान्ता रेतः समुद्रं वृत्वाऽतिष्ठन्नथेतराः पेयाः स्वाद्वः शान्तास्तास्तत्रैवाभ्यश्राम्यदभ्यतपत्, समतपत्, ताभ्यः श्रान्ताभ्यस्तप्ताभ्यः सन्तप्ताभ्यो यद्रेत आसीत्तदभृज्यत, यदभृज्यत तस्माद् भृगुः

१ ताभिरनन्दत् तदब्रवीत् आभिर्व्वा अहमिदं सर्व्वं धारयिष्यामि यदिदं किञ्चाभिर्वा अहमिदं सर्व्वं धारयिष्यामि यदिदं किञ्चेति तस्माद्धारा अभवंस्तद्धाराणां धारात्वमिति ख, ग, चिह्नितपुस्तकद्वयपाठः परन्त्वयं मध्ये खण्डित इत्यध्यवसीयते उपक्रमे अनुपात्तस्य अहमिदं सर्व्वं जनयिष्यामीत्यादिपाठस्य उपसंहारकाले दर्शनादिति।

२ ता आप इति क, घ,।

३ द्वैधतममभवन्निति ख, ग,।

समभवत्, तद् भृगो र्भृगुत्वं भृगुरिव वै स सर्वेषु लोकेषु भाति य एवं वेद ॥ ३ ॥

स भृगुं सृष्ट्वाऽन्तरधीयत, स भृगुः सृष्टः प्राङेजततं वागन्ववद-द्वायो वायो इति, सन्न्यवर्त्तत, स दक्षिणां दिशमेजततं वागन्ववदत् मातरिश्वन् मातरिश्वन्निति, स न्यवर्त्तत(१) स प्रतीचीं दिशमेजततं वागन्ववदत् पवमानः पवमान इति, स न्यवर्त्तत(२) स उदीचीन्दि-शमेजततं वागन्ववदद्वात वातेति, तमब्रवीन्नन्वविदामह इति, नहीत्य-थार्वाङेनमेताखेवाप्सुन्विच्छेति(३) तद्यदब्रवीदथार्वाङेनमेताखेवा-प्सुन्विच्छेति(४) तदथर्वाऽभवत्, तदथर्वणोऽथर्वत्वं (५)। तस्य ह वा एतस्य भगवतोऽथर्वण ऋषेर्यथैव ब्रह्मणो लोमानि यथाऽङ्गानि यथा प्राण एवमेवास्य सर्वं आत्मा समभवत्तमथर्वाणं ब्रह्माऽब्रवीत् प्रजापतेः प्रजाः सृष्ट्वा पालयस्वेति। तद्यदब्रवीत् प्रजापतेः प्रजाः सृष्ट्वा पालयस्वेति, तस्मात् प्रजापतिरभवत्, तत् प्रजापतेः प्रजा-पतित्वमथर्वा वै प्रजापतिः, प्रजापतिरिव ह वै स सर्वेषु लोकेषु भाति य एवं वेद ॥ ४ ॥

तमथर्वाणमृषिमभ्यश्राम्यदभ्यतपत्, समतपत्तस्माच्छ्रान्तात्तप्तात् सन्तप्तात् दशतयानथर्वण ऋषीन्निरमिमतैकर्चान् द्व्यर्चांस्तृचांश्चतु-र्ऋचान् पञ्चर्चान् षडर्चान् सप्तर्चानष्टर्चान्नवर्चान्दशर्चानिति। ता-

---

१ सन्न्यवर्त्तत इति ख, ।

२ सन्न्यवर्त्तत इति ख, ।

३ एताखेवास्वन्विच्छेति क, घ, ।

४ एताखेवास्वन्विच्छेति क, घ, ।

५ तदथर्वाणाथर्वत्वमिति क, ख, ग, ।

नथर्वण ऋषीनभ्यश्राम्यदभ्यतपत्समतपत्, तेभ्यः श्रान्तेभ्यस्तप्तेभ्यः सन्तप्तेभ्यो दशतयानाथर्वणानार्षेयान्निरमिमतैकादशान् द्वादशांस्त्रयोदशांश्चतुर्दशान् पञ्चदशान् षोडशान् सप्तदशानष्टादशान्नवदशान् विंशानिति। तानथर्वण ऋषीनाथर्वणांश्चार्षेयानभ्यश्राम्यदभ्यतपत् समतपत् तेभ्यः श्रान्तेभ्यस्तप्तेभ्यः सन्तप्तेभ्यो यान् मन्त्रानपश्यत् स आथर्वणो वेदोऽभवत्तमाथर्वणं वेदमभ्यश्राम्यदभ्यतपत्समतपत्तस्माच्छ्रान्तात् तप्तात् सन्तप्तादोमिति मन एवोर्द्धमक्षरमुदक्रामत्, स य इच्छेत्सर्वैरेतैरथर्वभिश्चाथर्वणैश्च कुर्वीयेत्थितयैव तं महाव्याहृत्या कुर्वीत। सर्वैर्ह वा अस्यैतैरथर्वभिश्चाथर्वणैश्च कृतं भवति य एवं वेद यश्चैवं विद्वानेवमेतया महाव्याहृत्या कुरुते॥ ५॥

स भूयोऽश्राम्यद्‌ भूयोऽतप्यद्‌ भूय आत्मानं समतपत् स आत्मत एव त्रींल्लोकान्निरमिमत पृथिवीमन्तरिक्षन्दिवमिति। स खलु पादाभ्यामेव पृथिवीं निरमिमतोदरादन्तरिक्षम्, मूर्द्ध्नो दिवं। स तांस्त्रींल्लोकानभ्यश्राम्यदभ्यतपत्समतपत्तेभ्यः श्रान्तेभ्यस्तप्तेभ्यः सन्तप्तेभ्यस्त्रीन् देवान् निरमिमताग्निं वायुमादित्यमिति। स खलु पृथिव्या एवाग्निं निरमिमतान्तरिक्षाद्वायुन्दिव आदित्यं। स तांस्त्रीन् देवानभ्यश्राम्यदभ्यतपत् समतपत्तेभ्यः श्रान्तेभ्यस्तप्तेभ्यः सन्तप्तेभ्यस्त्रीन् वेदान्निरमिमत ऋग्वेदं यजुर्व्वेदं सामवेदमिति, अग्नेऋग्वेदं,वायोर्यजुर्वेदमादित्यात्सामवेदं। स तांस्त्रीन् वेदानभ्यश्राम्यदभ्यतपत् समतपत् तेभ्यः श्रान्तेभ्यस्तप्तेभ्यः सन्तप्तेभ्यः स्तिस्रो महाव्याहृतीर्निरमिमत भूर्भुवःस्वरिति। भूरित्यृग्वेदात्, भुव इति यजुर्वेदात्,स्वरिति सामवेदात्। स य इच्छेत्सर्वैरेतैस्त्रिभिर्वेदैः कुर्वी-

येत्येताभिरेव तं महाव्याहृतिभिः कुर्वीत सर्वैर्ह वा अस्यैतैस्त्रिभिर्वेदैः कृतं भवति य एवं वेद यश्चैवं विद्वानेवमेताभिर्महाव्याहृतिभिः कुरुते ॥ ६ ॥

ता या अमू रेतः समुद्रं वृत्वाऽतिष्ठंस्ताः प्राच्यो दक्षिणाच्यः प्रतीच्य उदीच्यः समवद्रवन्त । तद्यत्समवद्रवन्त तस्मात्समुद्र उच्यते । ता भीता अब्रुवन् भगवन्तमेव वयं राजानं वृणीमह इति । यच्च वृत्वाऽतिष्ठंस्तद्वरणोऽभवत्(१) तं वा एतं वरणं सन्तं वरुण इत्याचक्षते । परोक्षेण परोक्षप्रिया इव हि देवा भवन्ति प्रत्यक्षद्विषः । स समुद्रादमुच्यत स मुच्युरभवत्तं वा एतं मुच्युं सन्तं मृत्युरित्याचक्षते । परोक्षेण परोक्षप्रिया इव हि देवा भवन्ति प्रत्यक्षद्विषः । तं वरुणं मृत्युमभ्यश्राम्यदभ्यतपत्समतपत्तस्य श्रान्तस्य तप्तस्य सन्तप्तस्य सर्वेभ्योऽङ्गेभ्यो रसोऽक्षरत् सोऽङ्गरसोऽभवत्तं वा एतमङ्गरसं सन्तमङ्गिरा इत्याचक्षते । परोक्षेण परोक्षप्रिया इव हि देवा भवन्ति प्रत्यक्षद्विषः ॥ ७ ॥

तमङ्गिरसमृषिमभ्यश्राम्यदभ्यतपत्समतपत्तस्माच्छ्रान्तात्तप्तात्सन्तप्ताद्विंशिनोऽङ्गिरस(२)ऋषीन्निरमिमत,तान् विंशिनोऽङ्गिरस ऋषीनभ्यश्राम्यदभ्यतपत्समतपत्, तेभ्यः श्रान्तेभ्यस्तप्तेभ्यः सन्तप्तेभ्यो दशतयानाङ्गिरसानार्षेयान्निरमिमत, षोड़शिनोऽष्टादशिनो द्वादशिन एकर्चांस्तृचांश्चतुर्ऋचान् पञ्चर्चान् षड़र्चान् सप्तर्चानिति । तानङ्गिरस ऋषीनाङ्गिरसांश्चार्षेयानभ्यश्राम्यदभ्यतपत्समतपत्तेभ्यः श्रान्तेभ्यस्तप्तेभ्यः सन्तप्तेभ्यो यान् मन्त्रानपश्यत्स आङ्गिरसो वेदोऽ-

---

१ वरणोऽभवत् इति ख, ग, ।

१ विंशिनोऽङ्गिरस इति ख, ग, ।

भवत्तमाङ्गिरसं वेदमभ्यश्राम्यदभ्यतपत्समतपत्तस्माच्छ्रान्तात्तप्तात् सन्तप्तात्जनदिति ह्येतमक्षरं व्यभवत्। स य इच्छेत्सर्वैरेतैरङ्गिरोभिश्चाङ्गिरसैश्च कुर्वीयेत्येतयैव तं महाव्याहृत्या कुर्वीत सर्वैर्ह वा अस्यैतैरङ्गिरोभिश्चाङ्गिरसैश्च कृतं भवति य एवं वेद यश्चैवं विद्वानेवमेतया महाव्याहृत्या कुरुते ॥ ८ ॥

स ऊर्द्ध्वोऽतिष्ठत् स इमांल्लोकान् व्यष्टभ्नात्, तस्मादङ्गिरसोऽधीयान ऊर्द्ध्वस्तिष्ठति, तद् व्रतं स मनसा ध्यायेद्यद् वा अहं किञ्चन मनसा ध्यास्यामि तथैव तद् भविष्यति तद्ध स्म तथैव भवति।

तदप्येतदृचोक्तं। श्रेष्ठो ह वेदस्तपसोऽधिजातो ब्रह्मज्यानां क्षितये सम्बभूव(१) ऋज्यद् भूतं(२) यदसृज्यतेदं निवेशनमनृणं दूरमस्येति।
ता वा एता अङ्गिरसां यामयो(३) यन्मेनयः करोति मेनिभिर्वीर्थिं य एवं वेद॥९॥

स दिशोऽन्वैक्षत प्राचीं दक्षिणां प्रतीचीमुदीचीं ध्रुवामूर्द्ध्वामिति। तास्तत्रैवाभ्यश्राम्यदभ्यतपत्समतपत्ताभ्यः श्रान्ताभ्यस्तप्ताभ्यः सन्तप्ताभ्यः पञ्च वेदान्निरमिमत सर्पवेदं पिशाचवेदमसुरवेदमितिहासवेदं पुराणवेदमिति। स खलु प्राच्या एव दिशः सर्पवेदं निरमिमत, दक्षिणस्याः पिशाचवेदं, प्रतीच्या असुरवेदमुदीच्या इतिहासवेदं, ध्रुवायाश्चोर्द्ध्वायाश्च पुराणवेदं(४)। स तान् पञ्च वेदानभ्यश्राम्यदभ्यतपत्समतपत्तेभ्यः श्रान्तेभ्यस्तप्तेभ्यः सन्तप्तेभ्यः पञ्च

१ स बभूव इति ख, ग, घ,।

२ ऋज्यृगभूत मिति ख, ग,।

३ अङ्गिरसां च यामय इति घ,।

४ ध्रुवायाश्चोर्द्ध्वायाः पुराणवेदमिति घ,।

महाव्याहृतीर्निरमिमत वृधत् करद् गुहन् महत् तदिति। वृधदिति सर्पवेदात्, करदिति पिशाचवेदात्, गुहदित्यसुरवेदात्, महदितीतिहासवेदात्, तदिति पुराणवेदात्, स य इच्छेत्सर्वैरेतैः पञ्चभिर्वेदैः कुर्वीयेत्येताभिरेव तं महाव्याहृतिभिः कुर्वीत सर्वैर्ह वा अस्यैतैः पञ्चभिर्वेदैः कृतं भवति य एवं वेद यश्चैवं विद्वानेवमेताभिर्महाव्याहृतिभिः कुरुते॥ १०॥

स आवतश्च परावतश्चान्वैक्षत, तास्तत्रैवाभ्यश्राम्यदभ्यतपत्समतपत्ताभ्यः श्रान्ताभ्यस्तप्ताभ्यः सन्तप्ताभ्यः ओमित्यूर्ध्वमक्षरमुदक्रामत्। स य इच्छेत्सर्वाभिरेताभिरावद्भिश्च परावद्भिश्च कुर्वीयेत्येतयैव तं महाव्याहृत्या कुर्वीत सर्वाभिर्ह वा अस्यैताभिरावद्भिश्च परावद्भिश्च कृतं भवति य एवं वेद यश्चैवं विद्वानेवमेतया महाव्याहृत्या कुरुते॥ ११॥

स भूयोऽश्राम्यत्, भूयोऽतप्यत्, भूय आत्मानं समतपत्स मनस एव चन्द्रमसन्निरमिमत, नखेभ्यो नक्षत्राणि, लोमभ्य ओषधिवनस्पतीन्, क्षुद्रेभ्यः प्राणेभ्योऽन्यान् बहून् देवान्। स भूयोऽश्राम्यद् भूयोऽतप्यत्, भूय आत्मानं समतपत् स एतं त्रिवृतं सप्ततन्तुमेकविंशतिसंस्थं यज्ञमपश्यत्।

तदप्येतदृचोक्तं। अग्निर्यज्ञं त्रिवृतं सप्ततन्तुमिति।

अथाप्येष प्राक्नोदितः श्लोकः प्रत्यभिवदति सप्त सुत्याः सप्त च पाकयज्ञा इति॥ १२॥

तमाहरत् येनायजत(१)तस्याग्निर्होताऽऽसीत्, वायुरध्वर्युः, सूर्य-

१ तमाहरत्तेनायजत इति ख' ग,।

उद्गाता, चन्द्रमा ब्रह्मा, पर्ज्जन्यः सदस्य, ओषधिवनस्पतयश्च-मसा, अध्वर्य्यवो विश्वेदेवा होत्रका, अथर्वाङ्गिरसो गोप्तारस्तं ह स्मै-तमेवं विद्वांसः पूर्वे श्रोत्रिया यज्ञं ततं सावसाय ह स्माहैत्यभि-व्रजन्ति, मा नोऽयं घर्म उद्यतः, प्रमत्तानाममृताः प्रजाः प्रसाची-दिति, तान् वायेतान्(१) परिरचकान् सदःप्रसर्पकानित्याचचते दक्षिणासमृद्धांस्तदु ह स्माह प्रजापतिर्यद्दै यज्ञेऽकुशला(२)ऋत्विजो भवन्त्यचरितिनो ब्रह्मचर्य्य(३)मपराग्या वा तद्वै यज्ञस्य विरिष्टमित्या-चचते। यज्ञस्य विरिष्टमनुयजमानो विरिष्यते, यजमानस्य विरिष्ट-मन्वृत्विजो विरिष्यन्त, ऋत्विजां विरिष्टमनुदक्षिणा विरिष्यन्ते, दक्षिणानां विरिष्टमनुयजमानः पुत्त्रपशुभिर्विरिष्यते, पुत्त्रपशूनां विरिष्टमनु यजमानः स्वर्गेण लोकेन विरिष्यते, स्वर्गस्य लोकस्य विरिष्टमनु तस्यार्द्धस्य योगचेमो विरिष्यते, यस्मिन्नर्द्धे यजन्त इति ब्राह्मणम् ॥ १२ ॥

तं ह स्मैतमेवं विद्वांसं ब्रह्माणं यज्ञविरिष्टौ वा यज्ञविरिष्टिनो वेत्युपाधावेरन् नमस्ते अस्तु भगवन् यज्ञस्य नो विरिष्टं सन्धेहीति, तद्यत्रैव विरिष्टं स्यात्तत्राग्नीनुपसमाधाय शान्त्युदकं कृत्वा पृथिव्यै श्रोत्रायेति त्रिरेवाग्नीन् सम्प्रोचति, त्रिः पर्य्युचति, त्रिः कारय-माणमाचामयति च, सम्प्रोचति च, यज्ञवास्तु च सम्प्रोचत्यथापि वेदानां रसेन यज्ञस्य विरिष्टं सन्धीयते, तद्यथा लवणेन सुवर्णं

---

१ तान् वा एतानिति ख, ग, घ, ।

२ यद्वै यज्ञाकुशला इति ख, ग, ।

३ ब्रह्मचर्य्यामिति घ, ।

सन्दध्यात्सुवर्णेन रजतं, रजतेन लोहं, लोहेन सीसं, सीसेन एवमेव-
मेवास्य यज्ञस्य विरिष्टं सन्धीयते, यज्ञस्य सन्धितिमनुयजमानः
सन्धीयते, यजमानस्य सन्धितिमन्वृत्विजः सन्धीयन्त, ऋत्विजां
सन्धितिमनुदक्षिणाः सन्धीयन्ते दक्षिणानां सन्धितिमनुयजमानः
पुत्रपशुभिः सन्धीयते, पुत्रपशूनां सन्धितिमनुयजमानः स्वर्गेण
लोकेन सन्धीयते, स्वर्गस्य लोकस्य सन्धितिमनु तस्यार्द्धस्य योग-
क्षेमः सन्धीयते, यस्मिन्नर्द्धे यजन्त इति ब्राह्मणम् ॥ १४ ॥

तदु ह स्माहाथर्वा देवो विजानन्यज्ञविरिष्टानन्दानीत्युपशम-
येरन् (१)यज्ञे प्रायश्चित्तिः क्रियतेऽपि च यदु बह्विव यज्ञे (२) विलोमः
क्रियते नचैवास्य काचनार्त्तिर्भवति न च यज्ञविष्कन्धमुपयात्यपहन्ति
पुनर्मृत्युमपात्येति पुनराजातिं कामचारोऽस्य सर्वेषु लोकेषु भाति
य एवं वेद यश्चैवं विद्वान् ब्रह्मा भवति यस्य चैवं विद्वान् ब्रह्मा
दक्षिणतः सदोऽध्यास्ते यस्य चैवं विद्वान् ब्रह्मा दक्षिणत उदङ्मुख
आसीनो यज्ञ आज्याहुतीर्जुहोतीति ब्राह्मणम् ॥ १५ ॥

ब्रह्म ह वै ब्रह्माणं पुष्करे ससृजे, स खलु ब्रह्मा सृष्टश्चिन्ता-
मापेदे केनाहमेकेनाक्षरेण सर्वांश्च कामान् सर्वांश्च लोकान्
सर्वांश्च देवान् सर्वांश्च वेदान् सर्वांश्च यज्ञान् सर्वांश्च शब्दान्
सर्वाश्च व्युष्टीः सर्वाणि च भूतानि स्थावरजङ्गमान्यनुभवेयमिति
स ब्रह्मचर्य्यमचरत् स ओमित्येतदक्षरमपश्यद् (३) द्विवर्णञ्चतुर्मात्रं
सर्वव्यापि सर्वविभ्वयातयामब्रह्म ब्राह्मीं व्याहृतिं ब्रह्मदैवतं तया

१ यज्ञविरिष्टानन्दानित्युपशमयेरन्निति घ, ।

२ य उ बह्विव यज्ञे इति ख, ग, ।

३ स तु ओमित्येतदक्षरमपश्यदिति ख, ग, ।

सर्वांश्च कामान् सर्वांश्च लोकान् सर्वांश्च देवान् सर्वांश्च वेदान् सर्वांश्च यज्ञान् सर्वांश्च शब्दान् सर्वाश्च व्युष्टीः सर्वाणि च भूतानि स्थावरजङ्गमान्यन्वभवत्तस्य प्रथमेन वर्णेनापस्नेहश्चान्वभवत्तस्य द्वितीयेन वर्णेन तेजो ज्योतींष्यन्वभवत् ॥ १६ ॥

तस्य प्रथमया स्वरमात्रया पृथिवीमग्निमोषधिवनस्पतीन् ऋग्वेदं भूरिति व्याहृतिर्गायत्रं(१) छन्दस्त्रिवृतं स्तोमं प्राचीं दिशं वसन्तमृतुं वाचमध्यात्मं जिह्वां रसमितीन्द्रियाण्यन्वभवत् ॥ १७ ॥

तस्य द्वितीयया स्वरमात्रयाऽन्तरिक्षं वायुं यजुर्वेदं भुव इति व्याहृतिस्त्रैष्टुभं (२) छन्दः पञ्चदशं स्तोमं प्रतीचीं दिशं ग्रीष्मऋतुं प्राणमध्यात्मन्नासिके गन्धघ्राणमितीन्द्रियाण्यन्वभवत् ॥ १८ ॥

तस्य तृतीयया स्वरमात्रया दिवमादित्यं सामवेदं स्वरिति व्याहृतिर्जागतं छन्दः सप्तदशं स्तोममुदीचीं दिशं वर्षाऋतुं ज्योतिरध्यात्मं चक्षुषी दर्शनमितीन्द्रियाण्यन्वभवत् ॥ १९ ॥

तस्य वकारमात्रयाऽपश्चन्द्रमसमथर्ववेदन्नक्षत्राण्यो३मिति स्वमात्मानं जनदित्यङ्गिरसामानुष्टुभं छन्द एकविंशं स्तोमं दक्षिणां दिशं शरदमृतुं मनोऽध्यात्मं ज्ञानं ज्ञेयमितीन्द्रियाण्यन्वभवत् ॥ २० ॥

तस्य मकारश्रुत्येतिहासपुराणं वाको वाक्यगाथानाराशंसीरुपनिषदोऽनुशासनानामिति वृधत् करद्रुहन् महत्तच्छमो३मिति व्याहृतीः स्वरशम्यनानातन्त्रीः (३) स्वरनृत्यगीतवादित्राण्यन्वभवच्चैत्ररथं दैवतं वैद्युतं ज्योतिर्बार्हतं छन्दस्तृणवत्त्रयस्त्रिंशौ स्तोमौ

१ व्याहृतिं गायत्रमिति ख, घ, ।

२ व्याहृतिं त्रैष्टुभमिति ख, घ, ।

३ स्वरशम्यनानातन्त्रीरिति ख, ग, घ, ।

भुवामूर्द्ध्वां दिशं हेमन्तशिशिरावृतू श्रोत्रमध्यात्मं शब्दश्रवणमितीन्द्रियाण्यन्वभवत् ॥ २१ ॥

सैषैकाचरर्क्तग् ब्रह्मणस्तपसोऽग्रे प्रादुर्बभूव ब्रह्म वेदस्याथर्वणं शुक्रमत एव मन्त्राः प्रादुर्बभूवुः स तु खलु मन्त्राणामतपसाशुश्रूषाऽनध्यायाध्ययनेन यदूनञ्च विरिष्टञ्च यातयामञ्च करोति तदथर्वणां तेजसा प्रत्याप्याययेन् मन्त्राश्च मामभिमुखीभवेयुर्गर्भा इव मातरमभिजिघांसुः पुरस्तादोङ्कारं प्रयुङ्क्त एतयैव तदृचा प्रत्याप्याययेदेषैव यज्ञस्य पुरस्ताद्युज्यत एषा पश्चात् सर्वत एतया यज्ञस्तायते ।

तदप्येतदृचोक्तं । या पुरस्ताद्युज्यत (१) ऋचोऽक्षरे परमे व्योमन्निति ।

तदेतदक्षरं ब्राह्मणो यं काममिच्छेत् त्रिरात्रोपोषितः प्राङ्मुखो वाग्यतो बर्हिष्युपविश्य सहस्रकृत्व आवर्त्तयेत् (२) सिद्धन्त्यस्यार्थाः सर्वकर्माणि चेति ब्राह्मणम् ॥ २२ ॥

वसोर्धाराणामैन्द्रनगर(३)न्तदसुराः पर्य्यवारयन्त, ते देवा भीता आसन् क इमानसुरानपहनिष्यतीति, त ओङ्कारं ब्रह्मणः पुत्रं ज्येष्ठं ददृशुस्ते तमब्रुवन् भवता मुखेनेमानसुरान् जयेमेति । स होवाच किं मे प्रतीवाहो भविष्यतीति वरं वृणीष्वेति वृणा इति स वरमवृणीत न मामनीरयित्वा ब्राह्मणा ब्रह्म वदेयुर्यदि वदेयुरब्रह्म तत्स्यादिति तथेति ते देवा देवयजनस्योत्तरार्द्धेऽसुरैः संयता आसंस्ता-

---

१ पुरस्ताद् युज्यन्त इति घ,

२ सहस्रकृत्व आवर्त्तयेदिति घ, ।

३ मैन्द्रं नगरमिति घ,

नोङ्कारेणाग्नीध्रीयाद्देवा असुरान् पराभावयन्त, तद्यत्पराभावयन्त तस्मादोङ्कारः पूर्वउच्यते(१)। यो ह वा एतमोङ्कारं न वेदावशः-स्यादित्यथ य एवं वेद ब्रह्म वशः स्यादिति तस्मादोङ्कार ऋच्यृग् भवति यजुषि यजुः साम्नि साम सूत्रे सूत्रं ब्राह्मण ब्राह्मणं श्लोके श्लोकः प्रणवे प्रणव इति ब्राह्मणम् ॥ २३ ॥

ओङ्कारं पृच्छामः को धातुः किं प्रातिपदिकं किं नामाख्यातं किं लिङ्गं किं वचनं का विभक्तिः कः प्रत्ययः कः स्वर उपसर्गो निपातः किं वै व्याकरणं को विकारः को विकारी कतिमात्रः कतिवर्णः कत्यक्षरः कतिपदः कः संयोगः किं स्थानानुप्रदानकरणं शिक्षुकाः किमुच्चारयन्ति किं छन्दः को वर्ण इति पूर्वे प्रश्ना, अथोत्तरे मन्त्रः कल्पो ब्राह्मणमृग्यजुः साम कस्माद्ब्रह्मवादिन ओङ्कारमादितः कुर्वन्ति किं देवतं किं ज्योतिषं किं निरुक्तं किं स्थानं का प्रकृतिः किमध्यात्ममिति षट्त्रिंशत् प्रश्नाः पूर्वोत्तराणां त्रयो वर्गा द्वादशका एतैरोङ्कारं व्याख्यास्यामः ॥ २४ ॥

इन्द्रः प्रजापतिमपृच्छद् भगवन्नभिसृय पृच्छामीति, पृच्छ वत्सेत्यब्रवीत्, किमयमोङ्कारः कस्य पुत्त्रः किञ्चैतच्छन्दः किञ्चैतद्वर्णः किञ्चैतद् ब्रह्मा ब्रह्म सम्पद्यते तस्माद् वै तद्भद्रमोङ्कारं पूर्व्वमालेभे स्वरितोदात्त एकाक्षर ओङ्कार ऋग्वेदे, त्रैस्वर्य्योदात्त एकाक्षर ओङ्कारो यजुर्वेदे, दीर्घप्लुतोदात्त एकाक्षर ओङ्कारः सामवेदे, ह्रस्वोदात्त एकाक्षर ओङ्कारोऽथर्ववेद उदात्तोदात्तद्विपद अ उ इत्यर्द्धचतस्रो मात्रा मकारे व्यञ्जनमित्याहुर्या सा प्रथमा मात्रा ब्रह्मदेवत्या

१. पर्वमुच्यते इति ख, ग, घ,।

रक्ता वर्णेन यस्तां ध्यायते नित्यं स गच्छेद् ब्राह्मं पदं,(१) या सा द्वितीया मात्रा विष्णुदेवत्या कृष्णा वर्णेन यस्तां ध्यायते नित्यं स गच्छेद् वैष्णवं पदं, या सा तृतीया मात्रैशानदेवत्या कपिला वर्णेन यस्तां ध्यायते नित्यं स गच्छेदैशानं पदं, या सार्धचतुर्थी मात्रा सर्वदेवत्या व्यक्तीभूता खं विचरति शुद्धस्फटिकसन्निभा वर्णेन यस्तां ध्यायते नित्यं स गच्छेत्पदमनामकमोङ्कारस्य चोत्पत्तिर्विप्रो यो न जानाति तत्पुनरुपनयनं तस्माद् ब्राह्मणवचनमादर्त्तव्यं यथा लातव्यो गोत्रो ब्रह्मणः पुत्रो गायत्रं छन्दः शुक्लो वर्णः पुंसो वत्सो रुद्रो देवता ओङ्कारो वेदानाम् ॥ २५ ॥

को धातुरित्याद्यर्धातुरवतिमप्येके रूपसामान्यादर्थसामान्यन्नेदीयस्तस्मादापेरोङ्कारः सर्वमाप्नोतीत्यर्थः कृदन्तमर्थवत् प्रातिपदिकमदर्शनं प्रत्ययस्य नाम सम्पद्यते निपातेषु चैनं वैयाकरणा उदात्तं समामनन्ति तदव्ययीभूतमन्वर्थवाची शब्दो न व्येति कदाचनेति।

सदृशं त्रिषु लिङ्गेषु सर्वासु च विभक्तिषु। वचनेषु च सर्वेषु यन्न व्येति तदव्ययं॥ को विकारी च्यवते प्रसारणमाप्नोतिरावात्प्रकारो विकार्यावादित ओङ्कारो विक्रियते द्वितीयो मकार एवं द्विवर्ण एकाक्षर ओमित्योङ्कारो निर्वृत्तः॥ २६ ॥

कतिमात्र इत्यादेस्तिस्रो मात्रा अभ्यादाने हि प्लवते मकारश्चतुर्थीं किं स्थानमित्युभावोष्ठौ स्थानं नादानुप्रदानकरणी च द्वयस्थानं सन्ध्यक्षरमवर्णलेशः कण्ठ्यो यथोक्तशेषः पूर्वो विवृतकरणस्थितश्च द्वितीयस्पृष्टकरणस्थितश्च न संयोगो विद्यत(२) आख्यातोप-

---

१ ब्राह्मसम्पदमिति ख, ग, ब्राह्मपदमिति घ,।

२ संयोगो विद्यत इति घ,।

सर्गानुदात्तस्वरितलिङ्गविभक्तिवचनानि च संस्थानाध्यायिन (१) आचार्य्याः पूर्वे बभूवुः श्रवणादेव प्रतिपद्यन्ते नकारणं पृच्छन्त्य-थापरपत्तीयाणां कविः पञ्चालचण्डः(२) परिपृच्छको बभूवां वु पृथगुन्नीथदोषान् भवन्तो ब्रुवन्त्विति तद्वाप्युपलचयेद्वर्णाचरपदा-ङ्क्शो विभक्त्यामृषिनिषेवितामिति वाचं स्तुवन्ति तस्मात् कारणं ब्रूमो वर्णानामयमिदं भविष्यतीति षड़ङ्गविदस्तत्तथाऽधीमहे। किञ्छन्द इति गायत्रं हि छन्दो गायत्री वै देवानामेकाचरा श्वेतवर्णा च व्याख्याता द्वौ द्वादशकौ वर्गावेतद्व वैयाकरणं (३) धात्वर्थवचनं शैच्यं (४) छन्दोवचनं चाथोत्तरौ द्वौ द्वादशकौ वर्गौ वेदरहसिकौ व्याख्याता मन्त्रः कल्पो ब्राह्मणमृग्यजुःसामाथर्व-णेषा व्याहृतिश्चतुर्णां वेदानामानुपूर्वेणोंभूर्भुवस्वरिति व्याहृ-तयः॥ २७॥

असमीच्यप्रवह्लितानि(५) श्रूयन्ते द्वापरादावृषीणामेकदेशो दोष-पतिरिह(६) चिन्तामापेदे त्रिभिः सोमः पातव्यः समाप्तमिव भवति तस्मादृग्यजुःसामान्यपक्रान्ततेजांस्यासंस्तत्र महर्षयः परिदेवयाञ्च-क्रिरे महच्छोकभयं प्राप्तास्मो न चैतत् सर्वैः समभिहितं ते वयं

---

१ सञ्क्रिन्नाध्यायिन इति ख, ग, सञ्छन्नाध्यायिन इति घ,।

२ पञ्चालपण्ड इति ग,।

३ एतद्वैयाकरणमिति घ,।

४ शैच्चमिति ख, ग, घ,।

५ असमीच्यप्रवह्लितानीति ख, ग, घ,।

६ दोषपतीच इति क,।

भगवन्तमेवोपधावाम(१) सर्वेषामेव शर्म भवानीति(२) तं तथेत्युक्त्वा तूष्णीमतिष्ठन्नानुपसन्नेभ्य इत्युपोपसीदामेति नीचैर्बभूवुः। स एभ्य उपनीय प्रोवाच मामिकामेव व्याहृतिमादितः आदितः कुरुध्वमित्येवं मामका आधीयन्ते।

नर्त्ते भृग्वङ्गिरोविद्भ्यः सोमः पातव्य ऋत्विजः पराभवन्ति यजमानो रजसापध्वस्यति श्रुतिश्चापध्वस्ता तिष्ठतीत्येवमेवोत्तरोत्तरायोगात्तोकं तोकमग्राध्वमित्येवं प्रतापो न पराभविष्यतीति तथाह तथाह भगवन्निति प्रतिपेदिर आप्याययंस्ते तथा वीतशोकभया बभूवुः। तस्माद् ब्रह्मवादिन ओङ्कारमादितः कुर्वन्ति॥२८॥

किन्देवतमित्यृचामग्निर्देवतन्तदेव ज्योतिर्गायत्रं छन्दः पृथिवी स्थानं। अ॒ग्निमी॑ले॒(३) पु॒रोहि॑तं य॒ज्ञस्य॑ दे॒वमृ॒त्विज॑म्। होता॑रं रत्न॒धात॑ममित्येवमादिं कृत्वा ऋग्वेदमधीयते।

यजुषां वायुर्देवतं तदेव ज्योतिः त्रैष्टुभं छन्दोऽन्तरिक्षं स्थानं। इषे (४) त्वोर्जे त्वा वायव स्थ देवो वः सविता प्रार्पयतु। श्रेष्ठतमाय कर्म्मण इत्येवमादिं कृत्वा यजुर्वेदमधीयते

साम्नामादित्यो देवतं तदेव ज्योतिर्जागतं छन्दो द्यौ स्थानं। अग्न आयाहि वीतये गृणानो हव्यदातये। निहोता सत्सि बर्हिषीत्येवमादिं कृत्वा सामवेदमधीयते।

अथर्वणां चन्द्रमा देवतं तदेव ज्योतिः

---

१ उपधावाम इति ख, ग,।

२ भवतीति इति घ,।

३ अग्निमीडे इति घ,।

४ इषे इति ख, ग, घ,।

सर्वाणि छन्दांस्यापः स्थानं। शन्नो देवीरभिष्टय इत्येवमादिं कृत्वा अथर्ववेदमधीयते। अद्भ्यः स्थावरजङ्गमो भूतग्रामः सम्भवति, तस्मात् सर्वमापोमयं भूतं सर्वं भृग्वङ्गिरोमयं। अन्तरैते त्रयो वेदा भृगूनङ्गिरसः श्रिता इत्यब्विति प्रकृतिरपामोङ्कारेण चैतस्माद् व्यासः पुरोवाच भृग्वङ्गिरोविदा संस्कृतोऽन्यान् वेदानधीयीत नान्यत्र संस्कृतो (१) भृग्वङ्गिरसोऽधीयीत अथ सामवेदे खिलश्रुतिः(२) ब्रह्मचर्येण चैतस्मादथर्वाङ्गिरसो ह यो वेदः स वेद सर्वमिति ब्राह्मणं॥ २९॥

अध्यात्ममात्मभैषज्यमात्मकैवल्यमोङ्कार आत्मानं निरुध्य सङ्गममात्रीं भूतार्थचिन्तां(३) चिन्तयेदतिक्रम्य वेदेभ्यः सर्वपरमाध्यात्मफलं प्राप्नोतीत्यर्थः सवितर्कं ज्ञानमयमित्येतैः प्रश्नैः प्रतिवचनैश्च यथार्थं पदमनुविचिन्त्य प्रकरणज्ञो हि प्रबलो विषयी स्यात् सर्वस्मिन्वाक्यो वाक्य इति ब्राह्मणम्॥ ३०॥

एतद्ध स्मैतद्विद्वांसमेकादशाक्षम्मौद्गल्यं ग्लावो मैत्रेयोऽभ्याजगाम स तस्मिन् ब्रह्मचर्यं वसतो विज्ञायोवाच किं स्विन्मर्या अयं तं मौद्गल्योऽध्येति यदस्मिन् ब्रह्मचर्यं वसतीति तद्धि मौद्गल्यस्यान्तेवासी शुश्राव सः आचार्यायाव्रज्याचचष्टे दुरधीयानं वा अयं भवन्तमवोचद्योऽयमद्यातिथिर्भवति किं सौम्य विद्वानिति। त्रीन् वेदान् ब्रूते भो३इति तस्य सौम्य यो विस्पष्टो विजिगीषोऽन्ते-

१ भृगवङ्गिरो विदा संस्कृतोऽन्यान् वेदानधीयीत नान्यत्र संस्कृत इति ख, ग,।

२ सामवेदेऽखिलश्रुतिरिति क,।

३ भूतार्थचिन्तार्थमिति क,।

४ एकादशाक्षं मौद्गल्यमिति घ,

षासी तस्मै ह्वयेति, तमाशुहाव तमभ्युवाचासाविति भो३इति किं सौम्य त आचार्य्योऽध्येतोति, त्रीन् वेदान् ब्रूते भो३इति, यन्नु खलु सौम्यास्माभिः सर्व्वं वेदा मुखतो गृहीताः कथन्त एवमाचार्य्यो भाषते कथं नु शिष्टाः शिष्टेभ्य एवं(१) भाषेरन् यं ह्येनमहं प्रश्नं प्रच्छामि न तं विवक्ष्यति न ह्येनमध्येतीति। स ह मौद्गल्यः स्वमन्तेवासिनमुवाच, परेहि सौम्य ग्लावं मैत्रेयमुपसीदाधीहि भोः सावित्रीं गायत्रीञ्चतुर्विंशतियोनिं द्वादशमिथुनां यस्या भृग्वङ्गिरसश्चक्षुर्यस्यां सर्व्वमिदं श्रितं, तां भवान् प्रब्रवीत्विति स चेत्सौम्य दुरधीयानो भविष्यत्याचार्य्योवाच ब्रह्मचारी ब्रह्मचारिणे सावित्रीं प्राहेति वक्ष्यति तत्त्वं ब्रूयात् दुरधीयानन्तं वै भवान् मौद्गल्यमवोचत् स त्वा यं प्रश्नमप्राक्षीन्न तं व्यवोचः पुरा संवत्सरादार्त्तिमाक्ष्यसीति(२) ॥ २१ ॥

स तत्राजगाम यत्रेतरो बभूव, तं ह पप्रच्छ स ह न प्रतिपेदे, तं होवाच दुरधीयानं तं वै भवान् मौद्गल्यमवोचत् स त्वा यं प्रश्नमप्राक्षीन्न तं व्यवोचः पुरा संवत्सरादार्त्तिमाक्ष्यसीति(३)। स ह मैत्रेयः(४) स्वानन्तेवासिन उवाच यथार्थं भवन्तो यथागृहं यथामनो विप्रसृज्यन्तां दुरधीयानं वा अहं मौद्गल्यमवोचं स मा यं प्रश्नमप्राक्षीन्न तं व्यवोचं तमुपेष्यामि(५) शान्तिं करिष्यामीति। स ह मैत्रेयः

१ शिष्टेभ्य इदमिति घ,

२ मारिष्यसीति ख, ग, । मार्ष्यसीति घ, ।

३ दार्त्तिमार्ष्यसीति ख, ।

४ स ह मौद्गल्य इति क, घ, ।

५ उपेष्याम ति ख, ग, घ, ।

प्रातः समित्पाणिर्मौद्गल्यमुपससादासावाग्रहं(१) भो मैत्रेयः किमर्थमिति दुरधीयानं वा अहं भवन्तमवोचं त्वं मा यम्मश्नमप्राचीर्न तं व्यवोचं त्वामुपेष्यामि शान्तिं करिष्यामीति,स होवाचात्र वा उपेतश्च सर्वञ्च कृतं पापकेन त्वा यानेन चरन्तमाहुरथोऽयं मम कल्याणस्तं ते ददामि (२) तेन याहीति। स होवाचैतदेवात्रात्विषञ्चानृशंस्यञ्च यथा भवानाहोपायामित्येवं भवन्तमिति तं होपेयाय तं होपेत्य पप्रच्छ किंस्विदाहुर्भोः सवितुर्वरेण्यं भर्गो देवस्य कवयः किमाहुर्धियो विचक्ष्व(३) यदि ताः प्रवेत्थ प्रचोदयात्सविता याभिरेतीति।

तस्मा एतत् प्रोवाच वेदाश्छन्दांसि सवितुर्वरेण्यं भर्गो देवस्य कवयोऽन्नमाहुः। कर्माणि धियस्तदु ते ब्रवीमि(४) प्रचोदयात्सविता याभिरेतीति।

तमुपसङ्गृह्य पप्रच्छाधीहि भोः कः सविता का सावित्री ॥३२॥

मन एव सविता, वाक् सावित्री, यत्र ह्येव मनस्तद् वाक्, यत्र वै वाक् तन्मन, इत्येते द्वे योनी एकं मिथुनम्, अग्निरेव सविता, पृथिवी सावित्री, यत्र ह्येवाग्निस्तत् पृथिवी यत्र वै पृथिवी तदग्निरित्येते द्वे योनी एकं मिथुनं, वायुरेव सविताऽन्तरिक्षं सावित्री यत्र ह्येव वायुस्तदन्तरिक्षं, यत्र वा अन्तरिक्षं तद्वायुरित्येते द्वे योनी एकं मिथुनम्, आदित्य एव सविता द्यौः सावित्री यत्र ह्येवादित्यस्तद्द्यौर्यत्र वै द्यौस्तदादित्य इत्येते द्वे योनी एकं मिथुनं, चन्द्रमा एव

---

१ उपससादासाया अहमिति क, घ, ।

२ दधामीति क, ।

३ धियो विचष्ट इति घ, ।

४ प्रब्रवीमीति ख, ग, घ, ।

सविता, नक्षत्राणि सावित्री, यत्र ह्येव चन्द्रमास्तन्नक्षत्राणि यत्र वै नक्षत्राणि तच्चन्द्रमा, इत्येते द्वे योनी एकं मिथुनम्, अहरेव सविता, रात्रिः सावित्री, यत्र ह्येवाहस्तद्रात्रिर्यत्र वै रात्रिस्तदहरित्येते द्वे योनी एकं मिथुनम्, उष्णमेव सविता, शीतं सावित्री, यत्र ह्येवोष्णं, तच्छीतं, यत्र वै शीतं तदुष्णमित्येते द्वे योनी एकं मिथुनम्, अभ्रमेव सविता, वर्षं सावित्री, यत्र ह्येवाभ्रन्तद्वर्षं यत्र वै वर्षं तदभ्रमित्येते द्वे योनी एकं मिथुनं, विद्युदेव सविता स्तनयित्नुः सावित्री यत्र ह्येव विद्युत् तत् स्तनयित्नुः यत्र वै स्तनयित्नुस्तद्विद्युदित्येते द्वे योनी एकं मिथुनं, प्राण एव सविता, अन्नं सावित्री, यत्र ह्येव प्राणस्तदन्नं यत्र वा अन्नं तत् प्राण इत्येते द्वे योनी एकं मिथुनं, वेदा एव सविता छन्दांसि सावित्री, यत्र ह्येव वेदास्तच्छन्दांसि यत्र वै छन्दांसि तद् वेदा इत्येते द्वे योनी एकं मिथुनं, यज्ञ एव सविता, दक्षिणा सावित्री, यत्र ह्येव यज्ञस्तत् दक्षिणा यत्र वै दक्षिणास्तद्यज्ञ इत्येते द्वे योनी एकं मिथुनम्, एतद्ध स्मैतद्विद्वांसमोपाकारिमासस्तुर्ब्रह्मचारी ते संस्थित इत्यथैत आसस्तुराचित इव चितो बभूवाथोत्थाय प्राव्राजीदित्येतद्वाऽहं वेद नैतासु योनिष्वित एतेभ्यो वा मिथुनेभ्यः सम्भूतो ब्रह्मचारी मम पुरायुषः प्रेयादिति ॥ ३२ ॥

ब्रह्म हेदं श्रियं प्रतिष्ठामायतनमैक्षत तत्तपस्व(१) यदि तद् व्रते ध्रियेत तत्सत्ये प्रत्यतिष्ठत् स सविता सावित्र्या ब्राह्मणं सृष्ट्वा तत्-सावित्रीं पर्यदधात्(२) तत् सवितुर्वरेण्यमिति सावित्र्याः प्रथमः पादः, पृथिव्यर्चं समदधादृचाऽग्निमग्निना श्रियं, श्रिया स्त्रियं,

१ तत्तपस्वेति ख, ग, ।

२ पर्यदध्यादिति ख, ग, ।

स्त्रिया मिथुनं, मिथुनेन प्रजां, प्रजया कर्म, कर्म्मणा तपस्तपसा सत्यं, सत्येन ब्रह्म, ब्रह्मणा ब्राह्मणं, ब्राह्मणेन व्रतं व्रतेन वै ब्राह्मणः संशितोभवत्यशून्यो भवत्यविच्छिन्नो भवत्यविच्छिन्नोऽस्य तन्तुरविच्छिन्नं जीवनं भवनं भवति(१) य एवं वेद यश्चैवं विद्वानेवमेतं सावित्र्याः प्रथमं पादं व्याचष्टे ॥ ३४ ॥

भर्गो देवस्य धीमहीति सावित्र्या द्वितीयः पादोऽन्तरिक्षेण यजुः समदधात्(२) यजुषा वायुं, वायुनाऽभ्रमभ्रेण वर्षं, वर्षेणौषधिवनस्पतीनोषधिवनस्पतिभिः पशून् पशुभिः कर्म्म कर्म्मणा तपस्तपसा सत्यं, सत्येन ब्रह्म, ब्रह्मणा ब्राह्मणं, ब्राह्मणेन व्रतं व्रतेन वै ब्राह्मणः संशितो भवत्यशून्यो भवत्यविच्छिन्नो भवत्यविच्छिन्नोऽस्य तन्तुरविच्छिन्नं जीवनं भवति य एवं वेद यश्चैवं विद्वानेवमेतं सावित्र्या द्वितीयं पादं व्याचष्टे ॥ ३५ ॥

धियो यो नः प्रचोदयादिति सावित्र्यास्तृतीयः पादो दिवा साम समदधा(३) त्साम्नाऽऽदित्यमादित्येन रश्मीन् रश्मिभिर्वर्षं, वर्षेणौषधिवनस्पतीनोषधिवनस्पतिभिः पशून् पशुभिः कर्म कर्मणा तपस्तपसा सत्यं सत्येन ब्रह्म, ब्रह्मणा ब्राह्मणं ब्राह्मणेन व्रतं व्रतेन वै ब्राह्मणः संशितो भवत्यशून्यो भवत्यविच्छिन्नो भवत्यविच्छिन्नोऽस्य तन्तुरविच्छिन्नं जीवनं भवति य एवं वेद यश्चैवं विद्वानेवमेतं सावित्र्यास्तृतीयं पादं व्याचष्टे ॥ ३६ ॥

तेन ह वा एवं विदुषा ब्राह्मणेन ब्रह्माभिपन्नं ग्रसितं परामृष्टं

१ जीवनं भवतीति ख, ग, ।

२ समदधादिति ख, ।

३ दिवा सा दधादिति ख, गग, ।

ब्रह्मणाऽऽकाशमभिपन्नं ग्रसितं परामृष्टमाकाशेन वायुरभिपन्नो ग्रसितः परामृष्टो, वायुना ज्योतिरभिपन्नं ग्रसितं परामृष्टं, ज्योतिषाऽपोऽभिपन्ना ग्रसिताः परामृष्टा अद्भिर्भूमिरभिपन्ना ग्रसिता परामृष्टा, भूम्याऽन्नमभिपन्नं ग्रसितं परामृष्टमन्नेन प्राणोऽभिपन्नो ग्रसितः परामृष्टः प्राणेन मनोऽभिपन्नं ग्रसितं परामृष्टं, मनसा वागभिपन्ना ग्रसिता परामृष्टा, वाचा वेदा अभिपन्ना ग्रसिताः परामृष्टा, वेदैर्यज्ञोऽभिपन्नो ग्रसितः परामृष्टस्तानि ह वा एतानि द्वादशमहाभूतान्येवं विधिप्रतिष्ठितानि(१) तेषां यज्ञ एव परार्द्ध्यः ॥ २७ ॥

तं ह स्मैतमेवं विद्वांसो मन्यन्ते विद्मैनमिति याथातथ्यमविद्वांसोऽयं यज्ञो वेदेषु प्रतिष्ठितो, वेदा वाचि प्रतिष्ठिता, वाङ् मनसि प्रतिष्ठिता, मनः प्राणे प्रतिष्ठितं, प्राणोऽन्ने प्रतिष्ठितो, ऽन्नं भूमौ प्रतिष्ठितं, भूमिरप्सु प्रतिष्ठिता, आपो ज्योतिषि प्रतिष्ठिता, ज्योतिर्वायौ प्रतिष्ठितं, वायुराकाशे प्रतिष्ठित, आकाशं ब्रह्मणि प्रतिष्ठितं, ब्रह्म ब्राह्मणे ब्रह्मविदि प्रतिष्ठितं, यो ह वा एवं वित् स ब्रह्मवित्, पुण्यां च कीर्त्तिं लभते सुरभींश्च गन्धान् सोऽपहतपाप्मानन्त्यश्रियमश्नुते(२) य एवं वेद यश्चैवं विद्वानेवमेतां वेदानां मातरं सावित्रीसम्पदमुपनिषदमुपास्त इति ब्राह्मणम् ॥ २८ ॥

आपो गर्भं जनयन्तीरित्यपाङ्गर्भः पुरुषः स यज्ञोऽग्नियँज्ञः प्रणीयमानः प्राङ्णायते, तस्मादाचमनीयं पूर्वमाहारयति स यदाचामति त्रिराचामति द्विः परिशुम्भत्यायुरवरुध्य पाप्मानं निर्णुदत्युपसाद्य यजुषोद्धृत्य मन्त्रान् प्रयुज्यावसाय प्राचीः शाखाः

---

१ एवं वेदिप्रतिष्ठितानीति ख, ग, ।

२ पाप्मामन्त्यश्रियमश्नुते इति घ, ।

स आचामति । स यत्पूर्व्वमाचामति सप्त प्राणांस्तानेतेनास्मिन्नाप्याययति या इमा बाह्याः शरीरान्मात्रास्तद्यथैतदग्निं वायुमादित्यं चन्द्रमसमपः पशूनन्यांश्च प्रजास्तानेतेनास्मिन्नाप्याययत्यापोऽमृतं । स यद् द्वितीयमाचामति सप्तापानांस्तानेतेनास्मिन्नाप्याययति या इमा बाह्याः शरीरान् मात्रा(१)स्तद्यथैतत्पौर्णमासीमष्टकाममावास्यां श्रद्धां दीक्षां यज्ञं दक्षिणास्तानेतेनास्मिन्नाप्याययत्यापोऽमृतं । स यत्तृतीयमाचामति सप्त व्यानांस्तानेतेनास्मिन्नाप्याययति या इमा बाह्याः शरीरान्मात्रा(२)स्तद्यथैतत् पृथिवीमन्तरीक्षं दिवन्नक्षत्राण्यृतूनार्त्तवान् संवत्सरांस्तानेतेनास्मिन्नाप्याययत्यापोऽमृतं पुरुषो ब्रह्मांथाप्रियनिगमो भवति तस्माद्वै विद्वान् पुरुषमिदं पुण्डरीकमिति प्राण एष स पुरि शेते संपुरिशंत इति । पुरिशयं सन्तं प्राणं पुरुष इत्याचक्षते । परोक्षेण परोक्षप्रिया इव हि देवा भवन्ति प्रत्यक्षद्विषः । स यत्पूर्व्वमाचामति पुरस्ताद्धोमांस्तेनास्मिन्नवरुन्धे सयद् द्वितीयमाचामत्याज्यभागौ तेनास्मिन्नवरुन्धे, स यत्तृतीयमाचामति संस्थितहोमांस्तेनास्मिन्नवरुन्धे,स यद्द्विःपरिमृजति तत्समित्संवर्हिः,स यत्सर्वाणि खानि सर्वं देहमाप्याययति यच्चान्यदातारं मन्त्रकार्य्यं यज्ञे स्कन्दति सर्वन्तेनास्मिन्नवरुन्धे, स यदीपूर्वान् मन्त्रान् प्रयुङ्क्त आसर्वमेधादेते क्रतव एत एवास्य सर्व्वेषु लोकेषु सर्व्वेषु देवेषु सर्व्वेषु वेदेषु सर्व्वेषु

१ मन्त्राइति क; ।

२ शरीरान्मन्त्रा इति क, ।

भूतेषु सर्वेषु सत्वेषु कामचारः कामविमोचनं भवत्यर्द्धंच न प्रमीयते(१) य एवं वेद।

तदप्येतदृचोक्तं। आपो भृग्वङ्गिरोरूपमापो भृग्वङ्गिरोमयं। सर्वमापोमयं भूतं सर्वं भृग्वङ्गिरोमयम्। अन्तरैते त्रयो वेदा भृगूनङ्गिरसोऽनुगाः।

अपां पुष्पं मूर्त्तिराकाशं पवित्रमुत्तम-मित्याचम्याभ्युक्ष्या-त्मानमनुमन्त्रयत इन्द्र जीवेति ब्राह्मणं॥ ३९॥

इति अथर्व्ववेदे गोपथब्राह्मणपूर्वभागे प्रथमः प्रपाठकः॥१॥

---

## अथ द्वितीयः प्रपाठकः।

ओं ब्रह्मचारीष्णंश्चरति रोदसी उभे इत्याचार्य्यमाह। तस्मिन् देवाः सम्मनसो भवन्तीति वायुमाह स सद्य एति पूर्वस्मादुत्तरं समुद्रमित्यादित्यमाह दीक्षितो दीर्घश्मश्रुरेष दीक्षित एष दीर्घश्मश्रुरेष एवाचार्य्यस्थाने तिष्ठन्नाचार्य्य इति स्तूयते, वैद्युतस्थाने तिष्ठन् वायुरिति स्तूयते, द्यौस्थाने तिष्ठन्नादित्य इति स्तूयते।

तदप्येतदृचोक्तं ब्रह्मचारीष्णन्निति ब्राह्मणम्॥१।

जायमानो ह वै ब्राह्मणः सप्तेन्द्रियाण्यभिजायन्ते, ब्रह्मवर्चसञ्च यशश्च स्वप्नञ्च क्रोधश्च श्लाघाञ्च रूपञ्च पुण्यमेव गन्धं सप्तमं। तानि ह वा अस्यैतानि ब्रह्मचर्य्यमुपेतोपक्रामन्ति, मृगानस्य ब्रह्मवर्चसं गच्छत्याचार्य्य यशोऽजगरं स्वप्नो वराहं क्रोधोपश्लाघं कुमारीं रूप-

१ भवत्यर्द्धेनेच न प्रमीयते इति घ,।

मोषधिवनस्पतीन् पुण्यो गन्धः स यन्मृगाजिनानि वस्ते तेन तद् ब्रह्मवर्च्चसमवरुन्धे, यदस्य मृगेषु भवति सह स्नातो ब्रह्मवर्च्चसी भवति स यदहरहराचार्य्याय कर्म करोति तेन तद्यशोऽवरुन्धे यदस्याचार्य्ये भवति स ह स्नातो यशस्वी भवति स यत्सुषुप्सुर्निद्रान्निनयति तेन तं स्वप्नमवरुन्धे योऽस्याजगरे भवति तं ह स्नातं स्वपन्तमाहुः स्वपितु मैनं बोबुधथेति स क्रुद्धो वाचा न कञ्चन हिनस्ति पुरुषात् पुरुषात् पापीयानिव मन्यमानस्तेन तं क्रोधमवरुन्धे, योऽस्य वराहे भवति तस्य ह स्नातस्य क्रोधा श्लाघीयसं विशन्तेऽथाह्निः श्लाघ्यमानो न श्लायात्तेन तं श्लाघामवरुन्धे, याऽस्याप्सु भवति सह स्नातः श्लाघीयोऽन्येभ्यः श्लाघ्यतेऽथैतद्ब्रह्मचारिणो रूपं यत्कुमार्य्यास्तान्नग्नाबोदीक्षेदेतिवेति मुखं विपरिधापयेत्तेन तद्रूपमवरुन्धे, य दस्य कुमार्य्यां भवति तं ह स्नातं कुमारीमिव निरीक्षन्तेऽथैद्ब्रह्मचारिणः पुण्यो-गन्धो य ओषधिवनस्पतीनां तासां पुण्यं गन्धं प्रच्छिद्य नोपजिघ्रेत्तेन तं पुण्यं गन्धमवरुन्धे, योऽस्यौषधिवनस्पतीषु भवति स ह स्नातः पुण्यगन्धिर्भवति ॥ २ ॥

स वा एष उपयंश्चतुर्द्धोपैत्यग्निं पादेनाचार्य्यं पादेन ग्रामं पादेन मृत्युं पादेन, स यदहरहः समिध आहृत्य सायं प्रातरग्निं परिचरेत्तेन तं पादमवरुन्धे, योऽस्याग्नौ भवति। स यदहरहराचार्य्याय कर्म करोति, तेन तं पादमवरुन्धे, योऽस्याचार्य्ये भवति। स यदहरहर्ग्रामं प्रविश्य भिक्षामेव परीप्सति न मैथुनन्तेन तं पादमवरुन्धे, योऽस्य ग्रामे भवति, स यत् क्रुद्धो वाचा न कञ्चन हिनस्ति पुरुषात् पुरुषात् पापीयानि मन्यमानस्तेनव तं पादमवरुन्धे, योऽस्य मृत्यौ भवति ॥ ३ ॥

पञ्च ह वा एते ब्रह्मचारिण्यग्नयो धीयन्ते, द्वौ पृथग्घस्तयोर्मुखे हृदय उपस्थ एव पञ्चमः । स यद्दक्षिणेन पाणिना स्त्रियन्न स्पृशति तेनाहरहर्य्याजिनां लोकमवरुन्धे, यत्सव्येन तेन प्रव्राजिनां, यन्मुखेन तेनाग्निप्रस्कन्दिनां, यद्धृदयेन तेन शूराणां, यदुपस्थेन तेन गृहमेधिनां, तैश्चेत् स्त्रियं पराहरत्यनग्निरिव शिष्यते । स यदहरहराचार्य्याय कुलेऽनुतिष्ठते सोऽनुष्ठाय ब्रूयाद्धर्मगुप्तो (१) मा गोपायेति धर्मो हैनं गुप्तो गोपायेति, तस्य ह प्रजा श्वः श्वः श्रेयसी श्रेयसी ह भवति, धाय्यैव प्रतिधीयते, स्वर्गे लोके पितॄन्निदधाति, तान्तवं न वसीत,यस्तान्तवं वस्ते क्षत्रं वर्द्धते न ब्रह्म, तस्मात्तान्तवं न वसीत ब्रह्म वर्द्धतां मा क्षत्रमिति, नोपर्य्यासीत यदुपर्य्यास्ते प्राणमेव तदात्मनोऽधरं कुरुते यद्याती वहति, अध एवासीत, अधः शयीत, अधस्तिष्ठेदधो व्रजेदेवं ह स्म वैतत् पूर्वे ब्राह्मणा ब्रह्मचर्य्यञ्चरन्ति तं ह स्म तत्पुत्रं भ्रातरं वोपतापिनमाहुरुपनयेतैनमित्यासमिद्धारात् स्वरेयन्तोऽन्नमद्यादथाह जघनमाहुः, स्नापयेतैनमित्यासमिद्धाराद्ध्येतानि व्रतानि भवन्ति, तं चेच्छयानमाचार्य्योऽभिवदेत्, स प्रतिसंहाय प्रतिशृणुयात्तं चेच्छयानमुत्थाय तच्चेदुत्थितमभिप्रक्रम्य (२) तं चेदभिप्रक्रान्तमभिपलायमानमेवं ह स्म वैतत् पूर्वे ब्राह्मणा ब्रह्मचर्य्यं चरन्ति, तेषां ह स्म वैषा पुण्या कीर्त्तिर्गच्छत्याह वा अयं सोऽद्य गमिष्यतीति ॥ ४ ॥

जनमेजयो(३) ह वै पारीक्षितो मृगयाञ्चरिष्यन् हंसाभ्यामभिस-

---

१ धर्मगुप्तगुप्तो इति क, घ, ।

२ दुत्थितमधिप्रक्रम्येति ग, ।

३ जन्मेजय इति क, ग, ।

नुपावतस्थ इति, तावूचतुर्जनमेजयं (१) पारीक्षितमभ्याजगाम, स होवाच नमो वां भगवन्तौ, कौ नु भगवन्ताविति, (२) तावूचतुर्द्दक्षिणाग्निश्चाहवनीयश्चेति, स होवाच नमो वां भगवन्तौ, तदाकीयतामितिह्योपाराममित्यपि किल देवा न रमन्ते न ह्वि देवा न रमन्तेऽपि चैकोपारामाद्देवा आराममुपसङ्क्रामन्तीति, स होवाच नमो वां भगवन्तौ, किं पुण्यमिति ब्रह्मचर्य्यमिति, किं लौक्यमिति(३) ब्रह्मचर्य्यमेवेति, तत् को वेद इति,(४) दन्ताबलो धौम्रोऽथ खलु दन्ताबलो धौम्रो यावति तावति काले पारीक्षितं जनमेजयमभ्याजगाम, तस्मा उत्थाय स्वयमेव विष्टरं निदधौ, तमुपसङ्गृह्य पप्रच्छाधीहि भो किं पुण्यमिति ब्रह्मचर्य्यमिति, किं लौक्यमिति ब्रह्मचर्य्यमेवेति, तस्मा एतत् प्रोवाचाष्टाचत्वारिंशद्वर्षं सर्ववेदब्रह्मचर्य्यं, तच्चतुर्द्धा वेदेषु व्यूह्य द्वादशवर्षं ब्रह्मचर्य्यं द्वादशवर्षाण्यवरार्द्धमपि स्नायंश्चरेद्यथाशक्त्यपरं। तस्मा उहस्पृषभो सहस्रन्ददावप्यपिकीर्त्तितमाचार्य्यो ब्रह्मचारीत्येक आहुराकाशमधिदैवतमथाध्यात्मं ब्राह्मणो व्रतवांश्चरणवान् ब्रह्मचारी ॥ ५ ॥

ब्रह्म ह वै प्रजा मृत्यवे सम्प्रयच्छत्, ब्रह्मचारिणमेव न सम्प्रददौ, स होवाचास्यामस्मिन्निति किमिति यां रात्रीं समिधमनाहृत्य वसेत्तामायुषोऽवरुन्धीयेति, तस्माद् ब्रह्मचार्य्यहरहः समिध आहृत्य सायं प्रातरग्निं परिचरेत्, नोपर्य्युपसादयेत्, अथ प्रतिष्ठापयेत् यद्

१ जन्मेजयमिति क,।

२ भवन्ताविति ख, ग,।

३ किं लौक्यमिति घ,।

४ वेदयति इति क,।

पर्य्युपसादयेज्जीमूतवर्षी तदहः, पर्ज्जन्यो भवति, ते देवा अब्रुवन् ब्राह्मणो वा अयं ब्रह्मचर्य्यञ्चरिष्यति ब्रूतास्मै भिक्षा इति, गृहपतिर्ब्रूत बहुचारी गृहपतना इति किमस्या वृञ्जीतादद्त्या इति, इष्टापूर्त्त-सुकृतद्रविणमवरुन्ध्यादिति, तस्माद् ब्रह्मचारिणेऽहरहर्भिक्षां दद्याद्गृहिणीमामेयुरिष्टापूर्त्तं (१) सुकृतद्रविणमवरुन्ध्यादिति। सप्तमीं नातिनयेत्सप्तमीमतिनयन्न ब्रह्मचारी भवति, समिद्भैक्षे सप्तरात्रमचरितवान् ब्रह्मचारी पुनरुपनेयो भवति॥ ६ ॥

नोपरि शायी स्यान्नगायनो न नर्त्तनो न सरणो न निष्ठीवेत् यदुपरि शायी भवत्यभीक्ष्णं निवासा जायन्ते, यद्गायनो भवत्यभीक्ष्णश आक्रन्दान्धावन्ते, यन्नर्त्तनो भवत्यभीक्ष्णशः प्रेताविर्हरन्ते, यत्सरणो भवत्यभीक्ष्णशः प्रजाः संविशन्ते, यन्निष्ठीवति मध्य एव तदात्मनो निष्ठीवति, स चेन्निष्ठीवेद्दिवो नु मां यदत्रापि मधोरहं यदत्रापि रसस्य म इत्यात्मानमनुमन्त्रयते। यदत्रापि मधोरहं निरिष्टविषमसृतं (२)। अग्निश्च तत्सविता च पुनर्मे जठरे धत्तां(३)। यदत्रापि रसस्य मे परापपातास्मि तं। तदिहोपह्वयामहे तन्म आप्यायतां पुनरिति। न श्मशानमातिष्ठेत्, स चेदभितिष्ठेदुदकं हस्ते कृत्वा यदीदमृतुकाम्येत्यभिमन्त्र्य जपंत्सम्प्रोक्ष्य परिक्रामेत् समयायोपरि व्रजेत् यदीदमृतुकाम्याघं रिप्रमुपेयिम अन्धः श्लोण-

१ गृहणीमामेयमिष्टापूर्त्त इति घ,।
२ निरष्टविषमसृतमिति ख, ग, घ,।
३ जठरेधत्तामिति ख, ग,।

इव हीयतां। मा नोऽन्वागादघं यत इति। अथ हैतद्देवानां परिषूतं यद् ब्रह्मचारी।

तदप्येतदृचोक्तं। देवानामेतत्परिषूतमनभ्यारूढं चरति रोचमानं तस्मिन् सर्वे पशवस्तत्र यज्ञास्तस्मिन्नन्नं सह देवताभिरिति ब्राह्मणम्॥७॥

प्राणापानौ जनयन्निति शङ्खस्य मूले महर्षेर्वसिष्ठस्य पुत्रः एतां वाचं ससृजे, शीतोष्णाविहोत्सौ (१) प्रादुर्भवेयातामिति तथा तच्छश्वदनुवर्त्तते, अथ खलु विपाणमध्ये वशिष्ठशिला नाम प्रथम आश्रमो, द्वितीयः कृष्णशिलास्तस्मिन् वसिष्ठः समतपद्वि-श्वामित्रजमदग्नी जामदग्ने तपतः, गौतमभरद्वाजौ सिंही प्रभवे तपतः गुङ्गुगुर्गुर्वासे तपत्यृषिर्त्रः षिद्रोणेऽभ्यतपदगस्त्योऽगस्त्यतीर्थे तपति दिव्यत्रिर्हं तपति स्वयम्भूः कश्यपः कश्यपतुङ्गेऽभ्यतपदुलूककच्छु-तरक्षुः श्वा वराहचिल्वटिबभ्रुकाः सर्पदंष्ट्रिनः संहनुकृण्वानाः कश्यपतुङ्गदर्शनात्सरणवाटात् सिद्धिर्भवति ब्राह्मं वर्षसहस्र-मृजिवने ब्रह्मचार्य्येकपादेनातिष्ठद् द्वितीयं वर्षसहस्रं मूर्द्धन्येवा-मृतस्य धारामधारयद् ब्राह्माण्यष्टाचत्वारिंशतं वर्षसहस्राणि सलिलस्य पृष्ठे शिवोऽभ्यतपत्तस्मात्तस्मात्तपसो भूय एवाभ्यतपत्। तदप्येता ऋचोऽभिवदन्ति प्राणापानौ जनयन्निति ब्राह्मणम्॥८॥

एकपाद् द्विपद इति वायुरेकपात्तस्याकाशं पादश्चन्द्रमा द्विपात्तस्य पूर्वपक्षापरपक्षौ पादावादित्यस्त्रिपात्तस्येमे लोकाः पादा अग्निः षट्पादस्तस्य पृथिव्यन्तरिक्षं द्यौराप ओषधिवनस्प-तय इमानि भूतानि पादास्तेषां सर्वेषां वेदा गतिरात्मा प्रति-

१ महर्षिर्वशिष्ठस्य पुत्र इति ख, ग, घ,।

ष्ठिताश्चतस्रो ब्रह्मणः शाखा, अथो आहुः षडिति मूर्त्तिराकाशस्येत्यृचा मूर्त्तिर्याजुषी गतिः साममयन्तेजो भृग्वङ्गिरसामापैतद् ब्रह्मैव यच्चतुष्पाद् द्विः संस्थित इति। तस्य भृग्वङ्गिरसः संस्थे अथो आहुरेकसंस्थित इति, यद्धोतर्चा मण्डलैः करोति पृथिवीं तेनाप्याययति एतस्यां ह्यग्निश्चरति ।

तदप्येतदृचोक्तम् । अग्निवासाः पृथिव्यसि तन्यूरिति ।

यदध्वर्य्युर्यजुषा करोत्यन्तरिक्षं तेनाप्याययति तस्मिन्वायुर्न निविशते कतमच्च नाह इति ।

तदप्येतदृचोक्तं । अन्तरिक्षे पथिभिर्ह्रीयमाणो (१) न निविशते कतमच्च नाहः । अपां योनिः प्रथमजा ऋतस्य क्व स्विज्जातः कुत आबभूवेति ।

यदुद्गाता साम्ना करोति दिवं तेनाप्याययति तत्र ह्यादित्यः शुक्रश्चरति ।

तदप्येतदृचोक्तं । उच्चायतं तमरुणं सुपर्णमिति । यद् ब्रह्मर्चा काण्डैः करोत्यपस्तेनाप्याययति चन्द्रमा ह्यप्सु चरति ।

तदप्येतदृचोक्तम् । चन्द्रमा अप्स्वन्तरिति । तासामोषधिवनस्पतयः काण्डानि, ततो मूलकाण्डपर्णपुष्पफलप्ररोहरसगन्धैर्यज्ञो वर्त्ततेऽद्भिः कर्माणि प्रवर्त्तन्तेऽद्भिः सोमो विषूयते, तद् यद् ब्रह्माणं कर्मणि कर्मण्यामन्त्रयत्यपस्तेनानुजानात्येषो ह्यस्य भागस्तद्यथा भोक्ष्यमाणोऽप एव प्रथममाचामयेदप उपरिष्टादेवं यज्ञोऽद्भिरेव प्रवर्त्ततेऽप्सु संस्थाप्यते तस्माद्

---

१ पथिभि र्ह्रीयमानं इति ख, घ, ।

ब्रह्मा पुरस्ताद्धोमसंस्थितहोमैर्यज्ञो वर्त्तते ऽन्तरा हि पुरस्ताद्धोमसंस्थितहोमैर्यज्ञं परिगृह्णात्यन्तरा हि भृग्वङ्गिरसः वेदानो दुह्य(१) भृग्वङ्गिरसः सोमपानं मन्यन्ते सोमात्मको ह्ययं वेद ।

तदप्येतदृचोक्तं । सोमं मन्यते पपिवानिति ।

तद्यथेमां पृथिवीमुदीर्णां ज्योतिषा धूमायमानां वर्षं शमयत्येवम् ब्रह्मा भृग्वङ्गिरोभिर्व्याहृतिभिर्यज्ञस्य विरिष्टं शमयत्यग्निरादित्याय म इत्येतेऽङ्गिरस एत इदं सर्वं समाप्नुवन्ति, वायुरापश्चन्द्रमा इत्येते भृगव एत इदं सर्वं समाप्याययन्त्येकमेव संस्थं भवतीति ब्राह्मणम् ॥ ८ ।

विचारी ह वै काबन्धिः कबन्धस्याथर्वणस्य पुत्रो मेधावी मीमांसकोऽनूचान आस, स ह स्वेनातिमानेन मानुषं वित्तं नेयाय, तं मातोवाच, त एवैतदन्नमवोचंस्त इममेषु कुरुपञ्चालेष्वङ्गमगधेषु काशिकौशल्येषु शाल्वमत्स्येषु शवसउशीनरेषूदीच्येष्वन्नमदन्तीत्यथ वयं तवैवातिमाने(२) नानाद्यास्मो वत्स वाहनमन्विच्छेति स मान्धातुर्यौवनाश्वस्य सार्वभौमस्य राज्ञः सोमं प्रसूतमाजगाम, स सदोऽनुप्रविश्यर्त्विजश्च यजमानञ्चामन्त्रयामास, तद्याः प्राच्यो नद्यो वहन्ति याश्च दक्षिणाच्यो याश्च प्रतीच्यो याश्च उदीच्यस्ताः सर्वाः पृथङ्नामधेयोरित्याचक्षते, तासां समुद्रमभिपद्यमानानां छिद्यते नामधेयं समुद्र इत्याचक्षते, एवमिमे सर्वे वेदा निर्मिताः सकल्पाः सरहस्याः सब्राह्मणाः सोपनिषत्काः सेतिहासाः सान्वाख्याताः

---

१ वेदान् दुह्य इति घ, ।

२ तवैनातिमानेन नामाद्यास्म इति क, ख, ।

सपुराणाः सस्वराः ससंस्काराः सनिरुक्ताः सानुशासनाः सानुमार्जनाः सवाकोवाक्यास्तेषां यज्ञमभिपद्यमानानां छिद्यते नामधेयं यज्ञ इत्येवाचक्षते ॥ ९ ॥

भूमिर्ह वै एतद्विच्छिन्नं देवयजनं यदप्राक्प्रवणं यदनुदक्प्रवणं यत् कृत्रिमं यत्समविषममिदं ह त्वेव देवयजनं यत्समं सम्मूलमविदग्धं प्रतिष्ठितं प्रागुदक्प्रवणं समं समास्तीर्णमिव भवति, यत्र ब्राह्मणस्य ब्राह्मणतां विद्याद् ब्रह्मा ब्रह्मत्वं करोतीति वोचे छन्दस्तन्न विन्दामो येनोत्तरमिमहीति। तान् ह पप्रच्छ किं विद्वान् होता हौत्रं करोति, किं विद्वानध्वर्य्युराध्वर्य्यवं करोति, किं विद्वानुद्गातौद्गात्रं करोति, किं विद्वान् ब्रह्मा ब्रह्मत्वं करोतीति वोचे छन्दस्तन्न विन्दामो येनोत्तरमिमहीति। ते ब्रूमो वागेव होता हौत्रं करोति वाचो हि स्तोमा स्र वषट्काराश्चाभिसम्पद्यन्ते, ते ब्रूमो वागेव होता वाग् ब्रह्म वाक् देव इति। प्राणापानाभ्यामेवाध्वर्य्युराध्वर्य्यवं करोति, प्राणः प्रणीतानि ह भूतानि प्राणः प्रणीताः प्रणीतास्ते ब्रूमः प्राणापानावेवाध्वर्य्युः प्राणापानौ ब्रह्म प्राणापानौ देव इति। चक्षुषैवोद्गाता औद्गात्रं करोति चक्षुषा हीमानि भूतानि पश्यन्त्यथो चक्षुरेवोद्गाता चक्षुर्ब्रह्म चक्षुर्देव इति। मनसैव ब्रह्मा ब्रह्मत्वं करोति मनसा हि तिर्य्यक् च दिश ऊर्द्ध्वं च यच्च किञ्च मनसैव करोति तद् ब्रह्म ते ब्रूमो मन एव ब्रह्मा मनो ब्रह्म मनो देव इति ॥ १० ॥

तद्यथा ह वा इदं यजमानश्च याजयितारश्च दिवं ब्रूयुः पृथिवीति, पृथिवीं वाक् द्यौरिति ब्रूयुस्तदन्यो नानुजानात्येतामेवं नानुजानाति यद्येतद् ब्रूयादथ नु कथमिति होतेत्येव होतारं ब्रूयाद्वा-

गिति वाचं, ब्रह्मेति ब्रह्म, देव इति देवमध्वर्य्युरित्येवाध्वर्य्युं ब्रूयात्, प्राणापानाविति प्राणापानौ, ब्रह्मेति ब्रह्म, देव इति देवमुद्गातेत्येवोद्गातारं ब्रूयाच्चक्षुरिति चक्षुर्ब्रह्मेति ब्रह्म, देव इति देवं ब्रह्मेत्येव ब्रह्माणं ब्रूयान्मन इति मनो ब्रह्मेति ब्रह्म देव इति देवम् ॥ ११ ॥

नाना प्रवचनानि ह वा एतानि भूतानि भवन्ति ये चैवासोमपं याजयन्ति ये च सुरापं ये च ब्राह्मणं विच्छिन्नं सोमयाजिनं तं प्रातः समित्पाणय उपोदेयुरुपायामो भवन्तमिति, किमर्थमिति यानेव नो भवांस्तां छ्वप्रश्नानपृच्छ्यानेवं नो भवान् व्याचक्षीयेति, तथेति तेभ्य एतान् प्रश्नान् व्याचष्टे, तद्येन ह वा इदं विद्यमानञ्चाविद्यमानञ्चाभिनिदधाति तद् ब्रह्म तद्यो वेद स ब्राह्मणोऽधीयानोऽधीत्याचक्षत इति ब्राह्मणम् ॥ १२ ॥

अथातो देवयजनान्यात्मा देवयजनं श्रद्धा देवयजनमृत्विजो देवयजनं भौमं देवयजनं तद्वा एतदात्मा देवयजनं यदुपव्यायच्छमानो वाऽनुपव्यायच्छमानो वा शरीरमधिवसत्येष यज्ञ एष यजत एतं यजन्त एतद्देवयजनमथैतत् श्रद्धा देवयजनं यदैव कदाचिदाद्यात् श्रद्धा त्वेवैनं नातोयात्तद्देवयजनमथैतदृत्विजो देवयजनं यत्र क्वचिद् ब्राह्मणो विद्यावान्मन्त्रेण करोति तद्देवयजनमथैतद्भौमं देवयजनं यत्रापस्तिष्ठन्ति यत्र स्यन्दन्ति प्रतदहन्त्युद्दहन्ति तद्देवयजनं यत्समं समूलमविदग्धं प्रतिष्ठितं प्रागुदक्प्रवणं समं समास्तीर्णमिव भवति यस्य श्वभ्रकूर्मौ वृक्षः पर्वतो नदी पन्था वा पुरस्तात्स्यान्न देवयजनमात्रं पुरस्तात्पर्य्यवशिष्येन्नोत्तरतोऽग्नेः पर्य्युपसीदेरन्निति ब्राह्मणम् ॥ १३ ॥

अदितिर्वै प्रजाकामौदनमपचत् तत उच्छिष्टमश्नात् सा गर्भमधत्त, तत आदित्या अजायन्त, य एष ओदनः पच्यत आरम्भणमेवैतत् क्रियते आक्रमणमेव प्रादेशमात्रीः समिधो भवन्त्येतावां ह्यात्मा प्रजापतिना सम्मितोऽग्नेर्वै या यज्ञिया तनूरखतथे तया समगच्छत एषा स्वधृत्या तनूर्यद् घृतं, यद् घृतेन समिधो अनक्ति ताभ्यामिवैनं तन्तनूभ्यां समर्द्धयति यन्निर्मार्गस्यादधात्यवक्लृत्या वै वीर्यं क्रियते यन्निर्मार्गस्यादधात्यवक्लृत्या एव संवत्सरो वै प्रजननमग्निः प्रजननमेतत् प्रजननं यत्संवत्सर ऋचाऽग्नौ समिधमादधाति, प्रजननादेवैनन्तत् प्रजनयिता प्रजनयत्यवत्यत्तुर्वै पुरुषो(१) न हि तद्वेद यदत्तुमभिजायते, यन्नचनं तदाप्नोति, य एष ओदनः पच्यते, योनिरेवैषा क्रियते, यत्समिध आधीयन्ते रेतस्तत् धीयते संवत्सरो वै रेतो हितं प्रजायते, ये संवत्सरे पर्य्येतेऽग्निमाधत्ते प्रजापतिरेवैनमाधत्ते, द्वादशसु रात्रीषु पुरा संवत्सरस्याधेयात्ता हि संवत्सरस्य प्रतिमा अथो तिसृष्वथो द्वयोरथो पूर्वेद्युराधेयात्, ते वा अग्निमादधानेनादित्या वा इत उत्तरमेव मेऽमुष्मिंल्लोक आयंस्ते पथि रक्षन्त इयन्तदु यच्यमाणं प्रतिनुदन्त उच्छेषणभाजा वा आदित्या यदुच्छिष्टं यदुच्छिष्टेन समिधो अनक्ति तेभ्य एव प्रोवाच तेभ्य एव प्रोच्य स्वर्गं लोकं यन्ति ॥ १५ ॥

प्रजापतिरथर्वा देवः स तपस्तप्त्वैतच्चातुष्प्राश्यं ब्रह्मौदनं निरमिमत, चतुर्लोकं चतुर्देवं चतुर्वेदं चतुर्होत्रमिति, चत्वारो वा इमे लोकाः पृथिव्यन्तरिक्षं द्यौराप इति, चत्वारो वा इमे देवा अग्निर्वायुरादित्यश्चन्द्रमाः, चत्वारो वा इमे वेदा ऋग्वेदो

१ प्रजनयत्यवत्सत्तुर्वै पुरुषः न हि तद्वेद यदत्त समभिजायते इति क, ख, ।

यजुर्वेदः सामवेदो ब्रह्मवेद इति, चतस्रो वा इमे होत्रा हौत्रमाध्वर्य्यवमौद्गात्रं ब्रह्मत्वमिति।

तदप्येतदृचोक्तम्। चत्वारि शृङ्गास्त्रयो अस्य पादा द्वे शीर्षे सप्त हस्तासो अस्य। त्रिधा बद्धो वृषभो रोरवीति महो देवो मर्त्त्यां आविवेश इति।

चत्वारि शृङ्गेति वेदा वा एत उक्ताः, त्रयो अस्य पादा इति सवनान्येव, द्वे शीर्षे इति ब्रह्मौदनप्रवर्ग्यावेव, सप्त हस्तासो अस्येति छन्दांस्येव, त्रिधा बद्ध इति मन्त्रः कल्पो ब्राह्मणं, वृषभो रोरवीत्येष ह वै वृषभ एष तद्रोरवीति यद्यज्ञेषु शस्त्राणि शंसत्यृग्भिर्यजुर्भिः सामभिर्ब्रह्मभिरिति, महोदेवो मर्त्त्यां आविवेशेत्येष ह वै महान् देवो यद्यज्ञ एष मर्त्त्यां आविवेश। यो विद्यात्सप्त प्रवत इति प्राणानाह सप्त विद्यात्परावत इत्यपानानाह। शिरो यज्ञस्य यो विद्यादित्येतद्वै यज्ञस्य शिरो यन्मन्त्रवान् ब्रह्मौदनो यो ह वा एतममन्त्रवन्तं ब्रह्मौदनमुपेयादपशिरसा ह वा अस्य यज्ञमुपेतो भवति तस्मान्मन्त्रवन्तमेव ब्रह्मौदनमुपेयान्नामन्त्रवन्तमिति ब्राह्मणम् ॥ १६ ॥

किमुपयज्ञ आत्रेयो भवतीत्यादित्यं हि तमो जग्राह, तदत्रिरपनुनोद तदत्रिरन्वपश्यत्।

तदप्येतदृचोक्तम्। स्तुताद्यमत्रिर्दिवमुन्निनाय दिवित्वाऽत्रिरधारयत् सूर्य्यामासाय कर्त्तव इति।

तं होवाच वरं वृणीष्वेति, स होवाच दक्षिणीया मे प्रजा स्यादिति, तस्मादात्रेयाय प्रथमदक्षिणा यज्ञे दीयन्त इति ब्राह्मणम् ॥ १७ ॥

प्रजापतिर्वेदानुवाच अग्नीनादधीयेति, तान्वागभ्युवाचाश्वो

वै सम्भाराणामिति, तद्घोरात् क्रूरात्सलिलात्सरस उदानिन्युस्ता-
न् वागभ्युवाचाश्वः शम्येतेति, तथेति तमृग्वेद एत्योवाचाहमश्वं
शमेयमिति तस्मा अविसृष्टाय महद्भयं ससृजे, स एतां प्राचीं दिश-
म्भेजे स होवाचाशान्तो न्वयमश्व इति । तं यजुर्वेद एत्योवाचाह-
मश्वं शमेयमिति तस्मा अविसृष्टाय महद्भयं ससृजे, स एतां
प्रतीचीन्दिशं भेजे स होवाचाशान्तो न्वयमश्व इति । तं साम-
वेद एत्योवाचाहमश्वं शमेयमिति, केन नु त्वं शमयिष्यसीति, रथ-
न्तरं नाम मे सामाघोरञ्चाक्रूरञ्च तेनाश्वमभिष्टूयते तस्मा-
अथ विसृष्टाय तदेव महद्भयं ससृजे, स एतामुदीचीन्दिशम्भेजे,
स होवाचाशान्तो न्वयमश्व इति । तान्वागभ्युवाच शंयुमाथर्वणं
गच्छथेति, ते शंयुमाथर्वणमासीनं प्राप्योचुर्नमस्ते अस्तु भगवन्नश्वं
शम्येतेति । तथेति स खलु कबन्धस्याथर्वणस्य पुत्रमामन्त्रयामास
विचारिन्निति, भगो इति हास्मै प्रतिश्रुतं प्रतिशुश्रावाश्वं शम्येतेति,
तथेति स खलु शान्त्युदकं चकाराथर्वणोभिश्चाङ्गिरसोभिश्चातनैर्मा-
तृनामभिर्वास्तोष्पत्यैरिति शमयति तस्य ह स्नातस्याश्वस्याभ्युक्षितस्य
सर्वेभ्यो रोमगर्तेभ्योऽङ्गारा आशीर्यन्त सोऽश्वस्तुष्टो नमस्कारं
चकार नमः शंयुमाथर्वणाय यो मा यज्ञमचोक्लृपदिति, भविष्यन्ति
ह वा अतोऽन्ये ब्राह्मणा लघुसम्भारतमास्त आदित्यस्य पद आधा-
स्यन्त्यनडुहो वत्सस्याजस्य श्रवणस्य ब्रह्मचारिणो वा एतद्वा आदि-
त्यस्य पदं यद्भूमिस्तथैव पद आहितं भविष्यतीति, सोऽग्नौ प्रणीय-
मानेऽश्वेऽन्वारब्धं ब्रह्मा यजमानं वाचयति यदक्रन्दः प्रथमं जायमान
इति पञ्च, तं ब्राह्मणा उपवहन्ति तद्ब्रह्मोपाकुरुते एष ह वै विद्वां-
स्सर्वविद्द ब्रह्मा यद्भृग्वङ्गिरोविदिति ब्राह्मणम् ॥ १८ ॥

देवाश्च ह वा असुराश्चास्पर्द्धन्त ते देवा इन्द्रमब्रुवन्निमन्नस्तावद्यज्ञं गोपाय, यावदसुरैः संयतामहा इति, स वै नस्तेन रूपेण गोपाय येन नो रूपेण भूयिष्ठं छादयसि येन शक्ष्यसि गोप्तु मिति, स ऋग्वेदो भूत्वा पुरस्तात्परीत्योपातिष्ठत्तं देवा अब्रुवन्नन्यत्तद्रूपं कुरुष्व नैतेन नो रूपेण भूयिष्ठं छादयसि नैतेन शक्ष्यसि गोप्तुमिति, स यजुर्वेदो भूत्वा पश्चात्परीत्योपातिष्ठत्तं देवा अब्रुवन्नन्यत्तद्रूपं कुरुष्व नैतेन नो रूपेण भूयिष्ठं छादयसि नैतेन शक्ष्यसि गोप्तुमिति, स सामवेदो भूत्वा उत्तरतः परीत्योपातिष्ठत् तं देवा अब्रुवन्नन्यदेव तद्रूपं कुरुष्व नैतेन नो रूपेण भूयिष्ठं छादयसि नैतेन शक्ष्यसि गोप्तुमिति, स इन्द्र उष्णीषी ब्रह्मवेदो भूत्वा दक्षिणतः परीत्योपातिष्ठत्तं देवा अब्रुवन्नेतत्तद्रूपं कुरुष्वैतेन नो रूपेण भूयिष्ठं छादयस्येतेन शक्ष्यसि गोप्तुमिति, तद्यदिन्द्र उष्णीषी ब्रह्मवेदो भूत्वा दक्षिणतः परीत्योपातिष्ठत्तद्ब्रह्माऽभवत्तद्ब्रह्मणो ब्रह्मत्वं तद्वा एतदथर्वणो रूपं यदुष्णीषी ब्रह्मा, तं दक्षिणतो विश्वेदेवा उपासीरंस्तं यद्दक्षिणतो विश्वेदेवा उपासीरंस्तत्सदस्योऽभवत्तत्सदस्यस्य सदस्यत्वं बलेर्ह वा एतद् बलमुपजायते यत्सदस्य आमयतो वै व्रजस्य बहुलतरं व्रजं विन्वन्ति,(१) घोरा वा एषा दिग्दक्षिणा शान्ता इतरास्तद्यानि स्तु-तानि ब्रह्माऽनुमन्त्रयते मनसैव तानि सदस्यो जनदित्येतां व्याहृतिं जपं चेत्यात्मानं जनयति नजित्यात्मानमपित्वे दधाति, तं देवा अब्रुवन्वरं वृणीष्वेति वृणा३ इति, स वरमवृणीतास्यामेव मां होत्रायामिन्द्रभूतं पुनन्तस्तुवन्तः शंसन्तः तिष्ठेयुरिति तं तस्यामेव होत्रायामिन्द्रभूतं पुनन्तस्तुवन्तः शंसन्तोऽतिष्ठंस्तं यत्तस्यामेव

१ विदन्तीति घ, ।

होत्रायामिन्द्रभूतं पुनन्तस्तुवन्तः शंसन्तस्तिष्ठंस्तद्ब्राह्मणाच्छंस्य-
भवत्तद्ब्राह्मणाच्छंसिनो ब्राह्मणाच्छंसित्वं सैषैन्द्री होत्रा यद् ब्राह्म-
णाच्छंसीया, द्वितीयं वरं वृणीष्वेति वृणा३ इति स वरमवृणीतास्या-
मेव मां होत्रायां वायुभूतं पुनन्तस्तुवन्तः शंसन्तस्तिष्ठेयुरिति
तं तस्यामेव होत्रायां वायुभूतं पुनन्तस्तुवन्तः शंसन्तोऽतिष्ठंस्तं यत्त-
स्यामेव होत्रायां वायुभूतं पुनन्तस्तुवन्तः शंसन्तस्तिष्ठंस्तत् पोताऽ
भवत्तत् पो.तुः पोतृत्वं सैषा वायव्या होत्रा यत् पोत्रिया, तृतीयं वरं
वृणीष्वेति वृणा३ इति स वरमवृणीतास्यामेव मां होत्राया-
मग्निभूतमिन्धानाः पुनन्तस्तुवन्तः शंसन्तस्तिष्ठेयुरिति तन्तस्या-
मेव होत्रायामग्निभूतमिन्धानाः पुनन्तस्तुवन्तः शंसन्तोऽतिष्ठंस्तं
यत्तस्यामेव होत्रायामग्निभूतमिन्धानाः पुनन्तस्तुवन्तः शंसन्त-
स्तिष्ठंस्तदाग्नीध्रोऽभवत्तदाग्नीध्रस्याग्नीध्रत्वं सैषाग्नेयी होत्रा
यदाग्नीध्रीयेति ब्राह्मणम् ॥ १९ ॥

ब्राह्मणो ह वा इममग्निं वैश्वानरं बभार । सोऽयमग्निर्वै-
श्वानरो ब्राह्मणेन भ्रियमाण(१) इमांल्लोकान् जनयतेऽथायमोच्चते-
ऽग्निर्जातवेदा ब्राह्मणद्वितीयो ह वा अयमिदमग्निर्वैश्वानरो
ज्वलति हन्ताहं यन्मयि तेज इन्द्रियं वीर्यन्तद्दर्शयास्युत वै मा
बिभ्रियादिति, स आत्मानमाप्याययेत्तं पयोधोक्तामिमं ब्राह्मणं
दर्शयित्वाऽऽत्मन्यजुहोत् सद्वितीयमात्मानमाप्याययेत्तं घृतमधोक्तामिमं
ब्राह्मणं दर्शयित्वा आत्मन्यजुहोत्, स तृतीयमात्मानमाप्याययेत्तदिदं
विश्वं विकृतमन्नाद्यमधोक्तामिमं ब्राह्मणं दर्शयित्वाऽऽत्मन्यजुहोत्, स
चतुर्थमात्मानमाप्याययेत्तेन ब्राह्मणस्य जायां विराजमपश्यत्

१ भ्रियमाण इति क, घ, ।

तामस्मै प्रायच्छत् स आत्मा अपित्वमभवत्तत इममग्निं वैश्वानरं धरास्युर्ब्राह्मणोऽग्निं जातवेदसमधत्त, सोऽयमब्रवीत् अग्ने जातवेदो अभिनिधेहि मेहीति तस्य हैतं नामाधत्ताघोरं चाक्रूरञ्च, सोऽश्वोऽभवत्तस्मादश्वो वहेत रथं न भवति(१) पृष्ठेन सादिनं, स देवानागच्छत्स देवेभ्योऽन्वातिष्ठत् तस्माद्देवा अबिभयुस्तं ब्रह्मणे प्रायच्छत्तमेतयर्चाऽशमयत् ॥ २० ॥

अग्निं त्वाहुर्वैश्वानरं सदनान् प्रदहन्वगाः । स नो देवत्राधिब्रूहि मारिषामा वयन्तवेति ।

तमेताभिः पञ्चभिर्ऋग्भिरुपाकुरुते यदक्रन्दः प्रथमं जायमान इति ।

सोऽशाम्यत्तस्मादश्वः पशूनां जिवत्नुतमो भवति वैश्वानरो ह्येष तस्मादग्निः पदमश्वं ब्रह्मणे ददाति ब्रह्मणे हि प्रत्तन्तस्य रसमपीडयत् स रसोऽभवद्रसो ह वा एष तं वा एतं रसं सन्तं रथ इत्याचक्षते, परोक्षेण परोक्षप्रिया इव हि देवा भवन्ति प्रत्यक्षद्विषः । स देवानागच्छत् स देवेभ्योऽन्वातिष्ठत्तस्माद्देवा अबिभयुस्तं ब्रह्मणे प्रायच्छत्तमेतयर्चाऽऽज्याहुत्याऽभ्यजुहोदिन्द्रस्यौजो मरुतामनीकमिति ।

रथमभिहुत्वा तमेतयर्चाऽतिष्ठद् वनस्पते वीड्वङ्गो हि भूया इति ।

तस्मादाग्न्याधेयिकं रथं ब्रह्मणे ददाति, ब्रह्मणे हि प्रत्तं तस्य तक्षाणस्तनूर्ज्येष्ठां दक्षिणां निरमिमत । तां पञ्चस्वपश्यदृचि यजुषि साम्नि शान्तेऽथ घोरे ।

१ तस्मादश्वो वहेत रथिन भवति इति क, ।

तासां द्वे ब्रह्मणे प्रायच्छद्वाचं च ज्योतिश्च, वाग्वै धेनुर्ज्योतिर्हिरण्यं तस्मादाग्न्याधेयिकां चातुष्प्राश्यां धेनुं ब्रह्मणे ददाति, ब्रह्मणे हि प्रत्ता पशुषु शाम्यमानेषु चक्षुर्हापयन्ति चक्षुरेव तदात्मनि धत्ते यद्वै चक्षुस्तद्धिरण्यं तस्मादाग्न्याधेयिकं हिरण्यं ब्रह्मणे ददाति, ब्रह्मणे हि प्रत्तं तस्यामन्नधत्त तेन प्राज्वलयद् यन्नाधत्त तदाग्लाऽभवत्तदाग्ला भूत्वा सा समुद्रं प्राविशत्सा समुद्रमदहत्तस्मात्समुद्रो दुर्गिरपि वैश्वानरेण हि दग्धः सा पृथिवीमुदैत्सा पृथिवीं व्यदहत्सा देवानागच्छत्सा देवानहिडत्ते देवा ब्रह्माणमुपाधावन् स नैवागायन्नानृत्यत् सैषाग्लैषा कारुविदा नाम तं वा एतमाग्लाहतं सन्तमाग्लागृध इत्याचक्षते, परोक्षेण परोक्षप्रिया इव हि देवा भवन्ति प्रत्यक्षद्विषः। य एष ब्राह्मणो गायनो वा नर्त्तनो वा भवति तमाग्लागृध इत्याचक्षते, तस्माद् ब्राह्मणो नैव गायेन्नानृत्येन्माग्लागृधः स्यात्तस्माद् ब्राह्मं पूर्वं हविरपरं प्राजापत्यं प्राजापत्यात् ब्राह्मणमेवोत्तममिति ब्राह्मणम् ॥ २१ ॥

अथर्वाणश्च ह वा आङ्गिरसश्च भृगुचक्षुषी तद् ब्रह्माभिव्यपश्यंस्तदजानन्वयं वा इदं सर्वं यद्भृग्वङ्गिरस इति। ते देवा ब्राह्मं हविर्यत्सान्तपनेऽग्नावजुहवुरेतद्वै ब्राह्मं हविर्यत्सान्तपनेऽग्नौ हूयते, एष ह वै सान्तपनोऽग्निर्यद् ब्राह्मणस्तस्योर्ज्जयोर्ज्जां देवा अभजन्त सुमनस एव स्वधां पितरः श्रद्धया स्वर्गं लोकं ब्राह्मणास्तेन सुन्वन्त्यपयोऽन्ततः स्त्रियः केवल आत्मन्यवारुन्धत वाह्या उभयेन सुन्वन्ति, यद्वै दद्ये ब्राह्मं हविर्न निरूप्येतानृजवः प्राजापत्यहविषो मनुष्या जायेरन्नसौ यांल्लोकान् शृणुति पिता ह्येष आह-

वनीयस्य गार्हपत्यस्य दक्षिणाग्नेर्योऽग्निहोत्रं जुहोतीति, देवा प्रिये धामनि मदन्ति तेषामेषोऽग्निः सान्तपनश्रेष्ठो भवत्येतस्य वाचि तृप्तायामग्निस्तृप्यति, प्राणे तृप्ते वायुस्तृप्यति, चक्षुषी तृप्त आदित्यस्तृप्यति, मनसि तृप्ते चन्द्रमास्तृप्यति, श्रोत्रे तृप्ते दिशश्चा-न्तर्देशाश्च तृप्यन्ति, स्नेहेषु तृप्तेष्वापस्तृप्यन्ति, लोमेषु तृप्तेष्वोषधि-वनस्पतयस्तृप्यन्ति, शरीरे तृप्ते पृथिवी तृप्यत्येवमेषोऽग्निः सान्त-पनः श्रेष्ठस्तृप्तः सर्वांस्तृप्तांस्तर्पयतीति ब्राह्मणम् ॥ २२ ॥

सान्तपना इदं हविरित्येष ह वै सान्तपनोऽग्निर्यद् ब्राह्मणो यस्य गर्भाधानपुंसवनसीमन्तोन्नयनजातकर्मनामकरणनिष्क्रमणान्न-प्राशनगोदानचूड़ाकरणोपनयनाप्लवनाग्निहोत्रव्रतचर्य्यादीनि कृता-नि भवन्ति, स सान्तपनोऽथ योऽयमनग्निकः स कुम्भे लोष्टः, तद्यथा कुम्भे लोष्टः प्रक्षिप्तो नैव शौचार्थाय कल्पते नैव शस्यं निर्वर्त्तयत्येव-मेवायं ब्राह्मणोऽनग्निकस्तस्य ब्राह्मणस्यानग्निकस्य नैव दैवं दद्यान्न पित्र्यं न चास्य स्वाध्यायाशिषो न यज्ञ आशिषः स्वर्गङ्गमा भवन्ति।

तदप्येतदृचोक्तम्। अग्निं दूतं वृणीमहे होतारं विश्ववेदसं। अस्य यज्ञस्य सुक्रतुमिति ब्राह्मणम् ॥ २३ ॥

अथ ह प्रजापतिः सोमेन यक्ष्यमाणो वेदानुवाच, कं वो होतारं वृणीयां, कमध्वर्य्युं, कमुद्गातारं, कं ब्रह्माणमिति। त ऊचु-र्ऋग्विदमेव होतारं वृणीष्व, यजुर्विदमध्वर्य्युं, सामविदमुद्गातार-मथर्वाङ्गिरोविदं ब्रह्माणं, तथा हास्य यज्ञश्चतुर्षु लोकेषु चतुर्षु देवेषु चतुर्षु वेदेषु चतसृषु होत्रासु चतुष्पाद् यज्ञः प्रतिष्ठति, प्रतितिष्ठति प्रजया पशुभिर्य एवं वेद, तस्मादृग्विदमेव होतारं वृणीष्व, स हि होत्रं वेदाग्निर्वै होता, पृथिवी वा ऋचामायतनमग्निर्देवता गायत्रं

छन्दः भूरिति शुक्रं तस्मात्तमेव होतारं वृणीष्वेत्येतस्य लोकस्य जितय एतस्य लोकस्य विजितय एतस्य लोकस्य सञ्जितय एतस्य लोकस्यावरुद्ध्य एतस्य लोकस्य व्यृद्ध्य एतस्य लोकस्य समृद्ध्य एतस्य लोकस्योदात्तय एतस्य लोकस्य व्याप्तय एतस्य लोकस्य पर्य्याप्तय एतस्य लोकस्य समाप्तये, अथ चेन्नैवंविदं होतारं वृणुते, पुरस्तादेवैषां यज्ञो रिच्यते। यजुर्विदमेवाध्वर्युं वृणीष्व स ह्याध्वर्य्यवं वेद, वायुर्वा अध्वर्य्युरन्तरिक्षं वै यजुषामायतनं वायुर्देवता त्रैष्टुभं छन्दो भुव इति शुक्रं तस्मात्तमेवाध्वर्युं वृणीष्वेत्येतस्य लोकस्येत्येवाथ चेन्नैवंविदमध्वर्य्युं वृणुते, पश्चादेवैषां यज्ञो रिच्यते। सामविदमेवोद्गातारं वृणीष्व स ह्यौद्गात्रं वेदादित्यो वा उद्गाता द्यौर्वै साम्नामायतनमादित्यो देवता जागतं छन्दः स्वरिति शुक्रं तस्मात्तमेवोद्गातारं वृणीष्वेत्येतस्य लोकस्येत्येवाथ चेन्नैवंविदमुद्गातारं वृणुते, उत्तर एवैषां यज्ञो रिच्यते। अथर्वाङ्गिरोविदमेव ब्रह्माणं वृणीष्व स हि ब्रह्मत्वं वेद चन्द्रमा वै ब्रह्मा आपो वै भृग्वङ्गिरसामायतनं चन्द्रमा देवता वैद्युतस्योष्णिक्ककुभे छन्दसी ओमित्यथर्वणां शुक्रं जनदित्यङ्गिरसां, तस्मात्तमेव ब्रह्माणं वृणीष्वेत्येतस्य लोकस्य जितय एतस्य लोकस्य विजितय एतस्य लोकस्य सञ्जितय एतस्य लोकस्यावरुद्ध्य एतस्य लोकस्य व्यृद्ध्य एतस्य लोकस्य समृद्ध्य एतस्य लोकस्योदात्तय एतस्य लोकस्य व्याप्तय एतस्य लोकस्य पर्य्याप्तय एतस्य लोकस्य समाप्तयेऽथ चेन्नैवंविदं ब्रह्माणं वृणुते, दक्षिणत एवैषां यज्ञो रिच्यते दक्षिणत एवैषां यज्ञो रिच्यते ॥ २४ ॥

इति अथर्व्ववेदे गोपथब्राह्मणपूर्व्वभागे
द्वितीयः प्रपाठकः समाप्तः।

## अथ तृतीयः प्रपाठकः।

ओं दक्षिणाप्रवणा भूमिर्दक्षिणत आपो वहन्ति तस्माद्यत्रा-स्तद्भूमेरुन्नततरमिव भवति यत्र भृग्वङ्गिरसो विष्ठास्तद्यथा(१) आप इमांल्लोकानभिवहन्त्येवमेव भृग्वङ्गिरसः सर्वान् देवानभिवहन्त्येव-मेवैषा व्याहृतिः सर्वान् वेदानभिवहन्त्यो३मिति ह्यर्चामो१मिति यजु-षामो१मिति साम्नामो१मिति सर्वस्याहाभिवादस्तं ह स्मैतदुत्तरं यज्ञे विद्वांसः कुर्वन्ति देवा ब्रह्माण आगच्छत आगच्छतेत्येते वै देवा ब्रह्माणो यद्भृग्वङ्गिरसस्तानेवैतद् गृणानांस्तान् वृणानां ह्वयन्तो(२) मन्यन्ते नान्यो भृग्वङ्गिरोविद् वृतो यज्ञमागच्छन् यज्ञस्य (३) तेजसा तेज आप्नोत्यूर्जयोर्जां यशसा यशो नान्यो भृग्व-ङ्गिरोविद्वृतो यज्ञमागच्छेन्नेद्यज्ञं परिमुष्णीयादिति, तद्यथापूर्वं वत्सोऽधीत्य गां धयेदेवं ब्रह्मा भृग्वङ्गिरोविद्वृतो यज्ञमागच्छेन्नेद्यज्ञं परिमुष्णीयादिति, तद्यथा गौर्वाऽश्वो वाऽश्वतरो वैकपात् द्विपात् त्रिपादिति स्यात्, किमभिवहेत् किमभ्यश्नुयादिति, तस्मादृग्विदमेव होतारं वृणीष्व, यजुर्विदमध्वर्युं, सामविदमुद्गातारमथर्वाङ्गिरो-विदं ब्रह्माणं, तथा हास्य यज्ञश्चतुर्षु लोकेषु चतुर्षु देवेषु चतुर्षु वेदेषु चतसृषु होत्रासु चतुष्पाद्यज्ञः प्रतिष्ठति, प्रतितिष्ठति प्रजया पशुभिर्य एवं वेद यश्चैवमृत्विजामार्त्विज्यं वेद यस्य यज्ञे यजनीयं वेदेति ब्राह्मणम् ॥ १ ॥

---

१ विष्ठासद् यथेति च, ।

२ तानेवैतद् गृणानंस्तान् वृणानं ह्वयन्त इति क, ।

३ यज्ञमागच्छन्नान्यस्येति क, ।

प्रजापतिर्यज्ञमतनुत, स ऋचैव हौत्रमकरोत्, यजुषाध्वर्य्यवं, साम्नौद्गात्रमथर्वाङ्गिरोभिर्ब्रह्मत्वं, तं वा एतं महावाद्यं कुरुते, यदृचैव हौत्रमकरोद्यजुषाध्वर्यवं साम्नौद्गात्रमथर्वाङ्गिरोभिर्ब्रह्मत्वं, स वा एष त्रिभिर्वेदैर्यज्ञस्यान्यतरः पक्षः संस्क्रियते मनसैव ब्रह्मा यज्ञस्यान्यतरं पक्षं संस्करोत्ययमु वै यः पवते स यज्ञस्तस्य मनश्च वाक् च वर्त्तनिर्मनसा चैव हि वाचा च यज्ञो वहत्यत एव मन इयमेव वाक् स यद्दन्नास्ति विद्यादर्द्धं मेऽस्य यज्ञस्यान्तरगादिति, तद्यथैकपात् पुरुषो यन्नेकचक्रो वा रथो वर्त्तमानो भ्रेषं न्येत्येवमेवास्य यज्ञो भ्रेषं न्येति, यज्ञस्य भ्रेषमनुयजमानो भ्रेषं न्येति, यजमानस्य भ्रेषमन्वृत्विजो भ्रेषं नियन्ति, ऋत्विजां भ्रेषमनुदक्षिणा भ्रेषं नियन्ति, दक्षिणानां भ्रेषमनुयजमानः पुत्रपशुभिर्भ्रेषं न्येति, पुत्रपशूनां भ्रेषमनुयजमानः स्वर्गेण लोकेन भ्रेषं न्येति, स्वर्गस्य लोकस्य भ्रेषमनु तस्यार्द्धस्य योगक्षेमो भ्रेषं न्येति, यस्मिन्नर्द्धे यजन्त इति ब्राह्मणम् ॥ २ ॥

तदु ह स्माह श्वेतकेतुरारुणेयो ब्रह्माणं दृष्ट्वा भाषमाणमर्द्धं मेऽस्य यज्ञस्यान्तरगादिति, तस्माद्ब्रह्मा स्तुते वहिःपवमाने वाचोयम्यमुपांश्वन्तर्य्यामाभ्यामथ ये पवमान उद्दूचुस्तेष्वथ यानि च स्तोत्राणि च शस्त्राण्यावषट्कारात्तेषु स यद्दत्तो भ्रेषन्नियच्छेद्दीं भूर्जनदिति गार्हपत्ये जुहुयात्, यदि यजुष्ट ओं भुवो जनदिति दक्षिणाग्नौ जुहुयात्, यदि सामत ओं स्वर्जनदित्याहवनीये जुहुयात्, यद्यनाज्ञाता ब्रह्मता ओं भूर्भुवः स्वर्जनदोमित्याहवनीय एव जुहुयात्, तद्यथा(?) वाक्यस्यर्चां यजुषां साम्नामथर्वाङ्गिरसामथापि वेदानां रसेन यज्ञस्य विरिष्टं सन्धीयते, तद्यथा लव-

णेनेत्युक्तं, तद्यथा उभयपात्पुरुषो यन्नुभयचक्रो वा रथो वर्त्तमानोऽभ्रेषं न्येत्येवमेवास्य यज्ञोऽभ्रेषं न्येति, यज्ञस्याभ्रेषमनु यजमानोऽभ्रेषं न्येति, यजमानस्याभ्रेषमन्वृत्विजोऽभ्रेषं नियन्ति, ऋत्विजामभ्रेषमनुदक्षिणा अभ्रेषं नियन्ति, दक्षिणानामभ्रेषमनुयजमानः पुत्त्रपशुभिरभ्रेषं न्येति, पुत्त्रपशूनामभ्रेषमनु यजमानः स्वर्गेण लोकेनाभ्रेषं न्येति, स्वर्गस्य लोकस्याभ्रेषमनु तस्यार्द्धस्य योगक्षेमोऽभ्रेषं न्येति, यस्मिन्नर्द्धे यजन्त इति ब्राह्मणम् ॥ ३ ॥

तद्यदौदुम्बर्य्यान्म आसिष्ट, हिङ्कृणोत् मे प्रास्तावीन्म उदके आसीत् मे सुब्रह्मण्यामाह्वासीदित्युद्गाते दक्षिणा नीयन्ते, ग्रहान् मेऽग्रहीत् प्राचारीन्मेऽश्रुश्रुवन् मे समनसस्कार्षीदयाक्षीन्मेऽशंसो न्मेऽवषट्कार्षीन्म इत्यध्वर्य्यवे होतृषदन आसिष्ट, अयाक्षीन्मेऽशंसो न्मेऽवषट्कार्षीन्म इति होत्रे देवयजनं मेऽचीक्लृपद् ब्रह्मा सादं मेऽसीसदद् ब्रह्मजपान्मेऽजपीत् पुरस्ताद्धोमसंस्थितहोमान्मेऽहौषी दयाक्षीन्मेऽशंसीन्मेऽवषट्कार्षीन् म इति(१) ब्रह्मणे भूयिष्ठेन मा ब्रह्मणाकार्षीदित्येतद्वै भूयिष्ठं ब्रह्म यद्भृग्वङ्गिरसः, येऽङ्गिरसो येऽङ्गिरसः स रसः, येऽथर्वाणो येऽथर्वाणस्तद्भेषजं, यद्भेषजं तदमृतं, यदमृतं तद् ब्रह्म, स वा एष पूर्वेषामृत्विजामर्द्धभागस्यार्द्धमितरेषामर्द्धं ब्रह्मण इति ब्राह्मणम् ॥ ४ ॥

देवाश्च ह वा असुराश्च सङ्ग्रामं समयतन्त, तत्रैतास्तिस्रो होत्रका जिह्मं प्रतिपेदिरे, तासामिन्द्र उक्थानि सामानि लुलोप, तानि

१ वषट्कारिषीन्म इतीति ख, ग, ॥

होत्रे प्रायच्छद्राज्यं ह वै होतुर्बभूव, प्रउगं पोतुर्वैश्वदेवं ह वै होतुर्बभूव, निष्केवल्यं नेष्टुर्मरुत्वतीयं ह वै होतुर्बभूव, आग्निमारुतमाग्नीध्रस्य, तस्मादेतदभ्यस्ततरमिव शस्यते, यदाग्निमारुतं यस्मादेते संशंसुका इव भवन्ति(१) यद्धोता पोता नेष्टाग्नीध्रो मुमोहे वसोत तद् बृह्मियसामिवास तासामर्द्धं प्रतिलुलोप प्रथमार्हणञ्च प्रथमपदञ्चैतद्दच्छिणाश्चैतत्परिशिषेदेदिति ब्राह्मणम् ॥ ५ ॥

उद्दालको ह वा आरुणिरुदीच्यान् वृतो धावयाञ्चकार, तस्य ह निष्क उपाहितो बभूव, उपवादाद् बिभ्यतो यो मा ब्राह्मणोऽनूचान उपवदिष्यति तस्मा एतं प्रदास्यामीति, तद्धोदीच्यान् ब्राह्मणान् भयं बिभेद उद्दालको ह वा अयमायाति, कौरुपाञ्चालो ब्रह्मा ब्रह्मपुत्रः स ऊर्द्धं वृतो न पर्य्यादधीत केनेमं वीरेण प्रति संयतामहा इति, तं यत एव प्रपन्नं दभ्रे तत एवमनुप्रतिपेदिरे, तं ह स्वैदायनं शौनकमूचुः, स्वैदायन त्वं वै नो ब्रह्मिष्ठोऽसीति त्वयेमं वीरेण प्रतिसंयतामहा इति, तं यत एव प्रपन्नं दभ्रे तत एवमनुप्रतिपेदिरे, तं ह स्वैदायना इत्यामन्त्रयामास, स हो गोतमस्य पुत्रेतीतिहास्मा असूयात्, प्रतिश्रुतं प्रतिशुश्राव, स वै गोतमस्य पुत्र ऊर्द्धं वृतोऽधावीत् ॥ ६ ॥

यस्तद्दर्शपूर्णमासयोरूपं विद्यात् कस्मादिमाः प्रजाः शिरस्तः प्रथमं लोमशा जायन्ते, कस्मादस्मात्परमिव श्मश्रूण्युपकचाण्यन्यानि लोमानि जायन्ते, यस्तद्दर्शपूर्णमासयोरूपं विद्यात् कस्मादिमाः प्रजाः शिरस्तः प्रथमं पलिता भवन्ति, कस्मादन्ततः सर्वा एव पलिता भवन्ति, यस्तद्दर्शपूर्णमास-

१ शंशंशका इव भवन्तीति क, ॥

योरूपं विद्यात् कस्मादिमाः प्रजा अदन्तिका जायन्ते, कस्मादासामपरमिव जायन्ते, यस्तद्दर्शपूर्णमासयोरूपं विद्यात् कस्मादासां सप्तवर्षाष्टवर्षाणां प्रभिद्यन्ते, कस्मादासां पुनरेव जायन्ते, कस्माद्दन्ततः सर्व्व एव प्रभिद्यन्ते, यस्तद्दर्शपूर्णमासयोरूपं विद्यात् कस्मादधरे दन्ताः पूर्व्वे जायन्ते, पर उत्तरे, यस्तद्दर्शपूर्णमासयो रूपं विद्यात् कस्मादधरे दन्ताः अणीयांसो ह्रसीयांसः प्रथीयांसो वर्षीयांस उत्तरे, यस्तद्दर्शपूर्णमासयोरूपं विद्यात् कस्मादिमौ दंष्ट्रौ दीर्घतरौ, कस्मात्समे इव जम्भे, (१) यस्तद्दर्शपूर्णमासयोरूपं विद्यात् कस्मादिमे श्रोत्रेऽन्ततः समे इव दीर्णे, यस्तद्दर्शपूर्णमासयोरूपं विद्यात् कस्मात् पुमांसः श्मश्रुवन्तोऽश्मश्रुवः स्त्रियः, यस्तद्दर्शपूर्णमासयोरूपं विद्यात् कस्मादासां सन्ततमिव शरीरं भवति, कस्मादासामस्थीनि दृढ़तराणीव भवन्ति, यस्तद्दर्शपूर्णमासयोरूपं विद्यात कस्मादासां प्रथमे वयसि रेतः सिक्तं न सम्भवति, कस्मादासां मध्यमे वयसि रेतः सिक्तं सम्भवति, कस्मादासामुत्तमे वयसि रेतः सिक्तं न सम्भवति, यस्तद्दर्शपूर्णमासयोरूपं विद्यात् कस्मादिदं शिश्नमुच्चश्च एति नोचीपद्यते कस्मात्सदपानम् ॥ ७ ॥

अथ यः पुरस्तादष्टावाज्यभागान् विद्यात् मध्यतः पञ्च हविर्भागाः, षट् प्राजापत्याः उपरिष्टादष्टावाज्यभागान् विद्यात् अथ यो गायत्रीं हरिणीं ज्योतिष्पक्षां सर्व्वांश्चैर्यजमानं स्वर्गं लोकमभिवहन्तीं विद्यात् अथ यः पङ्क्तिं पञ्चपदां सप्तदशाक्षरां सर्व्वांश्चैर्यज-

---

१ सम इमे जम्भे इति ख, ॥

मानं स्वर्गं लोकमभिवहन्तीं विद्यात् अस्मै ह निष्कं प्रयच्छन्नुवाचा-
नूचानो ह वै स्वैदायना स सुवर्णं वै सुवर्णविदे ददामीति तदुपयम्य
निश्चक्राम, तत्रापव्राज यत्रेतरो बभूव, तं ह पप्रच्छ किमेष गोतमस्य
पुत्र इत्येष ब्रह्मा ब्रह्मपुत्त्र इति होवाच, यदेनं कश्चिदुपवदेतोत
मीमांसेत ह वा मूर्द्धा वा अस्य विपतेत्, प्राणा वैनं जह्युरिति, ते
मिथ एव चिक्रन्देयुर्विं प्रापव्राज यत्रेतरो बभूवुस्ते प्रातः समित्पाणय-
उपोदेयुरुपायामो भवन्तमिति, किमर्थमिति यानेव नो भवांस्तां ह्य
प्रश्नानपृच्छद्यानेव नो भवान् व्याचक्षीयेति, तथेति तेभ्य एतान्
प्रश्नान् व्याचचष्टे ॥ ८ ॥

यत्पुरस्तात् वेदेः प्रथमं बर्हिस्तृणाति तस्मादिमाः प्रजाः
शिरस्तः प्रथमं लोमशा जायन्ते, यदपरमिव प्रस्तरमनुस्तृणाति तस्मा-
दासामपरमिव श्मश्रूण्युपकक्षाण्यन्यानि लोमानि जायन्ते, यत्
प्राग्बर्हिषः प्रस्तरमनुप्रहरति तस्मादिमाः प्रजाः शिरस्तः प्र-
थमं पलिता भवन्ति, यदन्ततः सर्वमेवानुप्रहरति तस्मादन्ततः
सर्वा एव पलिता भवन्ति, यत्प्रयाजा अपुरोऽनुवाक्यावन्तो भवन्ति
तस्मादिमाः प्रजा अदन्तिका जायन्ते, यद्धवींषि पुरोऽनुवाक्यावन्ति
भवन्ति तस्मादासामपरमिव जायन्ते, यदनुयाजा अपुरोऽनुवाक्या-
वन्तो भवन्ति तस्मादासां सप्तवर्षाष्टवर्षाणां प्रभिद्यन्ते, यत्पत्नी-
संयाजाः पुरोऽनुवाक्यावन्तो भवन्ति तस्मादासां पुनरेव जायन्ते,
यत्समिष्टयजुरपुरोऽनुवाक्यावद्भवति तस्मादन्ततः सर्व एव प्रभि-
द्यन्ते, यद्गायत्र्याऽनूच्य त्रिष्टुभा यजति तस्मादधरे दन्ताः पूर्वे
जायन्ते पर उत्तरे, यदृचाऽनूच्य यजुषा यजति तस्मादधरे दन्ता-
[illegible] श्लक्ष्णीयांसः प्रथीयांसो वर्षीयांस उत्तरे, यदाघारौ दीर्घ-

तरौ प्राञ्चावाघारयति तस्मादिमौ दंष्ट्रौ दीर्घतरौ, यत् संयाज्ये सच्छन्दसी तस्मात् समे इव जम्भे, यच्चतुर्थे प्रयाजे समानयति तस्मादिमे स्रोत्र अन्ततः समे इव दीर्णे, यज्जपं जपित्वाऽभिहिङ्कृणोति तस्मात् पुमांसः श्मश्रुवन्तोऽश्मश्रुव स्त्रियः, यत् सामिधेनीः सतत्त्वाह तस्मादासां सन्ततमिव शरीरं भवति, यत् सामिधेन्यः काष्ठहविषो भवन्ति तस्मादासामस्थीनि दृढ़तराणीव भवन्ति, यत् प्रयाजा आज्यहविषो भवन्ति तस्मादासां प्रथमे वयसि रेतः सिक्तं न सम्भवति, यन्मध्ये हविषां दध्ना च पुरोडाशेन च प्रचरन्ति तस्मादासां मध्यमे वयसिः रेतः सिक्तं सम्भवति, यदनुयाजा आज्यहविषो भवन्ति तस्मादासामुत्तमे वयसि रेतः सिक्तं न सम्भवति, यदुत्तमेऽनुयाजे सकृदपानिति तस्मादिदं शिश्नमुच्चश एति, नोचोपद्यते, यन्नापानेत् सकृच्छूनं स्याद्यन्मुहुरपानेत् सकृत्यन्नं स्यात्तस्मात् सकृदपानिति नेत् सकृच्छूनं स्यात् सकृत्यन्नं वेति ॥ ८ ॥

अथ ये पुरस्तादष्टावाज्यभागाः पञ्च प्रयाजा द्वावाघारौ द्वावाज्यभागावाग्नेया आज्यभागानां प्रथमः सौम्यो द्वितीयो हविर्भागानां हविर्ह्येव सौम्यमाग्नेयः पुरोडाशोऽग्निषोमीय उपांशुयाजोऽग्नीषोमीयः पुरोडाशोऽग्निः स्विष्टकृदित्येते मध्यतः पञ्च हविर्भागाः अथ ये षट् प्राजापत्या इडा च प्राशित्रञ्च यच्चाग्नीध्रायावद्यति, ब्रह्मभागो यजमानभागोऽन्वाहार्य्य एव षष्ठोऽथ य उपरिष्टादष्टावाज्यभागास्त्रयोऽनुयाजाश्चत्वारः पत्नीसंयाजाः समिष्टयजुरष्टममथ या गायत्री हरिणी ज्योतिष्पक्षा सर्वैर्यज्ञैर्यजमानं स्वर्गं लोकमभिवहति, वेदिरेव सा, तस्य ये पुरस्ता-

दष्टावाज्यभागाः स दक्षिणः पक्षोऽथ ये उपरिष्टादष्टावाज्यभागाः स उत्तरः पक्षः, हवींष्यात्मा, गार्हपत्यो जघनमाहवनीयः शिरः, सौवर्णराजतौ पक्षौ, तद्यदादित्यं पुरस्तात् पर्य्यञ्चं न पश्यन्ति तस्मादुज्योतिष्क उत्तरो भवति। अथ या पङ्क्तिः पञ्चपदा सप्तदशाक्षरा सर्वैर्यज्ञैर्यजमानं स्वर्गं लोकमभिवहति याज्येव सा, तस्या ओं श्रावयेति चतुरक्षरम्, अस्तु श्रौषडिति चतुरक्षरं, यजेति द्व्यक्षरं, येयजामह इति पञ्चाक्षरं, द्व्यक्षरो वै वषट्कारः, सैषा पङ्क्तिः पञ्चपदा सप्तदशाक्षरा सर्वैर्यज्ञैर्यजमानं स्वर्गं लोकमभिवहति, तद्यत्रास्यैश्वर्य्यं स्यादत्र वैनमभिवहेयुरेवंविदमेव तत्र ब्रह्माणं वृणीयान्नानेवंविदमिति ब्राह्मणम् ॥ १० ।

अथ ह प्राचीनयोग्य(१) आजगामाग्निहोत्रं भवन्तं पृच्छे गौतम इति, पृच्छ प्राचीनयोग्येति। किन्देवत्यं ते गवोडायां, किन्देवत्यमुपहूतायां, किन्देवत्यमुपसृष्टायां, किन्देवत्यं वत्समुन्नीयमानं, किन्देवत्यं वत्समुन्नीतं, किन्देवत्यं दुह्यमानं, किन्देवत्यं दुग्धं, किन्देवत्यं प्रक्रम्यमाणं, किन्देवत्यं क्रियमाणं, किन्देवत्यमधिश्रीयमाणं, किन्देवत्यमधिश्रितं, किन्देवत्यमभ्यवज्वाल्यमानं, किन्देवत्यमभ्यवज्वालितं, किन्देवत्यं समुदान्तं, किन्देवत्यं विष्यन्नं, किन्देवत्यमद्भिः प्रत्यानीतं, किन्देवत्यमुद्वास्यमानं, किन्देवत्यमुद्वासितं, किन्देवत्यमुन्नीयमानं, किन्देवत्यमुन्नीतं, किन्देवत्यं प्रक्रम्यमाणं, किन्देवत्यं क्रियमाणं, किन्देवत्यमुपसाद्यमानं, किन्देवत्यमुप-

१ अथ प्राचीनयोग्य इति ग, ।

सादितं, किन्देवत्या समित्, किन्देवत्यां प्रथमामाहुतिमहौषीः, किन्देवत्यं गार्हपत्यमवेचिष्ठाः, किन्देवत्योत्तराहुतिः, किन्देवत्यं हुत्वा स्रुचं विरुदस्रमुदैषीः, किन्देवत्यं बर्हिषि स्रुचन्निधायो-न्मृज्योत्तरतः पाणी निर्मार्क्षीः, किन्देवत्यं द्वितीयमुन्मृज्य पित्रुप-वीतं कृत्वा दक्षिणतः पितृभ्यः स्वधामकार्षीः, किन्देवत्यं प्रथमं प्राशीः, किन्देवत्यं द्वितीयं, किन्देवत्यमन्ततः सर्व्वमेवाप्राशीः,(१) किन्देवत्यमप्रक्षालितयोदकं स्रुचा न्यनैषीः, किन्देवत्यं प्रक्षा-लितया, किन्देवत्यमपरेणाहवनीयमुदकं स्रुचा न्यनैषीः, किन्दे-वत्यं स्रुवं स्रुचञ्च(२) प्रत्यताप्सीः, किन्देवत्यं रात्रौ स्रुगुदङ्गमव-मार्क्षीः, किन्देवत्यं प्रातरुन्मार्क्षीरित्येतच्चेद्वेत्थ, गोतम हुतं, चेदयद्यु न वेत्थाहुतं त इति ब्राह्मणम् ॥ ११ ॥

स होवाच, रौद्रं मे गवोडायां, मानव्यमुपहूतायां, वायव्यमुप-सृष्टायां, वैराजं वत्समुन्नीयमानं, जागतमुन्नीतम्, आश्विनं दुह्यमानं, सौम्यं दुग्धं, वार्हस्पत्यं प्रक्रम्यमाणं, द्यावापृथिव्यं क्रियमाणम्,(३) आग्नेयमधिश्रीयमाणं, वैश्वानरीयमधिश्रितं, वैष्णवमभ्यवज्वाल्य-मानं, मारुतमभ्यवज्वालितं, पौष्णं समुद्दान्तं, वारुणं विष्यन्नं, सारस्वतमद्भिः प्रत्यानीतं, त्वाष्ट्रमुद्दास्यमानं, धात्रमुद्दासितं, वैश्वदेव-मुन्नीयमानं, सावित्रमुन्नीतं, वार्हस्पत्यं प्रक्रम्यमाणं, द्यावापृथिव्यं(४) क्रियमाणम्, ऐन्द्रमुपसाद्यमानं, बलायोपसन्नम्, आग्नेयी समिद्, यां

---

१ सर्व्वमेव प्राशीरिति घ, ।

२ स्रुकस्रुवञ्चेति ख, ग, घ, ।

३ द्यावापृथिव्यां क्रियमाणमिति ख, घ, ।

४ द्यावापृथिव्यामिति ख, ग, ।

प्रथमामाहुतिमहौषं मामेव तत् स्वर्गे लोकेऽधां, यद्गार्हपत्यमवेक्षिष-मस्य लोकस्य सन्तत्यै, प्राजापत्योत्तराहुतिः, तस्मात् पूर्णतरा मनसैव सा, यद्धुत्वा स्रुचं निरुदस्यमुन्नैषं रुद्रांस्तेनाप्रैषं, यद्बर्हिषि स्रुचं निधायोन्मृज्योत्तरतः पाणी निर्मार्ज्मोषधिवनस्पतींस्तेनाप्रैषं, यद् द्वितीयमुन्मृज्य पितुरपवीतं कृत्वा दक्षिणतः पितृभ्यः स्वधामकार्षं पितृंस्तेनाप्रैषं, यत् प्रथमम्प्राशिषं प्राणांस्तेनाप्रैषं,(१) यद् द्वितीयं गर्भांस्तेन,(२) तस्मादनश्नन्तो गर्भा जीवन्ति, यदन्ततः सर्वमेवाप्राशिषं विश्वान्देवांस्तेनाप्रैषं, यदप्रक्षालितयोदकं स्रुचा न्यनैषं सर्पेतरजनांस्तेनाप्रैषं, यत् प्रक्षालितया सर्पपुण्यजनांस्तेन, यदपरेणाहवनीयमुदकं स्रुचा न्यनैषं गन्धर्वाप्सरसस्तेनाप्रैषं, यत् श्रुवं स्रुचञ्च प्रत्यतापसं सप्तऋषींस्तेनाप्रैषं, यद्रात्रौ स्रुग्दण्डमवमार्क्ष्यं ये रात्रौ संविशन्ति दक्षिणांस्तामुन्नैषं,(३) यत्प्रातरुन्मार्क्ष्यं ये प्रातः प्रव्रजन्ति दक्षिणां(४)स्तामुन्नैषमिति ब्राह्मणम् ॥ १२ ॥

एवमेवैतन्नो यथा भवानाह पृच्छामि त्वेव(५) भवन्तमिति, पृच्छ प्राचीनयोग्येति । यस्य सायमग्नय उपसमाहिता स्युः सर्वं ज्वलेयुः प्रक्षालितानि यज्ञपात्राण्युपसन्नानि स्युरथ चेद् दक्षिणाग्निरुद्वायात् किं वा ततो भयमागच्छेदिति, क्षिप्रमस्य पत्नी प्रैति, यो विद्वान्

१ प्राणंस्तेनाप्रैषमिति क, ख, ।

२ गर्भंस्तेनेति क, ख, ।

३ दक्षिणंस्तामुन्नैषमिति क, दक्षिणांस्तामुन्नैषमिति घ, ।

४ दक्षिणंस्तामुन्नैषमिति क, दक्षिणांस्तामुन्नैषमिति घ, ।

५ पृच्छामित्वेवमिति ख, ग, ।

जुहोति विद्यया त्वेवाहमभिजुहोमीति, का ते विद्या का प्रायश्चित्तिरिति गार्हपत्याद्धिदक्षिणाग्निं प्रणीय प्राचोऽङ्गारानुद्धृत्य प्राणापानाभ्यां स्वाहेति जुहुयादथ प्रातर्यथास्थानमग्नीनुपसमाधाय यथापुरं जुहुयात्सा मे विद्या सा प्रायश्चित्तिरिति। अथ चेदाहवनीय उद्वायात् किं वा ततो भयमागच्छेदिति क्षिप्रमस्य पुत्रः प्रैति, यो विद्वां जुहोति विद्यया त्वेवाहमभिजुहोमीति, का ते विद्या का प्रायश्चित्तिरिति गार्हपत्याद्ध्याहवनीयं प्रणीय प्रतीचोऽङ्गारानुद्धृत्य समानव्यानाभ्यां स्वाहेति जुहुयादथ प्रातर्यथास्थानमग्नीनुपसमाधाय यथापुरञ्जुहुयात् सा मे विद्या सा प्रायश्चित्तिरिति। अथ चेद्गार्हपत्य(१) उद्वायात् किं वा ततो भयमागच्छेदिति, क्षिप्रं गृहपतिः प्रैति, यो विद्वां जुहोति विद्यया त्वेवाहमभिजुहोमीति, का ते विद्या का प्रायश्चित्तिरिति सभस्मकमाहवनीयं दक्षिणेन दक्षिणाग्निं परिहृत्य गार्हपत्यस्यायतने प्रतिष्ठाप्य ततः आहवनीयं प्रणीय उदीचो(२)ऽङ्गारानुद्धृत्योदानरूपाभ्यां स्वाहेति जुहुयादथ प्रातर्यथास्थानमग्नीनुपसमाधाय यथापुरं जुहुयात् सा मे विद्या सा प्रायश्चित्तिरित्यथ चेत्सर्वेऽग्नय(३) उद्वायेयुः किं वा ततो भयमागच्छेदिति, क्षिप्रं गृहपतिः सर्वज्यानिञ्जीयते, यो विद्वां जुहोति विद्यया त्वेवाहमभिजुहोमीति, का ते विद्या का प्रायश्चित्तिरित्यानडुहेन शकृत्पिण्डेनाग्न्यायतनानि परिलिप्य होम्यमुपसाद्याग्निं निर्मथ्य

१ अथ प्रातर्यथास्थानमित्येवाथ चेद् गार्हपत्य इति ख, ग, घ, ।

२ प्रणीयोदुदीच इति ख, ग, प्रणीयेदुदीच इति घ, ।

३ अथ प्रातर्यथास्थानमित्येवाथ चेत् सर्वेऽग्नय इति ख, ग, घ, ।

प्राणापानाभ्यां स्वाहा समानव्यानाभ्यां स्वाहा उदानरूपाभ्यां स्वाहेति जुहुयादथ प्रातर्यथास्थानमग्नीनुपसमाधाय यथापुरञ्जुहुयात् सा मे विद्या सा प्रायश्चित्तिरित्यथ चेन्नाग्निं(१) जनयितुं शक्नुयुर्न कुतश्चन वातो वायात् किं वा ततो भयमागच्छेदिति मोघमस्येष्टं च हुतञ्च भवति, यो विद्वां जुहोति विद्यया त्वेवाहमभिजुहोमीति, का ते विद्या का प्रायश्चित्तिरित्यानडुहेनैव शकृत्पिण्डेनाग्न्यायतनानि परिलिप्य होम्यमुपसाद्यवात आवातु भेषजमिति सूक्तेनात्मन्येव जुहुयादथ प्रातरग्निं निर्मथ्य यथास्थानमग्नीनुपसमाधाय यथापुरं जुहुयात् सा मे विद्या सा प्रायश्चित्तिरिति ब्राह्मणम् ॥ १२ ॥

एवमेवैतद् भो भगवन् यथा भवानाहोपायामित्येव(२) भवन्तमित्येवं चेन्नावक्ष्यो मूर्द्धा ते व्यपतिष्यतीति(३) हन्त तु ते तद्वक्ष्यामि यथा ते न व्यपतिष्यतीति, यो ह वा एवंविद्वानश्नाति च पिबति च वाक् तेन तृप्यति, वाचि तृप्तायामग्निस्तृप्यत्यग्नौ तृप्ते पृथिवी तृप्यति, पृथिव्यां तृप्तायां यानि पृथिव्यां भूतान्यन्वायत्तानि तानि तृप्यन्ति, यो ह वा एवंविद्वानश्नाति च पिबति च प्राणस्तेन तृप्यति, प्राणे तृप्ते वायुस्तृप्यति, वायौ तृप्तेऽन्तरिक्षं तृप्यत्यन्तरिक्षे तृप्ते यान्यन्तरिक्षे भूतान्यन्वायत्तानि तानि तृप्यन्ति, यो ह वा एवंविद्वानश्नाति च पिबति च चक्षुस्तेन तृप्यति, चक्षुषो तृप्त आदित्यस्तृप्यत्यादित्ये तृप्ते द्यौस्तृप्यति, दिवि

१ अथ प्रातर्यथास्थानमित्येवाथ चेन्नाग्निमिति ख, ग, घ, ।

२ उपायामि त्वेवमिति ख, ग, ।

३ व्यपतिष्यदिति ख, ग, ।

तृप्तायां यानि दिवि भूतान्यन्वायत्तानि तानि तृप्यन्ति, यो ह वा एवं विद्वानश्नाति च पिबति च मनस्तेन तृप्यति, मनसि तृप्ते चन्द्रमास्तृप्यति, चन्द्रमसि तृप्त आपस्तृप्यन्त्यप्सु तृप्तासु यान्यप्सु भूतान्यन्वायत्तानि तानि तृप्यन्ति, यो ह वा एवंविद्वानश्नाति च पिबति च श्रोत्रं तेन तृप्यति, श्रोत्रे तृप्ते दिशश्चान्तर्देशाश्च तृप्यन्ति, दिक्षु चान्तर्देशेषु च तृप्तेषु च यानि दिक्षु चान्तर्देशेषु च भूतान्यन्वायत्तानि तानि तृप्यन्ति, यो ह वा एवं विद्वानश्नाति च पिबति च तस्यायमेव दक्षिणः पाणिर्जुहूः सव्य उपभृत् कण्ठो ध्रुवाऽन्नं हविः प्राणा ज्योतींषि सदेष्टं सदा हुतं सदाशितं पायितमग्निहोत्रं भवति य एवं वेद यश्चैवं विद्वानग्निहोत्रं जुहोतीति ब्राह्मणम् ॥ १४ ॥

प्रियमेधा ह वै भरद्वाजा यज्ञविदो मन्यमानास्ते ह स्म न कञ्चना वेदविदमुपयन्ति, ते सर्वमविदुस्ते सहैवाविदुस्तेऽग्निहोत्रमेव न समवादयन्त, तेषामेकः सकृदग्निहोत्रमजुहोत् द्विरेकस्त्रिरेकस्तेषां यः सकृदग्निहोत्रमजुहोत्तमितरावपृच्छतां कस्मै त्वं जुहोषीति एकधा वा, इदं सर्वं प्रजापतिः प्रजापतय एवाहं सायं जुहोमीति प्रजापतये प्रातरिति । तेषां यो द्विरजुहोत् तमितरावपृच्छतां काभ्यां त्वं जुहोषीति, अग्नये प्रजापतय इति सायं, सूर्य्याय प्रजापतय इति प्रातः । तेषां यस्त्रिरजुहोत्तमितरावपृच्छतां केभ्यस्त्वं जुहोषीत्यग्नये प्रजापतयेऽनुमतय इति सायं, सूर्य्याय प्रजापतये अग्नये स्विष्टकृत इति प्रातः । तेषां यो द्विरजुहोत्स आर्ध्नोत्स भूयिष्ठोऽभवत्प्रजया चेतरौ श्रिया चेतरावत्याक्रामत्तस्य ह प्रजामितरयोः प्रजासु या तत्तुमुपेयातां तस्माद् द्विर्होतव्यं, यजुषा चैव मनसा च

यामेव स ऋद्धिमार्प्नोति(१) तामाप्नोति य एवं वेद, यश्चैवंविद्वानग्निहोत्रं जुहोतीति ब्राह्मणम् ॥ १५ ॥

स्वाहा वै कुतः सम्भूता, केन प्रकृता, किं वाऽस्या गोत्रं, कत्यक्षरा, कतिपदा, किम्पूर्वावसाना, क्वचित् स्थिता, किमधिष्ठाना, ब्रूहि स्वाहाया यद्दैवतं रूपञ्च। स्वाहा वै सत्यसम्भूता, ब्रह्मणा प्रकृता, लामगायनसगोत्रा, द्वे अक्षरे, एकं पदं, त्रयश्च वर्णाः शुक्लः पद्मः सुवर्ण इति, सर्वच्छन्दसां वेदेषु समासभूतैकोच्छ्वासा वर्णान्ते चत्वारो वेदाः शरीरे, षडङ्गान्योषधिवनस्पतयो लोमानि, चक्षुषी सूर्य्याचन्द्रमसौ, सा स्वाहा सा स्वधा सैषा यज्ञेषु वषट्कारभूता प्रयुज्यते, तस्या अग्निर्दैवतं ब्राह्मणो रूपमिति ब्राह्मणम् ॥ १६ ॥

अथापि कारवो ह नाम ऋषयो अल्पस्वा आसंस्त इममेकगुमग्निष्टोमं ददृशुस्तमाहरंस्तेनायजन्त ते स्वर्ययुः, स य इच्छेत् स्वर्यायीति(२) स एतेनैकगुनाऽग्निष्टोमेन यजेतेति ब्राह्मणम् ॥ १७ ॥

अथातः सवनीयस्य पशोर्विभागं व्याख्यास्यामः। उद्धृत्यावदानानि, हनू सजिह्वे प्रस्तोतुः, कण्ठः सकाकुदः प्रतिहर्त्तुः, श्येनं वक्ष उद्गातुर्दक्षिणं पार्श्वं सांसमध्वर्य्योः, सव्यमुपगातॄणां, सव्योऽसः प्रतिप्रस्थातुर्दक्षिणा श्रोणिरथगास्ती ब्रह्मणोवरसकथं(३) ब्राह्मणाच्छंसिनः, ऊरुः पोतुः, सव्या श्रोणिर्होतुरवरसक्थं(४) मैत्राव-

१ सकृद्धिमार्प्नोतीति ख, ग, घ,।

२ स्वर्यामेति क,।

३ वरसक्थिमिति क,।

४ रवरसक्थिमिति क,।

रुणस्योरुरच्छावाकस्य, दक्षिणा दोर्नेष्टुः, सव्या सदस्यस्य, सदश्चानूकश्च गृहपतेर्जाघनी पत्न्यास्तां सा ब्राह्मणेन प्रतिग्राहयति, वनिष्टुर्हृदयं वृक्कौ चाङ्गुल्यानि दक्षिणो बाहुराग्नीध्रस्य, सव्य आत्रेयस्य, दक्षिणौ पादौ गृहपतेर्व्रतप्रदस्य,(१) सव्यौ पादौ गृहपत्न्या व्रतप्रदायाः,(२) सहैवैनयोरोष्ठस्तं गृहपतिरेवानुशास्ति मणिजांश्च स्कन्धास्तिस्रश्च कीकसा ग्रावस्तुतस्तिस्रश्चैव कीकसा अर्द्धञ्चापानस्योन्नेतुरत ऊर्द्ध्वं चमसाध्वर्य्यूणां क्लोमाः शमयितुः, शिरः सुब्रह्मण्यस्य, यश्च सुत्यामाह्वयते तस्य चर्म तद्वा खलु षट्त्रिंशत्सम्पद्यन्ते षट्त्रिंशदवदाना गौः षट्त्रिंशदक्षरा बृहती, वार्हतो वै स्वर्गो लोकः बृहत्या वै देवाः स्वर्गे लोके यजन्ते, बृहत्या स्वर्गे लोके प्रतिष्ठति, प्रतितिष्ठति प्रजया पशुभिर्य एवं विभजन्ते। अथ यदतोऽन्यथा शौलिको वा पापकृतो वा हुतादो वाऽन्यजना वाऽपि मथ्नीरन्नेवमेवैषां पशुर्विमथितो भवत्यस्वर्गोदेवता यो ह वा इमां श्रुतऋषिः पशोर्विभागं विदाञ्चकार, तामु ह गिरिजाय बाभ्रव्यायान्यो मनुष्येभ्यः(३) प्रोवाच, तत इयमर्वाङ् मनुष्येष्वासीदिति ब्राह्मणम्॥ १८॥

अथातो दीक्षाः। कस्मिन्निदतोर्दीक्षित इत्याचक्षते, श्रेष्ठां धियं क्षियतीति,(४) तं वा एतं दीक्षितं सन्तं दीक्षित इत्याचक्षते, परोक्षेण परोक्षप्रिया इव हि देवा भवन्ति प्रत्यक्षद्विषः।

---

१ व्रतपदस्येति ख, ग, ।

२ व्रतपदाया इति ख, ग, ।

३ अन्यो मनुष्ये मनुष्ये मनुष्यभ्य इति घ, ।

४ धियं क्षियन्तीति घ, ।

कस्यस्विद्धेतोर्दीक्षितोऽप्रत्युत्थायिको(१) भवत्यनभिवादुकः प्रत्युत्थे-
योऽभिवाद्यो ये प्रत्युत्थेयाभिवाद्यास्त एनमाविष्टाभवन्त्यथर्वाङ्गिरस-
स्तस्य किमाथर्वणमिति, यदात्मन्येव जुहोति न परस्मिन्नेवं ह्याथर्व-
णानामोदनसमानामात्मन्येव(२) जुह्वति न परस्मिन्नथास्य किमाङ्गि-
रसमिति, यदात्मनश्च परेषां च नामानि न गृह्णात्येवं ह तस्मिन्ना-
सादात्मनश्चैव(३) परेषां च नामानि न गृह्णन्ते, विचक्षणवतीं वाच-
श्चाषन्ते च न सितवतीं विचक्षयन्ति, ब्राह्मणं च न सयन्ति(४) प्राजा-
पत्यं, सैषा व्रतधुगथर्वाङ्गिरसस्तां ह्यन्वायत्ताः, कस्यस्विद्धेतोर्दी. क्षि-
तो नाश्यन्नो भवति नास्य नाम गृह्णन्त्यन्नस्थो नामस्थो भवतीत्या-
हुस्तस्य येऽन्नमदन्ति तेऽस्य पाप्मानमदन्त्यथास्य ये नाम गृह्णन्ति
तेऽस्य नाम्नः पाप्मानमपाघ्नतेऽथापि (५) वेदानां गर्भभूतो भव-
तीत्याहुस्तस्याजातस्याविज्ञातस्याक्रीतसोमस्याभोजनीयं भवती-
त्याहुः । स दीक्षाणां प्रातर्जायते सोमं क्रीणन्ति तस्य जातस्य
विज्ञातस्य क्रीतसोमस्य भोजनीयं भवतीत्याहुः । कस्यस्विद्धेतोः
संसवा परिजिहीर्षिता भवन्ति यतरो वीर्य्यवत्तमो भवति(६)स परस्य
यज्ञं परिमुष्णाति । कस्यस्विद्धेतोर्दैवे न ध्यायेत् संस्थिते नाधीयेतेति
संसवस्यैव हेतोरिति विद्योतमाने स्तनयत्यथो वर्षति वायव्य-

१ अप्रत्युत्थायुक इति ख, घ, ।

२ मोदनसवानामात्मन्येति ख, घ, ।

३ तस्मिन्नमादात्मनश्चैवेति ख, ग, ।

४ न च सयन्ति इति ख, ग, ।

५ तथापीति घ, ।

६ वीर्य्यवत्तो भवतीति क, वीर्य्यवत्तरो भवतीति ख, ग. ।

मभिषुण्वन्ति वै देवाः सोमञ्च भक्षयन्ति तदभिषुण्वन्ति ब्राह्मणाः शुश्रुवांसोऽनूचानास्तेषां सर्वरसभक्षाः पितृपितामहा भवन्ति, स दैवे न ध्यायेत् संस्थितेनाधीयेतेति(१) ब्राह्मणम् ॥ १९ ॥

समावृत्त आचार्य्या निषेदुस्तान् ह यज्ञो दीक्षिष्यमाणानां ब्राह्मणरूपं कृत्वोपोदेयायेत्यञ्चेद्दोपसमवत्सुर्हन्त वोऽहं मध्ये दीक्षा-इति, त ऊचुर्नैव त्वा विद्मः न जानीमः को ह्रीदविज्ञाय-मानेन सह दीक्षिष्यसीति, यन्निदं दीक्षिष्यध्वे भूयो न दी-क्षिष्यध्वे.थ वा उ एकन्दीक्षयिष्यथ सं वै तर्हि मोहिष्यथ मोहि-ष्यति वो यज्ञः(२) सर्वे ते दीक्षयिष्यतेत्यथ वा उ एकं दीक्षयिष्यथ ते वा अहीनर्त्विजो गृहपतयो भविष्यथ, ते तूष्णीं ध्यायन्त-आसाञ्चक्रिरे, सहोवाच किन्नु तूष्णीमाध्वे भूयो वः पृच्छामः पृच्छतेति, यन्निदं दीक्षिष्यध्व उपयेम एतस्मिन् संवत्सरे मिथुनं चरिष्यथ नोपेष्यथेति धिगिति होचुः, कथं नु दीक्षिता उपेष्यामो-नोपेष्यामहा इति, ते वै ब्राह्मणानामभिमन्तारो(३) भविष्यथ रेतो-ह वो य एतस्मिन् संवत्सरे ब्राह्मणास्तदभविष्यं(४) स्ते बोधिमता-भविष्यथेत्यथ वा उपेष्यामो नोपेष्यामहा इति, ते वै दीक्षिता अवकीर्णिनो भविष्यथ, न ह वै देवयानः पन्था प्रादुर्भविष्यति तिरो-वो देवयानः पन्था भविष्यतीति, ते वयं भगवन्तमेवोपधावाम यथा स्वस्ति संवत्सरस्योदृचं समश्नवामहा इति ब्राह्मणम् ॥ २० ॥

---

१ नाधीयीतेति ख, ।

२ मोहिष्यथ मोहिष्यति मो यज्ञ इति क, ।

३ अभिमन्तार इति घ, ।

४ स ह्नविग्रमिति क, नदभिभविष्य.मिति घ, ।

स होवाच, द्वादश ह वै वसूनि दीक्षितादुत्क्रामन्ति, न ह वै दीक्षितोऽग्निहोत्रं जुहुयात्, न पौर्णमासेन यज्ञेन यजेत, नामावास्येनाश्मिन्वसीत, न पितृयज्ञेन यजेत,न तत्र गच्छेद्यत्र मनसा जिगमिषेन्नेष्ट्या यजेत, न वाचा यथाकथाचिदभिभाषेत, न मिथुनं चरेत् नान्यस्य यथाकाममु युञ्जीत, न पशुबन्धेन यज्ञेन यजेत, न तत्र गच्छेद्यत्र चक्षुषा परापश्येत्, कृष्णाजिनं वसीत, कुरीरन्धारयेन्मुष्टोकुर्य्यादङ्गुष्ठप्रभृतयस्तिस्र उच्छ्रयेत्, मृगशृङ्गं गृह्णीयात्तेन कषेताथ(१) यस्य दीक्षितस्य वाग्वायता स्यात् मुष्टी वा विसृष्टी स एतानि जपेत्(२) ॥ २१ ॥

अग्निहोत्रञ्च मापौर्णमासश्च यज्ञः पुरस्तात् प्रत्यञ्चमुभौ कामप्रौ भूत्वा क्षित्या सहाविशतां, वसतिश्च माऽमावास्यश्च(३) यज्ञः पश्चात् प्राञ्चमुभाविति समानं, मनश्च मा पितृयज्ञश्च यज्ञो दक्षिणत-उदञ्चमुभाविति समानं, वाक् च मेष्टिश्चोत्तरतो दक्षिणाञ्चमुभाविति समानं, रेतश्च माऽन्नं चेत ऊर्द्ध्वञ्चमुभाविति समानं। चक्षुश्च मा पशुबन्धश्च यज्ञोऽमुतोर्वाञ्चमुभौ कामप्रौ भूत्वा क्षित्या सहाविशतामिति। खलु ह वै दीक्षितो य आत्मनि वसूनि धत्ते न चैवास्य काचनार्त्तिर्भवति, न च यज्ञविस्कन्धमुपयात्यपहन्ति पुनर्मृत्युमयात्येति पुनराजातिं, कामचारोऽस्य सर्वेषु लोकेषु भाति य एवं वेद, यश्चैवंविद्वान् दीक्षामुपैतीति ब्राह्मणम् ॥२२॥

---

१ कषेताथ इति क, ।

२ जपेदिति ख, घ, ।

३ वसतिश्च सामावास्येति ग, ।

अथ यस्य दीक्षितस्यर्त्तुमती जाया स्यात् प्रतिस्नावा प्रतिस्नावा सारूपवत्साया (१) गोः पयसि स्थालीपाकं श्रपयित्वाऽभिघार्य्योद्वास्योद्धृत्याभिहिङ्कृत्य गर्भवेदनपुंसवनैः सम्पातवन्तं(२) कृत्वा तं परैव प्राश्नीयाद्रेतो वा अन्नं वृषा हिङ्कार एवं ह्मीश्वराय दीक्षिताय दीक्षितो जाया पुत्रं लभेतेत्येतेनैव प्रक्रमेण यजेतेति ब्राह्मणम् ॥ २३ ॥

इत्यथर्व्ववेदे गोपथब्राह्मणपूर्व्वभागे तृतीयः प्रपाठकः समाप्तः ।

---

## अथ चतुर्थः प्रपाठकः ।

ओं अयं वै यज्ञो योऽयं पवते, तमेत इप्सन्ति ये संवत्सराय दीक्षन्ते । तेषां गृहपतिः प्रथमो दीक्षते, यं वै लोको गृहपतिरस्मिन् वा इदं सर्वं लोके प्रतिष्ठितं, गृहपता उ एव सर्वे सत्रिणः प्रतिष्ठिताः, प्रतिष्ठाया एवैनं तत् प्रतिष्ठित्यै दीक्षन्ते ॥ १ ॥

अथ ब्रह्माणं दीक्षयति, चन्द्रमा वै ब्रह्माऽधिदैवं, मनोऽध्यात्मं, मनसैव तदोषधीः सन्दधाति, तद्या ओषधीर्वेद स एव ब्रह्मौषधीस्तदनेन लोकेन सन्दधाति, तस्मादेतावन्तरेणान्यो न दीक्षेत, स यदेतावन्तरेणान्यो दीक्षेतेमं तं लोकमोषधिभिर्व्यापादयेदुच्छोषुका ह स्युस्तस्मादेतावन्तरेणान्यो न दीक्षेत ॥ २ ॥

---

१ प्रति स्नावा रूपवत्सायाा इति ख, ।

२ सम्पादवन्तमिति ख ।

अथोद्गातारं दीक्षयत्यादित्यो वा उद्गाताऽधिदैवं, चक्षुरध्यात्मं, पर्ज्जन्यः आदित्यः, पर्जन्यादधिवृष्टिर्जायते, वृष्टिरेव तदोषधीः सन्दधाति, तस्मादेतावन्तरेणान्यो न दीक्षेत, स यदेतावन्तरेणान्यो-दीक्षेतेमं तं लोकं वर्षेण व्यापादयेदवर्षका ह स्युस्तस्मादेतावन्त-रेणान्यो न दीक्षेत ॥ ३ ॥

अथ होतारं दीक्षयत्यग्निर्वैहोताऽधिदैवं, वागध्यात्ममन्नं वृष्टिः, वाचं चैव तदग्निं चान्नेन सन्दधाति, तस्मादेतावन्तरेणान्यो न दीक्षेत, स यदेतावन्तरेणान्यो दीक्षेतेमं तं लोकमन्नेन(१) व्यापा-दयेदग्ननायुका ह स्युस्तस्मादेतावन्तरेणान्यो न दीक्षेत ॥ ४ ॥

अथाध्वर्य्यं प्रतिप्रस्थाता दीक्षयति, वायुर्वा अध्वर्युरधिदैवं, प्राणोऽध्यात्ममन्नं वृष्टिर्वायुं चैव तत्प्राणं चान्नेन सन्दधाति,(२) तस्मादेतावन्तरेणान्यो न दीक्षेत, स यदेतावन्तरेणान्यो दीक्षेतेमं तं लोकं प्राणेन व्यापादयेत्, प्रमायुका ह स्युस्तस्मादेतावन्तरेणा-न्यो न दीक्षेत ॥ ५ ॥

अथ ब्रह्मणे ब्राह्मणाच्छंसिनं दीक्षयति। अथोद्गात्रे प्रस्तोतारं दीक्षयति। अथ होत्रे मैत्रावरुणं दीक्षयति। अथाध्वर्य्यवे प्रतिप्रस्था-तारं नेष्टा दीक्षयति। स हैनमन्वितरेषां वै नवानां क्लिप्तिरन्यतरे कल्पन्ते, नव वै प्राणाः, प्राणैर्यज्ञस्तायते। अथ ब्रह्मणे पोतारं दीक्ष-यति। अथोद्गात्रे प्रतिहर्त्तारं दीक्षयति। अथ होत्रेऽच्छावाकं दीक्ष-यति। अथाध्वर्य्यवे नेष्टारमुन्नेता दीक्षयति। स हैनमन्वथ ब्रह्मण आग्नीध्रं दीक्षयति। अथोद्गात्रे सुब्रह्मण्यं दीक्षयति। अथ होत्रे

१ लोकमन्येनेति क, घ, ।

२ चान्येन सन्दधातीति क, घ, ।

ग्रावस्तुतं दीक्षयति। अथ तमन्यस्नातको वा ब्रह्मचारी वा दीक्षयति, न पूतः पावयेदित्याहुः। सैषानुपूर्वं दीक्षा, तद्य एवं दीक्षन्ते दीक्षिष्यमाणा, एव ते सत्रिणां प्रायश्चित्तं न विन्दन्ते, सत्रिणां प्रायश्चित्तमनु तस्यार्द्धस्य योगक्षेमः कल्पते, यस्मिन्नर्द्धे दीक्षन्त इति ब्राह्मणम्॥ ६॥

श्रद्धाया वै देवा दीक्षणीयान्निरमिमत, अदितेः प्रायणीयां, सोमात् क्रयं, विष्णोरातिथ्यम् आदित्यात् प्रवर्ग्यं, स्वधाया उपसदोऽग्नीषोमाभ्यामौपवसथ्यमहः, प्रातर्य्यावभ्यो देवेभ्यः प्रातरनुवाकं वसुभ्यः, प्रातःसवनं, रुद्रेभ्यो माध्यन्दिनं सवनम्, आदित्येभ्यस्तृतीयसवनं, वरुणादवभृथम् अदितेरुदयनीयां, मित्रावरुणाभ्यामनूबन्ध्यां, त्वष्टुस्त्वाष्ट्रं देवीभ्यो दिविकाभ्यो,(१) देवता हवींषि, कामाद्दशातिरात्रं, स्वर्गलोकादुदवसानीयां, तद्वा एतदग्निष्टोमस्य जन्म स य एवमेतदग्निष्टोमस्य जन्म वेदाग्निष्टोमेन स आत्मा स लोको भूत्वा देवान् अप्येतीति ब्राह्मणम्॥ ७॥

अथ यद्दीक्षणीयया यजन्ते श्रद्धामेव तद्देवीं देवतां यजन्ते, श्रद्धा देवी देवता भवति, श्रद्धाया देव्याः सायुज्यं सलोकतां यन्ति य एतदुपयन्ति अथ यत् प्रायणीयया यजन्ते दितिमेव तद्देवीं देवतां यजन्तेऽदितिर्देवी देवता भवत्यदित्या देव्याः सायुज्यं सलोकतां यन्ति य एतदुपयन्ति अथ यत् क्रयमुपयन्ति सोममेव तद्देवं देवतां यजन्ते,सोमो देवो देवता भवति सोमस्य देवस्य सायुज्यं सलोकतां विश्वेभ्यो देवेभ्यः, दाशरात्रं दिग्भ्यो दशरात्रिकं पृष्ठ्यं षड़हमेभ्यो लोकेभ्यः, छन्दोमव्यहं संवत्सरात् दशममहः प्रजा-

१ देविकाभ्य इति क,।

यन्ति य एतदुपयन्ति अथ यदातिथ्यया यजन्ते विष्णुमेव तद्देवं देवतां यजन्ते, विष्णुर्देवो देवता भवति विष्णोर्देवस्य सायुज्यं सलोकतां यन्ति एतदुपयन्ति। अथ यत्प्रवर्ग्यमुपयन्त्यादित्यमेव तद्देवं देवतां यजन्ते, आदित्यो देवो देवता भवत्यादित्यस्य देवस्य सायुज्यं सलोकतां यन्ति य एतदुपयन्ति। अथ यदुपसदमुपयन्ति स्वधामेव तद्देवीं देवतां यजन्ते, स्वधा देवी देवता भवति स्वधाया देव्याः सायुज्यं सलोकतां यन्ति य एतदुपयन्ति। अथ यदौपवसथ्यमहरुपयन्त्यग्नीषोमावेव तद्देवौ देवते यजतोऽग्नीषोमौ देवौ देवते भवतोऽग्नीषोमयोर्देवयोः सायुज्यं सलोकतां यन्ति य एतदुपयन्ति। अथ यत् प्रातरनुवाकमुपयन्ति प्रातर्याव्ण(१) एव तद्देवां देवतां यजन्ते प्रातर्यावाणो, देवा देवता भवन्ति प्रातर्याव्णा देवानां सायुज्यं सलोकतां यन्ति य एतदुपयन्ति। अथ यत् प्रातःसवनमुपयन्ति वसूनेव तद्देवां देवतां यजन्ते, वसवो देवा(२) देवता भवन्ति वसूनां देवानां सायुज्यं सलोकतां यन्ति य एतदुपयन्ति। अथ यन्माध्यन्दिनं सवनमुपयन्ति रुद्रानेव तद्देवां देवतां यजन्ते, रुद्रा देवा देवता भवन्ति रुद्राणां देवानां सायुज्यं सलोकतां यन्ति य एतदुपयन्ति। अथ यत्तृतीयसवनमुपयन्त्यादित्यानेव तद्देवां देवतां यजन्ते, आदित्या देवा देवता भवन्त्यादित्यानां देवानां सायुज्यं सलोकतां यन्ति य एतदुपयन्ति। अथ यदवभृथमुपयन्ति वरुणमेव तद्देवं देवतां यजन्ते, वरुणो देवो देवता भवति वरुणस्य देवस्य सायुज्यं सलोकतां यन्ति य एतदुपयन्ति। अथ यदु-

१ प्रातर्यावाणोदेवो इति क, ख,।

२ वसवो देवो इति क, ख,।

दयनीयया यजन्ते दितिमेव तद्देवीं देवतां यजन्ते, दितिर्देवी देवता भवत्यदित्या देव्याः सायुज्यं सलोकतां यन्ति य एतदुपयन्ति। अथ यदनूबन्ध्यया यजन्ते मित्रावरुणावेव तद्देवौ देवते यजतो मित्रावरुणौ देवौ देवते भवतो मित्रावरुणयोर्देवयोः सायुज्यं सलोकतां यन्ति य एतदुपयन्ति। अथ यत् त्वाष्ट्रेण पशुना यजन्ते त्वष्टारमेव तद्देवं देवतां यजन्ते, त्वष्टा देवो देवता भवति त्वष्टुर्देवस्य सायुज्यं सलोकतां यन्ति य एतदुपयन्ति। अथ यद्देविकाहविर्भिश्चरन्ति या एता उपसत्सु भवन्त्यग्निः सोमो विष्णुरिति देव्यो देविका देवता भवन्ति देवीनां देविकानां देवतानां सायुज्यं सलोकतां यन्ति य एतदुपयन्ति। अथ यद्द्व्यातिरात्रमुपयन्ति काममेव तद्देवं देवतां यजन्ते, कामो देवो देवता भवति कामस्य देवस्य सायुज्यं सलोकतां यन्ति य एतदुपयन्ति। अथ यदुदवसानीयया यजन्ते स्वर्गमेव तं लोकं देवं देवतां यजन्ते स्वर्गो लोको देवो देवता भवति स्वर्गस्य लोकस्य देवस्य सायुज्यं सलोकतां यन्ति य एतदुपयन्ति। तद्वा एतदग्निष्टोमस्य जन्म स य एवमेतदग्निष्टोमस्य जन्म वेदाम्वेव तदग्निष्टोमं स्वर्गे लोके प्रतिष्ठति प्रतितिष्ठति प्रजया पशुभिर्य एवं वेदा अग्निष्टोमेन स आत्मा सलोको भूत्वा देवान् अप्येतीति ब्राह्मणम् ॥ ८ ॥

अहोरात्राभ्यां वै देवाः प्रायणीयमतिरात्रं निरमिमत अर्द्धमसेभ्यश्चतुर्विंशमहः, ब्रह्मणोऽभिप्लवं, क्षत्रात्पृष्ठ्यमग्नेरभिजितम् अद्भ्यः स्वरसामानः, सूर्य्याद्विषुवन्तमुक्ता आवृत्ताः स्वरसामान इन्द्राद्विश्वजितमुक्तौ पृष्ठ्याभिप्लवौ मित्रावरुणाभ्यां, गवायुषी

पतेर्महाव्रतं स्वर्गाल्लोकादुदयनीयमतिरात्रं तद्वा एतत् संवत्सरस्य जन्म, स य एवमेतत् संवत्सरस्य जन्म वेद संवत्सरेण स आत्मा सलोको भूत्वा देवमप्येतीति ब्राह्मणम् ॥ ८ ॥

अथ यत्प्रायणीयमतिरात्रमुपयन्त्यहोरात्रावेव तद्देवौ देवते यजतोऽहोरात्रौ देवौ देवते भवतोऽहोरात्रयोर्देवयोः सायुज्यं सलोकतां यन्ति य एतदुपयन्ति। अथ यच्चतुर्विंशमहरुपयन्त्यर्द्धमासानेव तद्देवां देवतां यजन्तेऽर्द्धमासा देवा देवता भवन्त्यर्द्धमासानां देवानां सायुज्यं सलोकतां यन्ति य एतदुपयन्ति। अथ यदभिप्लवमुपयन्ति ब्रह्माणमेव तद्देवं देवतां यजन्ते ब्रह्मा देवो देवता भवति ब्रह्मणो देवस्य सायुज्यं सलोकतां यन्ति य एतदुपयन्ति। अथ यत् पृष्ठ्यमुपयन्ति क्षत्रमेव तद्देवं देवतां यजन्ते क्षत्रं देवो देवता भवति क्षत्रस्य देवस्य सायुज्यं सलोकतां यन्ति य एतदुपयन्ति। अथ यदभिजितमुपयन्त्यग्निमेव तद्देवं देवतां यजन्तेऽग्निर्देवो देवता भवत्यग्नेर्देवस्य सायुज्यं सलोकतां यन्ति य एतदुपयन्ति। अथ यत्स्वरसाम्न उपयन्त्यप एव तद्देवीर्देवता यजन्त आपो देव्यो देवता भवन्त्यपान्देवीनां सायुज्यं सलोकतां यन्ति य एतदुपयन्ति। अथ यद्विषुवन्तमुपयन्ति सूर्य्यमेव तद्देवं देवतां यजन्ते सूर्य्यो देवो देवता भवति सूर्य्यस्य देवस्य सायुज्यं सलोकतां यन्ति य एतदुपयन्ति। उक्ता आवृत्ताः स्वरसामानः। अथ यद्विश्वजितमुपयन्तीन्द्रमेव तद्देवं देवतां यजन्त इन्द्रो देवो देवता भवतीन्द्रस्य देवस्य सायुज्यं सलोकतां यन्ति य एतदुपयन्ति। उक्तौ पृष्ठ्याभिप्लवावथ यद् गवायुषी उपयन्ति मित्रावरुणावेव तद्देवौ देवते यजतो मित्रावरुणौ देवौ देवते भवतो मित्रावरुणयोर्देवयोः सायुज्यं सलोकतां यन्ति य एतदुपयन्ति। अथ

यद्दशरात्रमुपयन्ति विश्वानेव तद्देवान्देवतां यजन्ते विश्वेदेवा देवता भवन्ति विश्वेषां देवानां सायुज्यं सलोकतां यन्ति य एतदुपयन्ति। अथ यद्दाशरात्रिकं पृष्ठ्यं षड़हमुपयन्ति दिश एव तद्देवीर्देवता यजन्ते दिशो देव्यो देवता भवन्ति दिशान्देवीनां सायुज्यं सलोकतां यन्ति य एतदुपयन्ति। अथ यच्छन्दोमत्र्यहमुपयन्तीमानेव तल्लोकां देवान् देवतां यजन्त इमे लोका देवा देवता भवन्ति एषां लोकानां देवानां सायुज्यं सलोकतां यन्ति य एतदुपयन्ति। अथ यद्दशममहरुपयन्ति संवत्सरमेव तद्देवं देवतां यजन्ते संवत्सरो देवो देवता भवति संवत्सरस्य देवस्य सायुज्यं सलोकतां यन्ति य एतदुपयन्ति। अथ यन्महाव्रतमुपयन्ति प्रजापतिमेव तद्देवं देवतां यजन्ते प्रजापतिर्देवो देवता भवति प्रजापतेर्देवस्य सायुज्यं सलोकतां यन्ति य एतदुपयन्ति। अथ यदुदयनीयमतिरात्रमुपयन्ति स्वर्गमेव तल्लोकं देवं देवतां यजन्ते स्वर्गो लोको देवो देवता भवति स्वर्गस्य लोकस्य देवस्य सायुज्यं सलोकतां यन्ति य एतदुपयन्ति तद् वा एतत्संवत्सरस्य जन्म स य एवमेतत्संवत्सरस्य जन्म वेदाप्त्वैतत्संवत्सरं स्वर्गे लोके प्रतिष्ठति प्रतितिष्ठति प्रजया पशुभिर्य एवं वेद संवत्सरेण स आत्मा सलोको भूत्वा देवाँ अप्येतीति (१) ब्राह्मणम्॥ १०॥

स वा एष संवत्सरोऽधिदेवं चाध्यात्मं च प्रतिष्ठितः स य एवमेतत् संवत्सरमधिदेवं चाध्यात्मं च प्रतिष्ठितं वेद प्रतिष्ठति प्रतितिष्ठति प्रजया पशुभिर्य एवं वेद स वा एष संवत्सरः॥ ११॥

स वा एष संवत्सरो बृहतीमभिसम्पन्नो द्वावचरावङ्गौ षड्हो

(१) देवम् अप्येतीति च,।

द्वौ पृष्ठ्याभिप्लवौ गवायुषी दशरात्रस्तथा खलु षट्त्रिंशत् सम्पद्यन्ते षट्त्रिंशदवदाना गौः षट्त्रिंशदक्षरा बृहती बार्हतो वै स्वर्गो लोको बृहत्या वै देवाः स्वर्गे लोके यजन्ते बृहत्याः स्वर्गे लोके प्रतिष्ठति प्रतितिष्ठति प्रजया पशुभिर्य एवं वेद स वा एष संवत्सरः ॥ १२ ॥

स वा एष संवत्सरस्त्रिमहाव्रतश्चतुर्विंशेन महाव्रतं विषुवति महाव्रतं महाव्रत एव महाव्रतं तं ह स्मैतमेवं विद्वांसः पूर्वे त्रिमहाव्रतमुपयन्ति ते तेजस्विन आसन् सत्यवादिनः संशितव्रता य एनमद्य तथोपेयुर्यथाऽऽमपात्रमुदक आसिक्तं निर्मृज्येदेवं यजमाना निर्मृज्येरन्नुपर्युपयन्ति तथा ह्यस्य सत्येन तपसा व्रतेन चाभिजितमवरुद्धं भवति य एवं वेद स वा एष संवत्सरः ॥ १३ ॥

अथ यच्चतुर्विंशमहरुपेत्यानुपेत्य विषुवन्तं महाव्रतमुपेयात् कथमनाकृत्यै भवतीति यमेवामुं पुरस्ताद्विषुवतोऽतिरात्रमुपयन्ति तेनेति ब्रूयादभिप्लवात् पृष्ठ्यो निर्मितः, पृष्ठ्यादभिजित्, अभिजितः स्वरसामानः, स्वरसामभ्यो विषुवान्, विषुवतः स्वरसामानः; स्वरसामभ्यो विश्वजित्, विश्वजितः पृष्ठ्याभिप्लवौ, पृष्ठ्याभिप्लवाभ्यां गवायुषी, गवायुर्भ्यां दशरात्रः, दशरात्राय महाव्रतं, महाव्रतादुदयनीयायातिरात्रायोदयनीयोऽतिरात्रः स्वर्गाय लोकायान्नाद्याय प्रतिष्ठित्यै य एवं वेद स वा एष संवत्सरः ॥ १४ ॥

अथ यच्चतुर्विंशमहरुपेत्यानुपेत्य विषुवन्तं महाव्रतमुपेयात् कथमनाकृत्यै भवतीति यमेवामुं पुरस्ताद्विषुवतोऽतिरात्रमुपयन्ति तेनेतिब्रूयादभिप्लवात् पृष्ठ्यो निर्मितः, पृष्ठ्यादभिजित्, अभिजितः स्वरसामानः, स्वरसामभ्यो विषुवान्, विषुवतः स्वरसामानः, स्वर-

सामभ्यो विश्वजित्, विश्वजितः पृष्ठ्याभिप्लवौ, पृष्ठ्याभिप्लवाभ्यां गवायुषी, गवायुर्भ्यां दशरात्रोऽथ ह देवेभ्यो महाव्रतं न तस्थे कथमूर्द्धः स्तोमैर्विषुवन्तमुपागातां हन्तैमामिति ते देवा इह सामिवास्त्रन्न तं यज्ञक्रतुं जानीमो य ऊर्द्ध्वस्तोमो येनैतदहरवाप्नुयामेति तत एतं द्वादशरात्रमूर्द्धस्तोमं ददृशुस्तमाहरंस्तेनायजन्त तत एभ्योऽतिष्ठांस्तिष्ठति हास्मै महाव्रतं महाव्रतं प्रतिष्ठति प्रतितिष्ठति प्रजया पशुभिर्य एवं वेद स वा एष संवत्सरः ॥ १५ ॥

अथ यच्चतुर्विंशमहरुपेत्यानुपेत्य विषुवन्तं महाव्रतमुपेयात् कथमनाकूत्यै भवतीति यमेवामुं पुरस्ताद्विषुवतोऽतिरात्रमुपयन्ति तेनेति ब्रूयात् तदाहुः कति संवत्सरस्य पराञ्च्यहानि भवन्ति, कत्यर्वाञ्चि, तद्यानि सकृत् सकृदुपयन्ति तानि पराञ्चि, अथ यानि पुनः पुनरुपयन्ति तान्यर्वाञ्चि, इत्येवैनां न्युपासीरन् षड़हयोर्ह्यावृत्तिमन्वावर्त्तन्ते य एवं वेद स वा एष संवत्सरः ॥ १६ ॥

अथ यच्चतुर्विंशमहरुपेत्यानुपेत्य विषुवन्तं महाव्रतमुपेयात् कथमनाकूत्यै भवतीति यमेवामुं पुरस्ताद्विषुवतोऽतिरात्रमुपयन्ति तेनेति ब्रूयादभिप्लवं पुरस्तात् विषुवतः पूर्वमुपयन्ति पृष्ठ्यमुपरिष्टात् पिता वा अभिप्लवः पुत्रः पृष्ठ्यस्तस्मात्पूर्वे वयसि पुत्राः पितरमुपजीवन्ति पृष्ठ्यं पश्चाद्विषुवतः पूर्वमुपयन्ति अभिप्लवमुपरिष्टात्पिता वा अभिप्लवः पुत्रः पृष्ठ्यस्तस्मादुत्तमे वयसि पुत्रान् पितोपजीवति य एवं वेद ।

तदप्येतदृचोक्तम् । शतमिन्नु शरदो अन्ति देवा यत्रा नश्चक्रा जरसं तनूनां । पुत्रासो यत्र पितरो भवन्ति मा नो मध्या रीरिषतायुर्गन्तोरिति ।

उप ह वा एनं पूर्वे वयसि पुत्राः पितरमुपजीवन्त्युपोत्तमे वयसि पुत्रान् पितोपजीवन्ति य एवं वेद स वा एष संवत्सरः ॥ १७ ॥

अथ हैष महासुपर्णस्तस्य यान् पुरस्ताद्विषुवतः षण्मासानुपयन्ति स दक्षिणः पक्षोऽथ यानावृत्तानुपरिष्टात् षडुपयन्ति स उत्तरः पक्षः आत्मा वै संवत्सरस्य विषुवानङ्गानि पक्षौ यत्र वा आत्मा तत्पक्षौ यत्र वै पक्षौ तदात्मा न वा आत्मा पक्षावतिरिच्येते नो पक्षावात्मानमतिरिच्यन्त इत्येवमु हैव तदपरेषां स्विदितमङ्गां परेषामित्यपरेषां चैव परेषां चेति ब्रूयात्स वा एष संवत्सरः ॥ १८ ॥

तदाहुर्यद्द्वादशमासाः संवत्सरोऽथ हैतदहरवाप्नुयामेति यद्वैषुवतमपरेषां स्विदितमङ्गां परेषामित्यपरेषां चैव परेषां चेति ब्रूयादात्मा वै संवत्सरस्य विषुवानङ्गानि मासौ यत्र वा आत्मा तदङ्गानि यत्राङ्गानि तदात्मा न वा आत्माऽङ्गान्यतिरिच्येते नोऽङ्गान्यात्मानमतिरिच्यन्त इत्येवमु हैव तदपरेषां स्विदितमङ्गां परेषामित्यपरेषां चैव परेषां चेति ब्रूयात्स वा एष संवत्सरः ॥ १९ ॥

तदाहुः कथमुभयतो ज्योतिषोऽभिप्लवा अन्यतरो(१)ज्योतिस्पृष्ट इत्युभयतो ज्योतिषो वा इमे लोका अग्निनेता आदित्येनामुत इत्येष ह वा एतेषां ज्योतिर्य एनं प्रस्रदीव तपति देवचक्रे ह वा एते पृष्ठे प्रतिष्ठिते पाप्मानं तृंहतो परिप्लवेते तद्य एवं विदुषां दीक्षितानां पापक कीर्त्तयेदेत एवास्य तद्देवचक्रे शिरश्छिन्दतो दशरात्रमुर्जि पृष्ठ्याभिप्लवो चक्रे दशरात्रमुर्जि पृष्ठ्याभिप्लवो चक्रे तन्वं कुर्वीतेति ह स्माह वास्युस्तयो स्तोत्राणि च शस्त्राणि च

(१) अन्यतरत इति क, ।

सञ्चारयेयः सञ्चारयेत्तस्मादिमे पुरुषे प्राणा नाना सन्त एकोदया-च्छरीरमधिवसति यत्र सञ्चारयेत् प्रमायुको ह यजमानः स्यादेष ह वै प्रमायुको योऽन्धो वा बधिरो वा न चाग्निष्टोमा मासि सम्पद्यन्ते न वै प्राणा प्राणैर्य्यज्ञस्तायत एकविंशतिरुक्थ्या एकोक्थ्यः षोड़श्यन्नं वा उक्थ्यं वीर्य्यं षोड़श्येव तया रूढ्वा स्वर्गं लोक-मध्यारोहन्ति ॥ २० ॥

अथातोऽङ्गामध्यारोहः। प्रायणीयेनातिरात्रेणोदयनीयमतिरात्र-मध्यारोहन्ति, चतुर्विंशेन महाव्रतमभिप्लवेन परमभिप्लवं, पृष्ठ्येन परं पृष्ठ्यमभिजिताऽभिजितं, स्वरसामभिः परान् स्वरसामानः ऽथ हैतदहरवाप्नुयामेति यद्वैषुवतमपरेषां स्विदितमङ्गां परेषामित्य-परेषां च परेषां चेति ब्रूयात्स वा एष संवत्सरः ॥ २१ ॥

अथातोऽङ्गां नोवाहः। प्रायणीयोऽतिरात्रश्चतुर्विंशायाङ्गे निवहति,(१) चतुर्विंशमहरभिप्लवाय, अभिप्लवः पृष्ठ्याय, पृष्ठ्योऽभि-जिते, अभिजित स्वरसामभ्यः, स्वरसामानो विषुवते, विषुवान् स्वरसामभ्यः, स्वरसामानो विश्वजिते, विश्वजित् पृष्ठ्याभिप्लवाभ्यां, पृष्ठ्याभिप्लवौ गवायुर्भ्यां, गवायुषो दशरात्राय, दशरात्रो महा-व्रताय, महाव्रतमुदयनीयायातिरात्राय, उदयनीयोऽतिरात्रः स्वर्गाय लोकायान्नाद्याय प्रतिष्ठित्यै य एवं वेद स वा एष संवत्सरः ॥ २२ ॥

आदित्याश्च ह वा आङ्गिरसश्च स्वर्गे लोकेऽस्पर्द्धन्त वयं पूर्वे स्वरे-ष्यामो वयं पूर्व इति त आदित्या लघुभिः सामभिश्चतुर्भिः स्तोमैर्द्वाभ्यां पृष्ठ्याभ्यां स्वर्गं लोकमभ्यप्लवन्त, यदभ्यप्लवन्त तस्मादभिप्लवोऽन्नञ्च एवा-ङ्गिरसः गुरुभिः सामभिः सर्वैः स्तोमैः सर्वैःपृष्ठैः स्वर्गं लोकमभ्य-

(१) अङ्गेन वहतीति क, घ,।

स्पृशन्त, यदभ्यस्पृशन्त तस्मात् पृष्ठ्यस्तंवा एतं स्पृशं सन्तं पृष्ठ्य इत्याचक्षते, परोक्षेण परोक्षप्रिया इव हि देवा भवन्ति प्रत्यक्षद्विषः। अभिप्लवात् पृष्ठ्यो निर्मितः, पृष्ठ्यादभिजित्, अभिजितः स्वरसामानः, स्वरसामभ्यो विषुवान्, विषुवतः स्वरसामानः, स्वरसामभ्यो विश्वजिद्विश्वजितः पृष्ठ्याभिप्लवौ, पृष्ठ्याभिप्लवाभ्यां गवायुषी, गवायुर्भ्यां दशरात्रस्तानहि वा एतानि यज्ञारण्यानि यज्ञकृत्तन्त्राणि तेषां शतं शतं रथानां न्यन्तरं तद्यथाऽरण्यान्यारूढ़ा अशनापिपासे ते पाप्मानं हंहतो परिप्लवेते एवं हैवैते प्रप्लवन्ते ये विद्वांस उपयन्त्यथ ये विद्वांसमुपयन्ति तद्यथा प्रवाहात् प्रवाहं स्थलात् स्थलं समात्समं सुखात्सुखमभयादभयमुपसङ्क्रामन्तीत्येवं हैवैते संवत्सरस्योदृचं समश्नवामहा इति ब्राह्मणम् ॥ २३ ॥

प्रेदिर्ह वै कौशाम्बेयः कौसुरविन्दुरुद्दालक आरुणौ ब्रह्मचर्य्यमुवाच तमाचार्य्यः पप्रच्छ कुमारः कति ते पिता संवत्सरस्याह्नान्यमन्यथेति कति त्वेवेति दशेति होवाच दश वा इति होवाच दशाक्षरा विराड् वैराजो यज्ञः कति त्वेवेति नवेति होवाच नव वा इति होवाच नव वै प्राणाः प्राणैः यज्ञस्तायते कति त्वेवेत्यष्टेति होवाचाष्ट वा इति होवाचाष्टाक्षरा गायत्री गायत्रो यज्ञः कति त्वेवेति सप्तेति होवाच सप्त वा इति होवाच सप्त छन्दांसि छन्दोभिर्यज्ञस्तायते कति त्वेवेति षड़िति होवाच षड् वा इति होवाच षड् वा ऋतव ऋतूनामाप्त्यै कति त्वेवेति पञ्चेति होवाच पञ्च वा इति होवाच पञ्चपदा पङ्क्तिः पाङ्क्तो यज्ञः कति त्वेवेति चत्वारीति होवाच चत्वारि वा इति होवाच चत्वारो वै वेदा वेदैर्यज्ञस्तायते कति त्वेवेति त्रीणीति होवाच

त्रीणि वा इति होवाच त्रिषवणो वै यज्ञः सवनैर्य्यज्ञस्तायते कति त्विवेति द्वे इति होवाच द्वे वा इति होवाच द्विपाद्वै पुरुषो द्विप्रतिष्ठः पुरुषः पुरुषो वै यज्ञः कति त्विवेत्येकमिति होवाचैकम् वा इति होवाचाहरहरित्येकमेव सर्वं संवत्सरम् (१)॥ २४॥

इति गोपथब्राह्मणपूर्व्वभागे चतुर्थः प्रपाठकः समाप्तः ।

---

## अथ पञ्चमः प्रपाठकः ।

ओं अभिप्लवः षडहः षडहानि भवन्ति ज्योतिर्गौरायुर्गौरायुर्ज्योतिरभिप्लवः पञ्चाहः पञ्च ह्येवाहानि भवन्ति यदेव प्रथममहस्तदुत्तममहरभिप्लवश्चतुरहश्चत्वारो हि स्तोमा भवन्ति त्रिवृत् पञ्चदशः सप्तदशैकविंश एवाभिप्लवस्त्र्यहस्त्र्यहावृत्तिर्ज्योतिर्गौरायुर्गौरायुर्ज्योतिरभिप्लवो द्व्यहो द्वे ह्येव सामनी भवतो बृहद्रथन्तरएवाभिप्लव एकाह एकाहस्य स्तोमै स्तायते चतुर्णामुक्थानां द्वादशस्तोत्राण्यतिरिच्यन्ते स सप्तमोऽग्निष्टोमस्तथा खलु सप्ताग्निष्टोमा मासि सम्पद्यन्ते इति ब्राह्मणम् ॥ १ ।

अथातो गाधप्रतिष्ठा समुद्रं वा एते प्रतरन्ति ये संवत्सराय दीक्षन्ते तेषां तीर्थमेव प्रायणीयोऽतिरात्रस्तीर्थेन हि प्रतरन्ति तद्यथा समुद्रं तीर्थेन प्रतरेयुस्तादृक् तद्गाधप्रतिष्ठा चतुर्विंशमहर्यथोपकक्षदघ्नं वा कण्ठदघ्नं वा यतो विश्रम्य प्रस्नायेयुस्तादृक् तत्प्रश्ने योऽभिप्लवः प्रश्ने यः पृष्ठ्योगाधप्रतिष्ठाभिजिद्यथोपकक्षदघ्नं वा

१ अहरह.रेत्येकमेव सर्वं संवत्सरमिति ख, ग।

कण्ठदघ्नं वा यतो विश्रम्य प्रप्नायेयुस्तादृक् तन्नीविदघ्न एव प्रथमः स्वरसामा जानुदघ्नो द्वितीयः कुल्युदघ्नस्तृतीयो द्वीपप्रतिष्ठा विषुवान्यथोपकक्षदघ्नं वा कण्ठदघ्नं वा यतो विश्रम्य प्रप्नायेयुस्तादृक् तत्कुल्युदघ्न एव प्रथमोऽर्वाक् स्वरसामा जानुदघ्नो द्वितीयो नीविदघ्नस्तृतीयो गाधप्रतिष्ठा विश्वजिद्यथोपकक्षदघ्नं वा कण्ठदघ्नं वा यतो विश्रम्य प्रप्नायेयुस्तादृक् तत्प्रश्ने यः पृष्ठ्यः प्रश्ने योऽभिप्लवः प्रश्नेयौ गवायुषी प्रश्ने यो दशरात्रो गाधप्रतिष्ठा महाव्रतं यथोपकक्षदघ्नं वा कण्ठदघ्नं वा यतो विश्रम्य प्रप्नायेयुस्तादृक् तत्तेषां तीर्थमेवोदनीयोऽतिरात्रस्तीर्थेन ह्युद्यन्ति तद्यथा समुद्रं तीर्थेनोदेयुस्तादृक्तदथ ह स्माह श्वेतकेतुरारुणेयः संवत्सरस्याहं दीक्षा इति तस्य ह पिता मुखमुदीक्ष्योवाच वेत्थ स्तत त्वमायुष्मान् संवत्सरस्य गाधप्रतिष्ठे इति वेदेत्येतद्ध स्मैतद्विद्वानाहेति ब्राह्मणम्॥ २॥

पुरुषो वाव संवत्सरस्तस्य पादावेव प्रायणीयोऽतिरात्रः पादाभ्यां हि प्रयन्ति (१) तयोर्यच्छुक्लं तदह्नो रूपं यत् कृष्णं तद्रात्रेः नखानि नक्षत्राणां रूपं लोमान्योषधिवनस्पतीनामूरू चतुर्विंशमहरुरोऽभिप्लवं पृष्ठं ग पृष्ठ्यः शिर एव त्रिवृत् त्रिवृत् ह्येव शिरो भवति त्वगस्थिमज्जामस्तिष्कं ग्रीवाः पञ्चदशस्तुर्दश ह्येवैतस्यां कराणि भवन्ति वीर्य्यं पञ्चदशं तस्मादियमाभिरण्वीभिः सतीभिर्गुरुं भारं (२)हरति तस्माद्ग्रीवाः पञ्चदश उरः सप्तदशौष्ठावन्ये यत्र वीष्ठावन्य उरः सप्तदशं तस्मादुरः सप्तदश-

(१) पादाभ्यां प्रयन्ति इति ख, ग,।

(२) गुरु भरमिति ख, ग,।

उदरमेकविंशो विंशतिर्ह्येवैतस्यान्तर उदरे उत्तापानि भवन्त्यु-
दरमेकविंशं तस्मादुदरमेकविंशः पार्श्वे त्रिणवस्त्रयोदशान्याः
पर्शवोऽन्याः पार्श्वे त्रिणवस्तस्मात् पार्श्वे त्रिणवोऽनूकं त्रयस्त्रिंशो
द्वात्रिंशतिर्ह्येवैतस्यां पृष्टी कुण्ड्री उलानि भवन्त्यनूकं त्रयस्त्रिंशः
तस्मादनूकं त्रयस्त्रिंशस्तस्यायमेव दक्षिणो बाहुरभिजित्तस्ये-
मे दक्षिणे त्रयः प्राणाः स्वरसामान आत्मा विषुवांस्तस्येमे
सव्ये त्रयः प्राणा अर्वाक् स्वरसामानस्तस्यायं सव्यो बाहुर्विश्व-
जिदुक्तौ पृष्ठ्याभिप्लवौ याववाञ्चौ प्राणौ तौ गवायुषी अङ्गानि
दशरात्रो मुखं महाव्रतं तस्य हस्तावेवोदयनीयोऽतिरात्रो
हस्ताभ्यां ह्युद्यन्ति य एवं वेद स वा एष संवत्सरः ॥ २ ॥

पुरुषो वाव संवत्सरः, तस्य प्राण एव प्रायणीयोऽति-
रात्रः प्राणेन हि प्रयन्ति वागारम्भणीयमहर्यद्यदारभते वागा-
रभते वाचैव तदारभते (१) तस्यायमेव दक्षिणः पाणिरभिप्लव-
स्तस्येदं प्रातःसवनमिदं माध्यन्दिनँ सवनमिदं तृतीयं
सवनं गायत्र्या आयतने तस्मादियमस्यै ह्रसिष्ठा तस्येदं
प्रातःसवनमिदं माध्यन्दिनं सवनमिदं तृतीयसवनं त्रिष्टुभ-
आयतने तस्मादियमस्यै वरिष्ठा तस्येदं प्रातःसवनमिदं
माध्यन्दिनं सवनमिदं तृतीयसवनं जगत्या आयतने तस्मादियमन-
योर्वरिष्ठा तस्येदं प्रातःसवनमिदं माध्यन्दिनँ सवनमिदं तृती-
यसवनं पङ्क्त्या आयतने पृथुरिव वै पङ्क्तिस्तस्मादियमासां
प्रतिष्ठा तस्येदं प्रातःसवनमिदं माध्यन्दिनँ सवनमिदं तृतीय-
सवनं विराज आयतनेऽन्नं वै श्रीः विराड़न्नाद्यस्य श्रियोऽवरुध्यै

(१) वाचैतदारभते इति क, ।

तस्मादियमासां वरिष्ठा तस्येदं प्रातःसवनमिदं माध्यन्दिनं सवनमिदं तृतीयसवनमतिच्छन्दसां आयतनेऽतिच्छन्दो वै छन्दसामायतनं तस्मादिदं प्रतिष्ठं फलकं तस्येदं प्रातःसवनमिदं माध्यन्दिनँ सवनमिदं तृतीयसवनं सैतः सैतोऽभिप्लवः सैत आत्मा पृष्ठाः प्लवतीवाभिप्लवस्तिष्ठतीव पृष्ठाः प्लवत इव ह्येवमङ्गैस्तिष्ठतीवात्मना तस्यायमेव दक्षिणः कर्णोऽभिजित् तस्य यद् दक्षिणमक्ष्णः शुक्लं स प्रथमस्स्वरसामा यत् कृष्णं स द्वितीयो यन्मण्डलं स तृतीयो नासिके विषुवान् मण्डलमेव प्रथमोऽर्वाक् स्वरसामा यत् कृष्णं स द्वितीयो यत् शुक्लं स तृतीयस्तस्यायं सव्यः कर्णो विश्वजिदक्षौ पृष्ठाभिप्लवौ यावर्वाञ्चौ प्राणौ तौ गवायुषी अङ्गानि दशरात्रो मुखं महाव्रतं तस्योदान एवोदयनीयोऽतिरात्र उदानेन ह्युद् यन्ति य एवं वेद स वा एष संवत्सरः ॥४॥

पुरुषो वाव संवत्सरः पुरुष इत्येकँ संवत्सरमित्येक इत्यत्र तत्समं, द्वे अहोरात्रे संवत्सरस्य द्वाविमौ पुरुषे प्राणा इत्यत्र तत्समं, त्रयो वा ऋतवः संवत्सरस्य त्रय इमे पुरुषे प्राणा इत्यत्र तत्समं, षड् वा ऋतवः संवत्सरस्य षडिमे पुरुषे प्राणा इत्यत्र तत्समं, सप्त वा ऋतवः संवत्सरस्य सप्तेमे पुरुषे प्राणा इत्यत्र तत्समं, द्वादशमासाः संवत्सरस्य द्वादशेमे पुरुषे प्राणा इत्यत्र तत्समं, त्रयोदशमासाः संवत्सरस्य त्रयोदशेमे पुरुषे प्राणा इत्यत्र तत्समं, चतुर्विंशतिरर्द्धमासाः संवत्सरस्य चतुर्विंशोऽयं पुरुषो विंशत्यङ्गुलिश्चतुरङ्ग इत्यत्र तत्समं, षड्विंशतिरर्द्धमासाः संवत्सरस्य षड्विंशोऽयं पुरुषः प्रतिष्ठे षड्विंश इत्यत्र तत्समं, त्रीणि च ह वै शतानि षष्टिश्च संवत्सर

स्याहोरात्राणीत्येतावन्त एव पुरुषस्य प्राणा इत्यत्र तत्-समं, सप्त च ह वै शतानि विंशतिश्च संवत्सरस्याहानि च रात्रयश्चेत्येतावन्त एव पुरुषस्यास्थीनि च मज्जानश्चेत्यत्र तत्-समं, चतुर्द्दश च ह वै शतानि चत्वारिंशच्च संवत्सरस्यार्द्धाह्याश्चार्द्धरात्रयश्चेत्येतावन्त एव पुरुषस्य स्नुरामांसानीत्यत्र तत् सममष्टाविंशतिश्च ह वै शतान्यशीतिश्च संवत्सरस्य पादाह्वाश्च पादरात्रयश्चेत्येतावन्त एव पुरुषस्य स्नावा बन्ध्या इत्यत्र तत् समं, दश च ह वै सहस्राण्यष्टौ च शतानि संवत्सरस्य मुहूर्त्ताः इत्येतावन्त एव पुरुषस्य पेशशरा इत्यत्र तत्समं, यावन्तो मुहूर्त्ताः पञ्चदशकृत्वस्तावन्तः प्राणा यावन्तः प्राणाः पञ्चदशकृत्वस्ता-वन्तोऽपाना: यावन्तोऽपानाः पञ्चदशकृत्वस्तावन्तो व्याना यावन्तो व्यानाः पञ्चदशकृत्वस्तावन्तः समाना यावन्तः समानाः पञ्चदश-कृत्वस्तावन्त उदाना यावन्त उदानाः पञ्चदशकृत्वस्तावन्त्येतादीनि यावन्त्येतादीनि तावन्ध्येतर्हीणि यावन्त्येतर्हीणि तावन्ति स्वेदाय-नानि यावन्ति स्वेदायनानि तावन्ति चिप्रायणानि यावन्ति चिप्रायणानि तावन्तो रोमकूपा यावन्तो रोमकूपाः पञ्चदश-कृत्वस्तावत्यो वर्षतो धारास्तदेतत् क्रोशशतिकम्परिमाणं ।

तदप्येतदृचोक्तम् । अस्मादन्यत्र परिवर्त्तमानश्चरत्यासीनो यदि वा स्वपन्नपि । अहोरात्राभ्यां पुरुषः क्षणेन कतिकृत्वः प्राणति चापानति च । शतं शतानि परिवत्सराणामष्टौ च शतानि मुहूर्त्तान् यान् वदन्ति (१) अहोरात्राभ्यां पुरुषः समेन कतिकृत्वः प्राणति चापानति चेति ब्राह्मणम् ॥ ५ ॥

(१) शतानि संवत् सरस्य मुहूर्त्तान यान् वदन्तीति ख, ग, ।

संवत्सरस्य समता वेदितव्येति ह स्मा ह वा स्वरेकमेव पुरस्ताद् विषुवतोऽतिरात्रमुपयन्त्येकमुपरिष्टात्त्रिपञ्चाशतमेव पुरस्ताद्विषुवतोऽग्निष्टोमानुपयन्ति त्रिपञ्चाशतमुपरिष्टाद्विंशतिशतमेव पुरस्ताद्विषुवत उक्थानुपयन्ति विंशतिशतमुपरिष्टात् षड़ेव पुरस्ताद्विषुवतः षोड़शिन उपयन्ति षडुपरिष्टात् त्रिंशदेव पुरस्ताद्विषुवतः षड़हानुपयन्ति त्रिंशदुपरिष्टात् सैषा संवत्सरस्य समता स य एवमेतां संवत्सरस्य समतां वेद संवत्सरेण स आत्मा सलोको भूत्वा देवानप्येतीति ब्राह्मणम् ॥ ६ ॥

अथातो यज्ञक्रमाः। अग्न्याधेयमग्न्याधेयात् पूर्णाहुतिः, पूर्णाहुतेरग्निहोत्रमग्निहोत्राद्दर्शपूर्णमासौ(१)दर्शपूर्णमासाभ्यामाग्रयणं, आग्रयणाच्चातुर्मास्यानि, चातुर्मास्येभ्यः पशुबन्धः, पशुबन्धादग्निष्टोमोऽग्निष्टोमाद्राजसूयो राजसूयाद्वाजपेयः, वाजपेयादश्वमेधः, अश्वमेधात्पुरुषमेधः, पुरुषमेधात्सर्वमेधः, सर्वमेधाद्दक्षिणावन्तो दक्षिणवद्भ्यो दक्षिणा अदक्षिणाः सहस्रदक्षिणे प्रत्यतिष्ठंस्ते वा एते यज्ञक्रमाः। स य एवमेतान् यज्ञक्रमान्वेद यज्ञेन स आत्मा सलोको भूत्वा देवानप्येतीति ब्राह्मणम् ॥ ७ ॥

प्रजापतिरकामयतानन्त्यमश्नूयेति(२) सोऽग्नीनाधाय पूर्णाहुत्या यजेत सोऽन्तमेवापश्यत्सोऽग्निहोत्रेणेष्ट्वाऽन्तमेवापश्यत् स दर्शपूर्णमासाभ्यामिष्ट्वाऽन्तमेवापश्यत् स आग्रयणेनेष्ट्वाऽन्तमेवापश्यत्स चातुर्मास्यैरिष्ट्वाऽन्तमेवापश्यत्स पशुबन्धेनेष्ट्वाऽन्तमेवापश्यत्सोऽग्निष्टोमेनेष्ट्वाऽन्तमेवापश्यत्स राजसूयेनेष्ट्वा राजेति नामाधत्त सोऽन्तमे-

(१) पौर्णमासाविति ख, ग, ।

(२) अनन्तमश्नूयेति ख, ग, ।

वापश्यत्स वाजपेयेनेष्ट्वा सम्राड़िति नामाधत्त सोऽन्तमेवापश्यत्सोऽश्वमेधेनेष्ट्वा स्वराडिति नामाधत्त सोऽन्तमेवापश्यत्स पुरुषमेधेनेष्ट्वा विराडिति नामाधत्त सोऽन्तमेवापश्यत्स सर्वमेधेनेष्ट्वा सर्वराडिति नामाधत्त सोऽन्तमेवापश्यत्सोऽहीनैर्दक्षिणावद्भिरिष्ट्वाऽन्तमेवापश्यत्सोऽहीनैरदक्षिणावद्भिरिष्ट्वाऽन्तमेवापश्यत्स सत्रेणोभयतोऽतिरात्रेणान्ततो यजेत वाचं ह वै होत्रे प्रायच्छत्प्राणमध्वर्य्यवे चक्षुरुद्गात्रे मनो ब्रह्मणेऽङ्गानि होत्रकेभ्य आत्मानं सदस्येभ्य एवमानन्त्यमात्मानं दत्वानन्त्यमश्नुयेति तद्या दक्षिणा अनयत्ताभिरात्मानं निष्क्रीणीय तस्मादेतेन ज्योतिष्टोमेनाग्निष्टोमेनात्मनिष्क्रयणेन सहस्रदक्षिणेन पृष्ठशमनीयेन त्वरेत यो ह्यनिष्ट्वा पृष्ठशमनीयेन प्रैत्यात्मानं सो निष्क्रीणीय प्रैतीति ब्राह्मणम् ॥ ८ ॥

यद्वै संवत्सराय संवत्सरसदो दीक्षन्ते कथमेषामग्निहोत्रमनन्तरितं भवति व्रतेनेति ब्रूयात्, कथमेषां दर्शोऽनन्तरितो भवति दध्ना च पुरोडाशेन चेति ब्रूयात्, कथमेषां पौर्णमासमनन्तरितं भवति आज्येन च पुरोडाशेन चेति ब्रूयात्, कथमेषामाग्रयणमनन्तरितं भवति सौम्येन चरुणेति ब्रूयात् कथमेषां चातुर्मास्यान्यनन्तरितानि भवन्ति पयसेति ब्रूयात्, कथमेषां पशुबन्धोऽनन्तरितो भवति पशुना च पुरोडाशेन चेति ब्रूयात्, कथमेषां सौम्योऽध्वरोऽनन्तरितो भवति ग्रहैरिति ब्रूयात्, कथमेषां गृहमेधोऽनन्तरितो भवति धानाकरम्भैरिति ब्रूयात्, कथमेषां पितृयज्ञोऽनन्तरितो भवत्यौपासनैरिति ब्रूयात्, कथमेषां मिथुनमनन्तरितं भवति हिङ्कारेणेति ब्रूयात्स्यैषा संवत्सरे यज्ञक्रतूनामुपैति स य एवमेतां

संवत्सरे यज्ञक्रतूनामुपैति वेद यज्ञेन स आत्मा सलोको भूत्वा देवाꣳअप्येतीति ब्राह्मणम् ॥ ९ ॥

देवा ह वै सहस्रसंवत्सराय दिदीक्षिरे, तेषां पञ्चशतानि संवत्सराणां पर्युपेतान्यासन्नथेदं सर्वं शुश्रुवुर्ये स्तोमा यानि पृष्ठानि यानि शस्त्राणि ते देवा इह सामिवासुरुप तं यज्ञक्रतुं जानीमो यः सहस्रसंवत्सरस्य प्रतिमा को हि तस्मै मनुष्यो यः सहस्रसंवत्सरेण यजेतेति तद्यातयाममभ्ये यज्ञस्यापश्यंस्तेनायातयाम्यायापेदे व्युष्टिरासीत्तां पञ्चस्वपश्यदृचि यजुषि साम्नि शान्तेऽथ घोरे, ता वा एताः पञ्च व्याहृतयो भवन्ति ओं आवयास्तु औषड् यज ये यजामहे वौषडिति ते देवा इह सामिवासुरुप तं यज्ञक्रतुं जानीमो यः सहस्रसंवत्सरस्य प्रतिमा को हि तस्मै मनुष्यो यः सहस्रसंवत्सरेण यजेतेति तत एतन्त्वापश्चितं सहस्रसंवत्सरस्याञ्जस्यमपश्यंस्ते ह्येव स्तोमा भवन्ति तानि पृष्ठानि तानि शस्त्राणि स खलु द्वादशमासां दीक्षाभिरेति द्वादशमासानुपसद्भिर्द्वादशमासां सुत्याभिरथ यद् द्वादशमासां दीक्षाभिरेति द्वादशमासानुपसद्भिस्तेनैतावग्न्यर्कावाप्नोति अथ यद् द्वादशमासां सुत्याभिस्तेनेदं महदुक्थमवाप्नोति ते देवा इह सामिवासुरुप तं यज्ञक्रतुं जानीमो यः सहस्रसंवत्सरस्य प्रतिमा को हि तस्मै मनुष्यो यः सहस्रसंवत्सरेण यजेतेति तत एतं संवत्सरन्त्वापश्चित्तस्याञ्जस्यमपश्यं स्ते ह्येव स्तोमा भवन्ति तानि पृष्ठानि तानि शस्त्राणि ते देवा इह सामिवासुरुप तं यज्ञक्रतुं जानीमो यः सहस्रसंवत्सरस्य प्रतिमा को हि तस्मै मनुष्यो यः सहस्रसंवत्सरेण यजेतेति तत एतं द्वादशाहं संवत्सरस्याञ्जस्यमपश्यंस्ते ह्येव स्तोमा भवन्ति तानि पृष्ठानि तानि श-

स्त्राणि स खलु द्वादशाहं दीक्षाभिरेति द्वादशाहमुपसद्भिर्द्वादशाहं सुत्याभिरथ यद् द्वादशाहं दीक्षाभिरेति द्वादशाहमुपसद्भिस्ते-नैतावन्नरक्षांवाप्नोत्यथ यद् द्वादशाहं सुत्याभिस्तेनेदं महदुक्थ-मवाप्नोति ते देवा इह सामिवासुरुप तं यज्ञक्रतुं जानीमो यः सहस्रसंवत्सरस्य प्रतिमा को हि तस्मै मनुष्यो यः सहस्रसंवत्सरेण यजेतेति तत एतं पृष्ठ्यः षड़हं द्वादशाहस्याञ्जस्यमपश्यं स्ते ह्येव स्तोमा भवन्ति तानि पृष्ठानि तानि शस्त्राणि ते देवा इह सामि-वासुरुप तं यज्ञक्रतुं जानीमो यः सहस्रसंवत्सरस्य प्रतिमा को हि तस्मै मनुष्यो यः सहस्रसंवत्सरेण यजेतेति तत एतं विश्वजितं पृष्ठ्यं षड़हस्याञ्जस्यमपश्यंस्ते ह्येव स्तोमा भवन्ति तानि पृष्ठानि तानि शस्त्राणि ते देवा इह सामिवासुरुप तं यज्ञक्रतुं जानीमो यः सहस्रसंवत्सरस्य प्रतिमा को हि तस्मै मनुष्यो यः सहस्रसंवत्सरेण यजेतेति स वा एष विश्वजिद् यः सहस्रसंवत्सरस्य प्रतिमैष ह प्रजानां प्रजापतिर्यद्विश्वजिदिति ब्राह्मणम् ॥ १० ॥

पुरुषं ह वै नारायणं प्रजापतिरुवाच यजस्व यजस्वेति स होवाच यजस्व यजस्वेत्येवं ह्यात्थमालिरयच्चतेमे वसवः प्रातःसवने-नागू रुद्रा माध्यन्दिने सवन आदित्यास्तृतीयसवने यज्ञवास्तु-न्येव पर्य्यशिषो यज्ञवास्तुमित्येवमाशिषोऽहं वा एतद्वेद यज्ञे वसवः प्रातःसवनेनागू रुद्रा माध्यन्दिने सवन आदित्यास्तृतीयसवने यज्ञवास्तुन्येव पर्य्यशिषो यज्ञवास्तुमित्येवमाशिषो विद्वांसो नूनं त्वा याजयेयुरेते ह वा अविद्वांसो यत्रानृग्विद् होता भवत्ययजु-र्विदध्वर्युरसामविदुद्गाता भृग्वङ्गिरोविद्ब्रह्मा यजस्वैव हन्त तु ते तद्वक्ष्यामि यथा सूत्रे मणिरिव सूत्रमेतान्युक्थाहानि भवन्ति

सूत्रमिव वा मणाविति तस्माद्य एव सर्वविंत्स्यात् तं ब्रह्माणं कुर्वीतैष ह वै विद्वान् सर्वविद्ब्रह्मा यद्भृग्वङ्गिरोविदेते ह वा अस्य सर्वस्य शमयितारः पालयितारस्तस्माद्ब्रह्मा स्तुते बहिः-पवमाने वाचयति ॥ ११ ॥

श्येनोऽसि गायत्रच्छन्दा अनु त्वारभे स्वस्ति मा सम्पारयेति स यदाह श्येनोऽसीति सोमं वा एतदाहैष ह वा अग्निर्भूत्वाऽस्मिं लोके संश्यायति तद्यत्संश्यायति तस्माच्छ्येनस्तच्छ्येनस्य श्येनत्वं स यदाह गायत्रच्छन्दा अनु त्वारभ इति गायत्रेण च्छन्दसा वसुभिर्दैवैः प्रातःसवनेऽस्मिं लोकेऽग्निं सन्तमन्वारभते स यदाह स्वस्ति मा सम्पारयेति गायत्रेणैव च्छन्दसा वसुभिर्दैवैः प्रातः-सवनेऽस्मिं लोकेऽग्निना देवेन स्वस्ति सम्पारयेति गायत्रेणैवैनन्त-च्छन्दसा वसुभिर्दैवैः प्रातःसवनेऽस्मिं लोकेऽग्निना देवेन स्वस्ति सम्पद्यते य एवं वेद ॥ १२ ॥

अथ माध्यन्दिने पवमाने वाचयति सम्राडसि त्रिष्टुप्छन्दा-अनु त्वारभे स्वस्ति मा सम्पारयेति स यदाह सम्राडसीति सोमं वा एतदाहैष ह वै वायुर्भूत्वाऽन्तरिक्षलोके सम्राजति तद्यत् सम्राजति तस्मात्सम्राट् तत् सम्राजस्य सम्राट्त्वं स यदाह त्रिष्टुप्-छन्दा अनु त्वारभ इति त्रैष्टुभेण छन्दसा रुद्रैर्दैवैर्माध्यन्दिने सवनेऽन्तरिक्षे लोके वायुं सन्तमन्वारभते स यदाह स्वस्ति मा सम्पारयेति त्रैष्टुभेणैव च्छन्दसा रुद्रैर्दैवैर्माध्यन्दिने सवनेऽन्तरिक्ष-लोके वायुना देवेन स्वस्ति मा सम्पारयेति त्रैष्टुभेणैवैनं तच्छ-न्दसा रुद्रैर्दैवैर्माध्यन्दिने सवनेऽन्तरिक्षलोके वायुना देवेन स्वस्ति सम्पद्यते य एवं वेद ॥ १३ ॥

अथार्भवे पवमाने वाचयति स्वरोऽसि गयोऽसि जगच्छन्दा अनु-त्वारभे स्वस्ति मा सम्पारयेति स यदाह स्वरोऽसीति सोमं वा एतदाहैष ह वै सूर्य्यो भूत्वाऽमुष्मिं लोके स्वरति तद्यत् स्वरति तस्मात् स्वरस्तत् स्वरस्य स्वरत्वं स यदाह गयोऽसीति सोमं वा एतदाहैष ह वै चन्द्रमा भूत्वा सर्वां लोकान् गच्छति तद् यद् गच्छति तस्माद्गयस्तद्गयस्य गयत्वं स यदाह जगच्छन्दा अनु त्वारभ इति जागतेन छन्दसाऽऽदित्यैर्देवैस्तृतीयसवनेऽमुष्मिन् लोके सूर्यं सन्तमन्वारभते स यदाह स्वस्ति मा सम्पारयेति जागतेनैव च्छन्दसाऽऽदित्यैर्देवैस्तृतीयसवनेऽमुष्मिं लोके सर्येण देवेन स्वस्ति सम्पारयेति जागतेनैवैनन्तच्छन्दसाऽऽदित्यैर्देवैस्तृतीयसवनेऽमुष्मिं लोके सूर्येण देवेन स्वस्ति सम्पद्यते य एवं वेद ॥ १४ ॥

अथ संस्थिते संस्थिते सवने वाचयति मयि भर्गो मयि महो मयि यशो मयि सर्वमिति पृथिव्येव भर्गो ऽन्तरिक्ष एव महो द्यौरेव यशोऽप एव सर्वमग्निरेव भर्गो वायुरेव मह आदित्य एव यशश्चन्द्र-मा एव सर्वं वसव एव भर्गो रुद्रा एव मह आदित्या एव यशो विश्वेदेवा एव सर्वं गायत्र्येव भर्गस्त्रिष्टुबेव महो जगत्येव यशोऽनु-ष्टुवेव सर्वं प्राच्येव भर्गः प्रतीच्येव मह उदीच्येव यशो दक्षिणैव सर्वं वसन्त एव भर्गो ग्रीष्म एव महो वर्षा एव यशः शरदेव सर्वं त्रिवृदेव भर्गः पञ्चदश एव महः सप्तदश एव यश एकविंश एव सर्व्वमृग्वेद एव भर्गो यजुर्वेद एव महः सामवेद एव यशो ब्रह्मवेद एव सर्वं होतैव भर्गोऽध्वर्युरेव मह उद्गातैव यशो ब्रह्मैव सर्वं वागेव भर्गः प्राण एव महश्चक्षुरेव यशो मन एव सर्वम् ॥ १५ ॥

स यदाह मयि भर्ग इति पृथिवीमेवैतं लोकानामाहाग्निं देवानां वसून् देवां देवगणानां गायत्रं छन्दसां प्राचीन्दिशां वसन्तमृतूनां त्रिवृतं स्तोमानामृग्वेदं वेदानां हौत्रं होत्रकाणां वाचमिन्द्रियाणाम् ॥ १६ ॥

स यदाह मयि महं इत्यन्तरिक्षमेवैतल्लोकानामाह(१) वायुं देवानां रुद्रां देवां देवगणानान्त्रैष्टुभं छन्दसां प्रतीचीन्दिशां ग्रीष्ममृतूनां पञ्चदशं स्तोमानां यजुर्वेदं वेदानामाध्वर्यवं होत्रकाणां प्राणमिन्द्रियाणाम् ॥ १७ ॥

स यदाह मयि यश इति दिवमेवैतल्लोकानामाहादित्यं(२) देवानामादित्यां देवां देवगणानां जागतं छन्दसामुदीचीन्दिशां वर्षां ऋतूनां सप्तदशं स्तोमानां सामवेदं वेदानामौद्गात्रं होत्रकाणां चक्षुरिन्द्रियाणाम् ॥ १८ ॥

स यदाह मयि सर्वमित्यप एवैतल्लोकानामाह(३) चन्द्रमसन्देवानां विश्वां देवां देवगणानामानुष्टुभं छन्दसां दक्षिणां दिशां शरदमृतूनामेकविंशं स्तोमानां ब्रह्मवेदं वेदानां ब्रह्मत्वं होत्रकाणां मन इन्द्रियाणाम् ॥ १९ ॥

स वा एष दशधा चतुः सम्पद्यते, दश च ह वै चतुर्विराजोऽक्षराणि तद्गर्भा उपजीवन्ति श्रीर्वै विराड्यशोऽन्नाद्यं श्रियमेव तद्विराजं यशस्यन्नाद्ये प्रतिष्ठापयति प्रतिष्ठन्तीरिदं सर्वमनुप्रतिष्ठति प्रतितिष्ठति प्रजया पशुभिर्य एवं वेद ॥ २० ॥

---

(१) एतं लोकानामाहेति क, ।

(२) एतं लोकानामाहादित्यमिति क, ।

(३) एतं लोकानामाहेति क, ।

अनर्वाणं ह वै देवं दध्यङ्ङाङ्गिरसमुपसीदं ह यज्ञस्य शुष्टिं समश्नवामहा इति स दध्यङ्ङाङ्गिरसोऽब्रवीद्यो वै सप्तदशं प्रजापतिं यज्ञेऽन्वितं वेद नास्य यज्ञो रिष्यति न यज्ञपतिं रिष्यन्त इति ता वा एताः पञ्च व्याहृतयो भवन्त्यों श्रावयास्तु श्रौषड् यज येयजामहे वौषडिति स दध्यङ्ङाङ्गिरसोऽब्रवीन्न वयं विद्मो यदि ब्राह्मणा स्मो यद्यब्राह्मणा स्मो यदि तस्य ऋषे स्मो यदि नान्यस्येत्यनर्वाणस्य ह वा ऋतावन्तस्य पितरः स्वधायामाहृषायन्त वयं वदामहै २वयं वदामहा १ इति सोऽयात् स्वायम्भुवो वा ऋतावन्तो मदेयातां न वयं वदामहा २ इति तस्मात्प्रवरे प्रव्रियमाणे वाचयेद्देवाः पितर इति तिस्रो य एति संयजति स भवति यस्य न ब्रूते यस्य न ब्रूत इति ब्राह्मणम् ॥ २१ ॥

सावित्रं ह स्म वैतं पूर्वं पुरस्तात् पशुमालभन्त इति मे तर्हि प्राजापत्यं यो ह्येव सविता स प्रजापतिरितिवदन्तस्तस्मादु समोऽथाग्नींस्तेन यजेरंस्ते समानधिष्ण्या एव स्युरीषा सम्भरणीया या उषा सम्भरणीया यां विन्द्युष्याग्नींस्तया यजेरंस्तेनानाधिष्ण्या एव स्युरादीक्षिणीया या दीक्षिणीया यां सन्द्युष्याग्नींस्तेन यजेरंस्ते समानधिष्ण्या एव स्युरोदवसानीया या उदवसानीया यां विन्द्युष्याग्नीं स्तया यजेरंस्तेनानाधिष्ण्या एव स्युरथ यदि यजमानस्योपतपेत्यार्ध्वतोऽग्नीनाधाय तावदासीत यावद्दग्धः स्याद्यदि प्रेयात्स्वैरेव तमग्निभिर्दहेद् दग्ध वा अग्निभिरितरे यजमाना आसत इति वदन्तस्तस्य तदेव ब्राह्मणं यददः पुरःसवने पितृमेध आशिषो व्याख्याताः ॥ २२ ॥

सायं प्रातर्होमौ स्थालीपाको नवश्च यः । बलिश्च पितृ-

यज्ञश्चाष्टका सप्तमः पशुरित्येते पाकयज्ञाः । अग्न्याधेयमग्निहोत्रं पौर्णमास्यमावास्ये । नवेष्टिश्चातुर्मास्यानि पशुबन्धोऽत्र सप्तम-इत्येते हविर्यज्ञाः । अग्निष्टोमोऽत्यग्निष्टोम उक्थ्यः षोडशिमांस्ततः । वाजपेयोऽतिरात्रश्चाप्तोर्यामात्र सप्तम इत्येते सुत्याः । केस्विद्देवाः प्रवोवाजाः केस्विद्देवा अभिद्यवः । केस्विद्देवा हविष्मन्तः किंस्विज्जिगाति सुम्नयुः । ऋतव एव प्रवोवाजा मासा देवा अभिद्यवः । अर्द्धमासा हविष्मन्तस्तज्जिगाति सुम्नयुः । कतिस्विद्रात्रयः कत्यहानि कति स्तोत्राणि कतिशस्त्राण्यस्य । कतिचित्सवनाः संवत्सरस्य स्तोत्रियाः पदाक्षराणि कत्यस्य । द्वावतिरात्रौ षट्शतमग्निष्टोमा द्वेविंशतिशते उक्थ्यानां । द्वादशषोड़शिनः षष्टिः षडहा वैषुवतञ्च । अहान्यस्य विंशतिशतानि त्रीण्यहश्चैकं तावदस्य । संवत्सरस्य सवनाः सहस्रमशीति त्रीणि च संस्तुतस्य । षट्षष्टिश्च द्वे च शते च भवत स्तत शस्त्राणामयुतं चैकमस्य । स्तोत्रियाश्च नवतिसहस्रा द्वे नियुते नवतिश्चातिषट् च । अष्टौ शतान्ययुतानि त्रिंशच्चतुर्नवतिश्च पदान्यस्य । संवत्सरस्य कविभिर्मितस्यैतावती मध्यमा देवमात्रा । अयुतमेकं प्रयुतानि त्रिंशद् द्वे नियुते तथा ह्यनुसृष्टाः । अष्टौ शतानि नव चाक्षराण्येतावानात्मा परमः प्रजापतेः । आद्यं वषट्कारः प्रदानान्तमेतमग्निष्टोमे पर्वशः स.धु क्लृप्तं । सोभिषजं छन्द ईप्सन्यदग्नौ चतुःशतं बहुधा हूयते यत् । प्रातःसवनस्तुत-एकविंशो गायत्रस्तोममित एक एव । माध्यन्दिनः सप्तदशेन क्लृप्तस्त्वर्यस्त्रिंशेन सवनं तृतीयं

श्रद्धायां रेतस्तपसा तपस्वी वैश्वानरः सिषिचेऽपत्यमीप्सन्। ततो यज्ञे लोकजित्सोमजम्भा ऋषेर्ऋषिरङ्गिराः सम्बभूव। ऋषेर्यत्तसा चतुर्विधस्य श्रद्धां यः श्रेयसीं लोकममुं जिगाय। यस्मै वेदाः प्रसृताः सोमबिन्दुयुक्ता वहन्ति सुकृतामु लोकं। ऋचोऽस्य भागांश्चतुरो वहन्त्युक्थशस्त्रैः प्रमुदो मोदमानाः। ग्रहैर्हविर्भिश्च कृताकृतश्च यजूंषि भागांश्चतुरो वहन्ति। औदुम्बर्यां सामघोषेण तावत् सविष्टुतिभिश्च स्तोमैः छन्दसा। सामानि भागांश्चतुरो वहन्ति गीत्या स्तोमेन सह प्रस्तावेन च। प्रायश्चित्तैर्भेषजैः संस्तवन्तोऽथर्वाणोऽङ्गिरसश्च शान्ताः। ब्रह्मा ब्रह्मत्वेन प्रमुदो मोदमाना असंसृष्टान् भागांश्चतुरो वहन्ति। यो ब्रह्मवित् सोऽभिकरोऽस्तु वः शिवो धिया धीरो रक्षतु धर्ममेतं। मा वः प्रमत्तामनृताच्च यज्ञात् कर्माच्च येनानङ्गिरसोऽपियासीत्। मायुं दग्धं मारुशस्ताः प्रमिष्ठा मा भे भूर्युक्ता विदहाथ लोकान्। दिव्यं भयं रक्षत धर्ममुद्यतं यज्ञं कलाशस्तुतिगोपलायनं। होता च मैत्रावरुणश्च पादमच्छावाकः सह ग्रावस्तैकं। ऋग्भिस्तुवन्तो अहरहः पृथिव्याः अग्निं पादं ब्रह्मणा धारयन्ति। अध्वर्युः प्रतिप्रस्थाता नेष्टोन्नेता निहितं पादमेकं। समन्तरिक्षं यजुषा स्तवन्तो वायुं पादं ब्रह्मणा धारयन्ति। साम्नोद्गाता च्छादयन्त प्रमत्त औदुम्बर्यां स्तोभदेयः सगद्गदः। विद्वान् प्रस्तोता विदहाथ सुष्टुतिं सुब्रह्मण्यः प्रतिहर्त्ताऽथ यज्ञे। साम्ना दिव्येकं निहितं निस्तुवन्तः सूर्यं पादं ब्रह्मणा धारयन्ति। ब्रह्माहैकं ब्राह्मणाच्छंसिनः सह पोताऽऽग्नीध्रो निहितं पादमेकं। अथर्व-

भिरङ्गिरोभिश्च गुप्तोऽपस्सु चन्द्रं पादं ब्रह्मणा धारयन्ति। षोडशिकं होत्रका अभिष्टुवन्ति वेदेषु युक्ताः प्रपृथक् चतुर्धा। मनीषिणो दीक्षिताः श्रद्दधाना होतारो गुप्ता अभिवहन्ति यज्ञं। दक्षिणतो ब्रह्मणस्यां जनदित्येतां व्याहृतिं जपन्। सप्तदशं सदस्यं तं कीर्त्तियन्ति पुरा विदुः। अष्टादशी दीक्षितो दीक्षितानां यज्ञे पत्नी श्रद्दधानेह युक्ता। एकोनविंशः शमिता बभूव विंशो यज्ञे गृहपतिरेव सुन्वन्। एकविंशतिरेवैषां संस्थायामङ्गिरो वह। वेदैरभिष्टुतो लोको नानाविशापराजितः॥ २४॥

सप्त सुत्याः सप्त च पाकयज्ञाः हविर्यज्ञाः सप्त तथैकविंशति। सर्वे ते यज्ञा अङ्गिरसोऽपियन्ति नूतना यानृषयो सृजन्ति ये च सृष्टाः पुराणैः। एतेषु वेदेष्वपि चैकमेवापव्रजमृत्विजां सम्भरन्ति। कूटस्तृपात् सचते तामशस्तं विस्कन्धमेनं विघ्नतं प्रजासु। निवर्त्तन्ते दक्षिणा नीयमानाः सुते सोमे वितते यज्ञतन्त्रे। मोघाशिषो यन्त्यनिवर्त्तमाना अनिष्टयज्ञा न तरन्ति लोकान्। द्वादशवर्षं ब्रह्मचर्य्यं पृथग्वेदेषु तत् स्मृतम्। एवं व्यवस्थिता वेदाः सर्व एव स्वकर्मसु। इति चैषां समानाः मन्त्राः कल्पाश्च ब्राह्मणानि च। व्यवस्थानन्तु तत्सर्वं पृथग्वेदेषु तत् स्मृतम्। ऋग्वेदस्य पृथिवी स्थानमन्तरिक्षस्थानो ऽध्वरः। द्यौः स्थानं सामवेदस्यापो भृग्वङ्गिरसां स्मृतं। अग्निदैवत ऋग्वेदस्य यजुर्वेदो वायुदेवतः। आदित्यः सामवेदस्य चन्द्रमा वैद्युतश्च भृग्वङ्गिरसाम्। त्रिवृत् स्तोम ऋग्वेदस्य यजूंषि पञ्चदशेन सह जज्ञिरे। सप्तदशेन सामवेद एकविंशो ब्रह्म-

सम्मितः। वागध्यात्ममृग्वेदस्य यजुषां प्राण उच्यते। चक्षुषी सामवेदस्य मनो भृग्वङ्गिरसां स्मृतम्। ऋग्भिः सह गायत्रं जागतमाहुर्यजूंषि त्रैष्टुभेन सह जज्ञिरे। उष्णिक्ककुब्भ्यां भृग्वङ्गिरसो जगत्या सामानि कवयो वदन्ति। ऋग्भिः पृथिवीं यजुषाऽन्तरिक्षं साम्ना दिवं लोकजित्सोमजम्भाः। अथर्वभिरङ्गिरोभिश्च गुप्तो यज्ञश्चतुष्पाद्दिवमुद्वदेह। ऋग्भिः सुशस्तो यजुषा परिष्कृतः सविष्टुतः सामजित् सोमजम्भाः। अथर्वभिरङ्गिरोभिश्च गुप्ता यज्ञश्चतुष्पाद्दिवमारुरोह। ऋचो विद्वान् पृथिवीं वेद सम्प्रति यजूंषि विद्वान् बृहदन्तरिक्षं। दिवं वेद सामगो यो विपश्चित् सर्वान् लोकान् यद्भृग्वङ्गिरोवित्। यांश्च ग्रामे यांश्चारण्ये जपन्ति मन्त्रान् नानार्थान् बहुधा जनासः। सर्वे ते यज्ञा अङ्गिरसोऽपियन्ति नूतना सा हि गतिर्ब्रह्मणो याऽवरार्ध्या। त्रिपिष्टपन्त्रिदिवन्नाकमुत्तमं तमेतया त्रय्या विद्ययेति। अत उत्तरे ब्रह्मलोका महान्तोऽथर्वणामङ्गिरसाञ्च सा गतिरथर्वणामङ्गिरसाञ्च सा गतिरिति ब्राह्मणम्॥ २५॥

इत्यथर्ववेदे गोपथब्राह्मणपूर्वभागे पञ्चमः प्रपाठकः समाप्तः॥५॥

समाप्तमिदं गोपथब्राह्मणपूर्वार्द्धं।

---

ओं श्रीब्रह्मवेदाय नमः ।

# गोपथब्राह्मणोत्तरभागे

## १ प्रपाठकः ।

अथ यद् ब्रह्मसदनात्तृणं निरस्यति शोधयत्येवैनं तदथोप-
विशतीदमहमर्वाग्वसोः सदने सीदामीत्यर्वाग्वसुर्ह वै देवानां ब्रह्मा
पराग्वसुरसुराणां तमेवैतत् पूर्वं सादयत्यरिष्टं यज्ञन्तनुतादि-
त्यथोपविश्य जपति बृहस्पतिर्ब्रह्मेति बृहस्पतिर्वा आङ्गिरसो
देवानां ब्रह्मा तस्मिन्नेवैतदनुज्ञामिच्छति प्रणीतासु प्रणीयमाना-
सु वाचं यच्छत्या हविष्कृत उद्वादनादेतद्वै यज्ञस्य द्वारं तदेतद-
शून्यं करोतीष्टे च स्विष्टकृत्यानुयाजानां प्रसवादित्येतद्वै यज्ञस्य
द्वितीयं द्वारन्तदेवैतदशून्यं करोति यत् परिधयः परिधीयन्ते
यज्ञस्य गोपीथाय परिधीन् परिधत्ते यज्ञस्य सात्मत्वाय
परिधीन् संमार्ष्टि पुनात्येवैनं त्रिर्मध्यमं त्रय इमे प्राणाः प्राणा-
नेवाभिजयति त्रिर्दक्षिणार्द्धं त्रयो वै लोका लोकानेवाभिजयति
त्रिरुत्तरार्द्धं त्रयो वै देवलोका देवलोकानेवाभिजयति त्रिरुप
वा जयति त्रयो वै देवयानाः पन्थानस्तानेवाभिजयति ते वै
द्वादश भवन्ति द्वादश ह वै मासाः संवत्सरः संवत्सरमेव तेन
प्रीणात्यथो संवत्सरमेवात्मा उपदधाति स्वर्गस्य लोकस्य
समष्ट्यै ॥ १ ॥

प्रजापतिर्वै रुद्रं यज्ञान्निरभजत् सोऽकामयत मेऽयमस्मा-आकूतिः समृद्धिर्यो मा यज्ञान्निरमाचीदिति। स यज्ञमभ्या-यम्याविध्य तदाविद्धं निरकृन्तत् तत् प्राशित्रमभवत्तदुदयकृत्त-द्भगाय पर्य्यहरंस्तत्प्रतीक्षेत। तस्य चक्षुः परापतत्तस्मादाहु-रन्धो वै भग इत्यपिहतं नेच्छेद्यमिच्छति तत् सवित्रे पर्य्यहरंस्तत् प्रत्यगृह्णात् तस्य पाणी प्रतिच्छेद तस्मै हिरण्मयौ प्रत्यदधुस्त-स्माद्धिरण्यपाणिरिति स्तुतस्तत्पूष्णे पर्य्यहरंस्तत् प्राश्नात्तस्य दन्ताः परोप्यन्त तस्मादाहुरदन्तकः पूषा पिष्टभाजन इति तदिध्मा-याङ्गिरसाय पर्य्यहरंस्तत् प्राश्नातस्य शिरो व्यपतत् तं यज्ञ एवा-कल्पयत् स एष इध्मः समिधो ह पुरातनस्तद्वर्हिषे आङ्गिरसाय पर्य्यहरंस्तत्प्राश्नात्तस्याङ्गा पर्वाणि व्यस्रंसन्त तं यज्ञ एवाकल्पयत्त-देतद्वर्हिः प्रस्तरो ह पुरातनस्तद्बृहस्पतय आङ्गिरसाय पर्य्यहरत् सोऽबिभेत् बृहस्पतिरित्थं वा मार्त्तिमाकृष्यसीति स एतं मन्त्रमपश्यत् सूर्य्यस्य त्वा चक्षुषा प्रतीक्ष इत्यब्रवीन्न हि सूर्य्यस्य चक्षुः किञ्चन हिनस्ति सोऽबिभेत्प्रतिगृह्णन्तं माहिंसिष्यतीति देवस्यत्वा सवितुः प्रसवेऽश्विनोर्बाहुभ्यां पूष्णो हस्ताभ्यां प्रसूतः प्रशिषा प्रतिगृह्णामी-त्यब्रवीत्सवितृप्रसूत एवैनं तद्देवताभिः प्रत्यगृह्णात्तद्धूर्द्ध्वतृणानि प्रागग्दण्डं स्थण्डिले निदधाति पृथिव्यास्त्वा नाभौ सादयामीति पृथिवी वान्तानां शमयित्री तयैवैतच्छमयाञ्चकार सोऽबिभे-त्प्राश्नन्तं माहिंसिष्यतीत्यग्नेष्ट्वास्ये न प्राश्नामीत्यब्रवीन्नह्यग्नेरास्यं किञ्चन हिनस्ति सोऽबिभेत्प्राशितं माहिंसिष्यतीतीन्द्रस्य त्वा जठरे सादयामीत्यब्रवीन्नहीन्द्रस्य जठरं किञ्चन हिनस्ति वरुण-स्योदर इति न हि वरुणस्योदरं किञ्चन हिनस्तीति ॥२॥

अथो आहुर्ब्राह्मणसोदर इत्यात्माऽस्यात्मनाऽऽत्मानं मे माहिंसीः स्वाहेत्यन्नं वै सर्वेषां भूतानामात्मा तेनैवैतच्छमयाञ्चकार प्राशित्रमनुमन्त्रयते। योऽग्निर्नृमणा नाम ब्राह्मणेषु प्रविष्टः तस्मिन् म एतत् सुहुतमस्तु प्राशित्रं तन्मा माहिंसीत् परमे व्योमन्निति तत्सर्वेण ब्रह्मणा प्राश्नात्तत एनं नाहिनत्तस्माद्यो ब्रह्मिष्ठः स्यात्तं ब्रह्माणं कुर्वीत बृहस्पतिर्वै सर्वं ब्रह्म सर्वेण ह वा एतद् ब्रह्मणा यज्ञं दक्षिणत उद्यच्छतेऽप एव वा एतस्मात् प्राणाः क्रामन्ति य आविद्धं प्राश्नात्यद्भिर्मार्जयित्वा प्राणान् संस्पृशते वाङ्म आस्यं नित्यमृतं वै प्राणा अमृतमापः प्राणानेव यथास्थानमुपाह्वयते तदु हैक आहुरिन्द्राय पर्यहरन्निति ते देवा अब्रुवन्निन्द्रो वै देवानामोजिष्ठो बलिष्ठस्तस्मा एतत्परिहरन्तीति तत्तस्मै पर्यहरंस्तत्सद् ब्रह्मणा(१) शमयाञ्चकार तस्मादाहुरिन्द्रो ब्रह्मेति यवमात्रं भवति यवमात्रं वै विषस्य न हिनस्ति यदधस्तादभिघारयति तस्मादधस्तात् प्रचरणं प्रजा अरुर्न हिनस्ति यदुपरिष्टादभिघारयति तस्मादुपरिष्टात् प्रचरणं प्रजा अरुर्न हिनस्ति यदुभयतोऽभिघारयत्युभयतोऽभिघारि प्रजा अरुर्घातुकं स्याद्यच्छमयाभिहरेदनभिविद्धं यज्ञस्याभिविद्धेत्॥ २ ॥

अग्रेण परिहरति तीर्थेनैव परिहरति वै वा एतद्यज्ञश्छिद्यते यत् प्राशित्रं परिहरति यदाह ब्रह्मन् प्रस्थास्यामीति बृहस्पतिर्वै सर्वं ब्रह्म सर्वेण ह वा एतद् ब्रह्मणा यज्ञं दक्षिणतः सन्दधात्यथोऽत्र वा एतर्हि यज्ञः श्रितो यत्र ब्रह्मा तत्रैव यज्ञः श्रितस्तत एवैनमालभते यद्धस्तेन प्रमीयेद्वेपनः स्याद्यच्छीर्ष्णा शीर्षक्तिमां-

(१) तत् स ब्रह्मणेति क,।

स्याद्यत्तूष्णीमासीदासम्प्रत्तो यज्ञः स्यात् प्रतिष्ठेत्येव ब्रूयाद्वाचि वै यज्ञः श्रितो यत्र ब्रह्मा तत्रैव यज्ञःश्रितस्तत एवैनं सम्प्रयच्छत्याग्नीध्र आदधात्यग्निमुखानेवर्त्तून् प्रीणात्यथोत्तरासामाहुतीनां प्रतिष्ठित्या ऽथो समिद्धत्येव जुहोति परिधींस्सम्मार्ष्टि पुनात्येवैनां सकृत् सकृत् सम्मार्ष्टि पराङिव ह्येतर्हि यज्ञश्चतुः सम्पद्यतेऽथो चतुष्पादः पशवः पशूनामाप्त्यै देव सवितरेतत्ते प्राहेत्याह प्रसूत्यै बृहस्पतिः ब्रह्मेत्याह स हि ब्रह्मिष्ठः स यज्ञं पाहि स यज्ञपतिं पाहि स मामाम्याहि स मां पाहि स मां कर्मण्यं पाहीत्याह यज्ञाय च यजमानाय च पशूनामाप्त्यै ॥ ४ ॥

न वै पौर्णमास्यां नामावास्यायां दक्षिणा दीयन्ते य एष ओदनः पच्यते दक्षिणैषा दीयते यज्ञस्यर्ध्या इष्टी वा एतेन यद्यजतेऽथो वा एतेन पूर्त्ती य एष ओदनः पच्यत एष हवा इष्टापूर्त्ती य एनं पचति ॥ ५ ॥

द्वया वै देवा यजमानस्य गृहमागच्छन्ति सोमपा अन्येऽसोमपा अन्ये हुतादोऽन्ये अहुतादोन्य एते वै देवा अहुतादो यद् ब्राह्मणा एतद्देवत्य ऋषयः पुरानीजान एते ह वा एतस्य प्रजायाः पशूनामीशते ते ऽस्याप्रीता इषमूर्जमादायापक्रामन्ति यदन्वाहार्यमन्वाहरति तानेव तेन प्रीणाति दक्षिणतः सद्भाः परिहृत्त्वा आह दक्षिणाहृतेनैव यज्ञेन यजत आहुतिभिरेव देवान् हुतादः प्रीणाति दक्षिणाभिर्मनुष्यदेवांस्तेऽस्मै प्रीता इषमूर्जं नियच्छन्ति ॥ ६ ॥

देवाश्च ह वा असुराश्चास्पर्द्धन्त, ते देवाः प्रजापतिमेवाभ्ययजन्त अन्योऽन्यस्यासन्न सुरा अजुहवुस्ते देवा एतमोदनमपश्यंस्तं

प्रजापतये भागमनुनिरवपंस्तं भागं पश्यन् प्रजापतिर्देवानुपावर्त्तत ततो देवा अभवन् परासुराः स य एवं विद्वानेतमोदनं पचति भवत्यात्मना परास्याप्रियो भ्रातृव्यो भवति प्रजापतिर्वै देवेभ्यो भागधेयानि व्यकल्पयत्सोऽमं मन्यत आत्मानमन्तरगादिति स-एत मोदनमभक्तमपश्यत्तमात्मने भागन्निरवपत् प्रजापतेर्वा एष भागो परिमितः स्यादपरिमितो हि प्रजापतिः प्रजापतेर्भागोसूर्ज-स्वान्पयस्वानचितोऽस्य चित्यै त्वा मामेचेष्ठाः। अमुत्रामुष्मिं लोक इह च प्राणापानौ मे पाहि समानव्यानौ मे पाह्युदानरूपे मे पाह्यूर्गस्यूर्जं मे धेहि कुर्वतो मे माचेष्ठाः। ददतो मे मोपदसः प्रजापतिमहन्त्वया सम्रुचसृध्या सजिति प्रजापतिमेव समृचमृध्नोति य एवं वेद य एवं वेद ॥ ७॥

ये वा इह यज्ञैरार्ध्नुवंस्तेषामेतानि ज्योतींषि यान्यमूनि नक्ष-त्राणि तन्नक्षत्राणां नक्षत्रत्वं यन्न क्षियन्ति दर्शपूर्णमासौ वै यज्ञस्या-वसानदर्शौ ये वा अनिष्ट्वा दर्शपूर्णमासाभ्यां सोमेन यजन्ते तेषा-मेतानि ज्योतींषि यान्यमूनि नक्षत्राणि पतन्तीव तद्यथाह वा इदमस्यष्टावसानेनेहावसास्यसि नेहावसासप्तसीति नोऽनुद्यन्त एवं हैवैतेऽमुष्मान् लोकान् नो नुद्यन्ते त एते प्रच्यवन्ते ॥ ८॥

यस्य हविर्निरुप्तं पुरस्ताच्चन्द्रमा अभ्युदियात्तांस्त्रेधा तण्डुला-न्विभजेद्ये मध्यमास्तानग्नये दात्रेऽष्टाकपालान्निर्वपेत् ये स्थविष्ठास्तानिन्द्राय प्रदात्रे दधनि चरुं ये क्षोदिष्ठास्तान्विष्णवे शिपिविष्टाय शृते चरुमाप्नवो वा एतेऽतिरिच्यन्ते तानेवाप्नोति तानवरुन्धेऽग्निर्वै मध्यमस्य दाता इन्द्रो वै ज्येष्ठस्य प्रदाता यदेवेदं क्षुद्रं पशूनां तद्विष्णोः शिपिविष्टं तदेवाप्नोति पशूनेवावरुन्धे ॥९॥

या पूर्वा पौर्णमासी सानुमतिर्योत्तरा सा राका या पूर्वा साऽमावास्या सा सिनीवाली योत्तरा सा कुहूश्चन्द्रमा एव धाता च विधाता च यत् पूर्णोऽन्यां वसत् पूर्णोन्यान्तत् मिथुनं यत् पश्यत्यन्यान्नान्यान्तन्मिथुनं यदमावास्यायाश्चन्द्रमा अधिप्रजायते तन्मिथनन्तस्मादेवास्मै मिथनात् पशून्प्रजनयते ॥ १० ॥

न द्वे यजेत यत् पूर्व्वया सम्प्रति यजेतोत्तरया छं वषट् कुर्य्याद्यदुत्तरया सम्प्रति यजेत पूर्वया छं वषट्कुर्य्यान्नेष्टिर्भवति न यज्ञस्तदनुह्योतामुख्यमुपगल्भोऽजायत एकामेव यजेत प्रगल्भो हैव जायते न हत्यन्त द्वे यजेत यज्ञमुखमेव पूर्वमालभते यजत उत्तरया देवता एवं पूर्वयाप्रीतीन्द्रियमुत्तरया देवलोकमेव पूर्वयाऽवरुन्धे मनुष्यलोकमुत्तरया भूयसो यज्ञक्रतूनामुपैत्येष ह वै सुमनानामेष्टिर्यं मध्ये याने पश्चाचन्द्रमा अभ्युदियादस्मा अस्मिन् लोक आर्धुकं भवति ॥ ११ ॥

आग्नावैष्णवमेकादशकपालं निर्वपेद् दर्शपूर्णमासावारिप्समाणोऽग्निर्वै सर्वा देवता विष्णुर्यज्ञो देवताश्चैव यज्ञं चारभत ऋध्या ऋध्नोत्येवोभौ सहारभ्भावित्याहुरुदिनु शृङ्गे श्रितो मुच्यत इति दर्शो वा एतयोः पूर्वः पौर्णमास उत्तरोऽथ यत् परस्तात्पौर्णमास आरभ्यते तद्यथापूर्वं क्रियते तद्यत्पौर्णमासमारभमाणः सरस्वत्यै चरुं निर्वपेत्सरस्वते द्वादशकपालममावास्या वै सरस्वती पौर्णमासः सरस्वानित्युभावेवैतौ सहारभत ऋध्या ऋध्नोत्येव ॥ १२ ॥

अग्नये पथिकृतेऽष्टाकपालं निर्वपेद्यस्य प्रज्ञातेष्टिरिति पद्यते वहिष्पथं वा एष एति यस्य प्रज्ञातेष्टिरिति पद्यते वैऽग्नि

देवानां पथिकृत्तमेव भागधेयेनोपासरत्स एनं पन्थानमपि नयत्यनड्वा दक्षिणा स हि पन्थानमभिवहति ॥ १३ ॥

अग्नये व्रतपतयेऽष्टाकपालं निर्वपेद् य आहिताग्निः सन्प्रवसे-द् वहुवा एष व्रतमतिपातयति य आहिताग्निः सन्प्रवसति व्रत्येऽ-हनि स्त्रियं वोपैति मांसं वा अश्नात्यग्निर्वै देवानां व्रतपतिरग्नि-मेतस्य व्रतमगात्तस्मादेतस्य व्रतमालम्भयते ॥ १४ ॥

अग्नये व्रतभृतेऽष्टाकपालं निर्वपेद्य आहिताग्निरार्त्ति-जमश्रु कुर्य्यादानीतो वा एष देवानां य आहिताग्निस्तस्मा-देतेनाश्रु न कर्त्तव्यं न हि देवा अश्रु कुर्वन्त्यग्निर्वै देवानां व्रतभृदग्निमेतस्य व्रतमगात्तस्मादेतस्य व्रतमालम्भयते ॥ १५ ॥

ऐन्द्राग्नमुत्सृष्टमनुसृष्टमालभेत यस्य पिता पितामहः सोमं न पिवेदिन्द्रियेण वा(१)एष वीर्य्येण व्यध्यते(२)यस्य पितापितामहः सोमं न पिवति यदैन्द्र इन्द्र इन्द्रियेणैवैनं तद्वीर्य्येण समर्द्धयति देव-ताभिर्वा एष वीर्य्येण व्यध्यते (३) यस्य पिता पितामहः सोमं न पिवति यदाग्नेयोऽग्निर्वै सर्वा देवताः सर्वाभिरेवैनन्तद् देवताभिः समर्द्धयत्यनुसृष्टो भवत्यनुसृष्ट इव ह्येतस्य सोमपीथो यस्य पिता पितामहः सोमं न पिवति तस्मादेष एव तस्या देव-तायाः पशूनां समृद्धः ॥ १६ ॥

देवा वा ओषधीषु पक्वास्वजिमयुः स इन्द्रो वेदाग्निर्वा वैमाः प्रथम उज्जेष्यतीति सोऽब्रवीद्यतरो नौ पूर्व उज्जयात्तं नौ

(१) इन्द्रियेण ह वेति ख, ।

(२) वीर्य्येण विवृध्यत इति ख, ग, ।

(३) एष वीर्य्येण विवृध्यते इति ख, ग, ।

सहेति ता अग्निरुदजयत्तदिन्द्रो नोदजयत स एष ऐन्द्राग्नः सन्नाग्नेन्द्र एका वै तर्हि यवस्य श्रुष्टिरासीदेका व्रीहेरेका माषस्यैका तिलस्य तद्विश्वे देवा अब्रुवन् वयं वा एतत् प्रथयिष्यामो भागो नोऽस्त्विति तद्भूम एव वैश्वदेवोऽथो प्रथयत्येतेनैव पयसि स्याद्वैश्वदेवत्वाय वैश्वदेवं हि पयोऽथेमे अब्रूतां नवा ऋतआवाभ्यामिवैतद्यूयं प्रथयत मयि प्रतिष्ठितमसौ वृष्ट्या पचति नैतद्वितोऽभ्युज्जेष्यतीति भागो नावस्त्विति ताभ्यां वा एष भागः क्रियत उज्जित्या एवाथो प्रतिष्ठित्या एव ये द्यावापृथिवीयः सोमोर्वा ओषधी सोम ओषधीनामधिराजो याश्च ग्राम्या याश्चारण्या स्तासामेष उद्धारो यच्छ्यामाको यच्छ्यामाकः सौम्यस्तमेव भागिनं कृणुते यदकृत्वाऽऽग्रयणं नवस्याश्नीयाद् देवानां भागं प्रतिक्लृप्तमद्यात्संवत्सराद्वा एतदधिप्रजायते यदाग्रयणं संवत्सरं वै ब्रह्मा तस्माद् ब्रह्मा पुरस्ताद्धोमसंस्थितहोमेष्वावर्पं तैकहायनो दक्षिणा स हि संवत्सरस्य प्रतिमा रेत एव ह्येषो प्रजातः प्रजात्यै ॥ १७ ॥

अथ हैतदप्रतिरथमिन्द्रस्य बाहू स्थविरौ वृषाणावित्येतेन ह वा इन्द्रोऽसुरानप्रत्यजयदप्रतिह भवत्येतेन यजमानो भ्रातृव्यञ्जयति सङ्ग्रामे जुहुयादप्रतिह भवत्येतेन ह वै भरद्वाजः प्रतर्दनं समनह्यत् स राष्ट्र्यभवद्यं कामयेत राष्ट्री स्यादिति तमेतेन सन्नह्येद्राष्ट्रो ह भवत्येतेन ह वा इन्द्रो विराजमभ्यजयद्दशैतान्वाह दशाक्षरा विराड्वैराजं वा एतेन यजमानो भ्रातृव्यं हङ्क्ते तदु हैक एकादशान्वाहुरेकादशाक्षरा वै त्रिष्टुप् त्रैष्टुभो वज्रो वज्रेणैवैतद्रक्षांस्यपसेधति दक्षिणतो वै देवानां यज्ञं रक्षां-

ध्यजिवांस्ᳯस्तान्यप्रतिरथेनापाघ्नत, तस्माद्ब्रह्मा अप्रतिरथञ्जपन्नेति। यद्ब्रह्मा अप्रतिरथञ्जपन्नेति, यज्ञस्याभिजित्यै रक्षसामपहत्यै रक्षसामपहत्यै ॥ १८ ॥

अथातश्चातुर्मास्यानां(१) चातुर्मास्यानां प्रयोगः, फाल्गुन्यां पौर्णमास्यां चातुर्मास्यानि प्रयुञ्जीत। मुखं वा एतत्संवत्सरस्य, यत् फाल्गुनी पौर्णमासी, मुखम् उत्तरे फल्गुन्यौ, पुच्छं पूर्वे, तद्यथाप्रवृत्तस्यान्तौ समेतौ स्याताम्, एवमेवैतत्संवत्सरस्यान्तौ समेतौ भवतः। तद्यत् फाल्गुन्यां पौर्णमास्यां चातुर्मास्यैर्यजते, मुखत एवैतत् संवत्सरं प्रयुङ्क्ते। अथो भैषज्ययज्ञा वा एते, यच्चातुर्मास्यानि। तस्मादृतुसन्धिषु प्रयुज्यन्ते, ऋतुसन्धिषु वै व्याधिर्जायते। तान्येतान्यष्टौ हवींषि भवन्ति, अष्टौ वै चतसृणां पौर्णमासीनां हवींषि भवन्ति, चतसृणां वै पौर्णमासीनां वैश्वदेवं समासः। अथ यदग्निं मन्थन्ति, प्रजापतिर्वै वैश्वदेवं प्रजात्या एव(२)। अथैनं देवं गर्भं प्रजनयति। अथ यत् सप्तदशसामिधेन्यः, सप्तदशो वै प्रजापतिः, प्रजापतेराप्त्यै। अथ यत्सद्वन्ताव्वाज्यभागावसिसन्तीति वै सद्वन्तौ भवतः। अथ यद्विराजौ संयाज्ये, अन्नं वै श्रीर्विराड्, अन्नाद्यस्य श्रियोवरुध्यै। अथ यन्नव प्रयाजा नवानुयाजा अष्टौ हवींषि वाजिनन्नवमं, तन्नाचरीयां विराजमाप्नोति। अथो आहुर्द्दशिनीं विराजमिति प्रयाजानुयाजा हवींष्याघारावाज्यभागाविति ॥ १९ ॥

अथ यदग्नीषोमौ प्रथमं देवतानां यजति, अग्नीषोमौ वै देवा-

---

१ ट, चिह्नितपुस्तके चातुर्मास्यानामिति वारत्रयमनुक्रम्।

२ प्राजापत्या एवेति ख०, ग० च।

नां मुखं, मुखत एव तद्देवान् प्रीणाति । अथ यत्सवितारं यजति, असौ वै सविता, योऽसौ तपति, एतमेव तेन प्रीणाति । अथ यत् सरस्वतीं यजति, वाग् वै सरस्वती, वाचमेव तेन प्रीणाति । अथ यत् पूषणं यजति, असौ वै पूषा, योऽसौ तपति, एतमेव तेन प्रीणाति । अथ यन्मरुतः स्वतवसो यजति, घोरा वै मरुतः स्वतवसः, तानेव तेन प्रीणाति । अथ यद्विश्वान् देवान्यजति, एते वै विश्वे देवाः, यत्सर्वे देवाः, तानेव तेन प्रीणाति । अथ यद् द्यावापृथिव्यौ यजति, प्रतिष्ठे वै द्यावापृथिव्यौ, प्रतिष्ठित्या एव । अथ यद्वाजिनो यजति, पशवो वै वाजिनः, पशूनेव तेन प्रीणाति । अथो ऋतवो वै वाजिनः, ऋतूनेव तेन प्रीणाति । अथो छन्दांꣳसि वै वाजिनः, छन्दांꣳस्येव तेन प्रीणाति । अथो देवाश्वा वै वाजिनः, अत्र देवाः साश्वा अभीष्टाः प्रीता भवन्ति । अथ यत्परस्तात् पौर्णमासेन यजते, तथा ह्यस्य पूर्वपक्षे वैश्वदेवेनेष्टं भवति ॥ २० ॥

वैश्वदेवेन वै प्रजापतिः प्रजा असृजत, ताः सृष्टा अप्रसूता वरुणस्य यवां जक्षुः(१) । ताः वरुणो वरुणपाशैः प्रत्यबध्नात्(२), ताः प्रजाः प्रजापतिं पितरमेत्योपावदन्, उप तं यज्ञक्रतुं जानीहि, येनेष्ट्वा वरुणमप्रीणात् । स प्रीतो वरुणो वरुणपाशेभ्यः सर्वस्मात्पाप्मनः(३) सम्प्रमुच्यन्त इति । तत एतं प्रजापतिं यज्ञक्रतुमपश्यत्, वरुणप्रघासं तमाहरत्, तेनायजत, तेनेष्ट्वा वरुणमप्रीणात् । स

१ वरुणस्यां यवाश्वतक्षुरिति ख० । वरुणस्य वांचक्षुरिति क० भ० च । वरुणस्य यवां चक्षुरिति ट० । वरुणास्यां वाचतक्षुरिति ग० ।

२ प्रत्याबध्नादिति भ० । ३ सर्वस्माच्च इति ख० ।

प्रीतो वरुणो वरुणपाशेभ्यः सर्वस्मात्पाप्मनः(१) प्रजाः प्रामुञ्चत्।
प्र ह वा एतस्य प्रजा वरुणपाशेभ्यः सर्वस्माच्च पाप्मनो मुच्यन्ते।
य एवं वेद। अथ यदग्निं प्रणयन्ति, यमेवामुं वैश्वदेवे मन्थन्ति(२)
तमेव तत् प्रणयन्ति। यन्मथ्यते, तस्योक्तं ब्राह्मणम्। अथ यत्
सप्तदशसामिधेन्यः, सद्वन्तावाज्यभागौ, विराजौ संयाज्ये, तेषामुक्तं
ब्राह्मणम्। अथ यन्नव प्रयाजाः, नवानुयाजाः, नवैतानि हवींषि
समानानि त्वेव पञ्च सञ्चराणि(३) हवींषि भवन्ति पौष्णान्तानि,
तेषामुक्तं ब्राह्मणम्॥ २१॥

अथ यदैन्द्राग्नो द्वादशकपालो भवति, बलं वै तेजः इन्द्राग्नी,
बलमेव तत्तेजसि प्रतिष्ठापयति। अथ यद्वारुण्यामिक्षा, इन्द्रो वै वरुणः,
स उ वै पयोभाजनः,(४) तस्माद् वारुण्यामिक्षा। अथ यन्मारुती पयस्या,
अप्सु वै मरुतः श्रितः, आपो हि पयः। अथेन्द्रस्या
वै मरुतः श्रितः, ऐन्द्रं पयः, तस्मान्मारुती पयस्या। अथ यत्
काय एककपालः, प्रजापतिर्वै कः, प्रजापतेराप्त्यै। अथो सुखस्य वा
एतन्नामधेयङ्कमिति, सुखमेव तदध्यात्मन्धत्ते। अथ यत् मिथुनौ
गावौ ददाति, प्रजात्यै; रूपमुक्थ्या वाजिनः। अथ यदप्सु वरुणं
यजति, स्व एवैनन्तदायतने प्रीणाति। अथ यत्परस्तात् पौर्णमासेन यजते, तथा ह्यस्य पूर्वपक्षे वरुणप्रघासैरिष्टं भवति॥ २२॥

१ सर्वस्माच्च पाप्मन इति ख०, ग०, च० च।

२ मन्थन्ति इति ख०, च०, छ० च।

३ पञ्च संवत्सराणीति ख०। पञ्चमं संवत्सराणीति ग०।

४ स उवै पयोभाजिन इति क०। स एवै पयोभाजन इति ख०। स एवै पयोभोजन इति ग०। स उ वै पयोभासिन इति ङ०।

ऐन्द्रो वा एष यज्ञक्रतुः, यत् साकमेधाः, तद्यथा महाराजः पुरस्तात् सेनानीकानि व्यूह्याभयं पन्थानमन्वियात्, एवमेवैतत् पुरस्ताद् देवता यजन्ते, तद् यथैवादः सोमस्य महाव्रतम्, एवमेवैतदिष्टिमहाव्रतम्। अथ यदग्निमनीकवन्तं प्रथमं देवतानां यजति, अग्निर्वै देवानां मुखं, मुखत एव तद्देवान् प्रीणाति। अथ यन्मध्यन्दिने मरुतः सान्तपनान् यजति(१), इन्द्रो वै मरुतः सान्तपनाः, ऐन्द्रं माध्यन्दिनं, तस्मादेनानिन्द्रेणोपसंहितान् यजति। अथ यत् सायं गृहमेधीयेन चरन्ति,(२) पुष्टिकर्म्म वै गृहमेधीयः, सायम्पोषः पशूनां, तस्मात् सायं गृहमेधीयेन चरन्ति। अथ यच्छ्वोभूते गृहमेधीयस्य(३) निष्कासमिश्रेण पूर्णादर्व्या(४) चरन्ति, पूर्वेद्युः कर्म्मणैवैतत् प्रातःकर्मोपसन्तन्वन्ति। अथ यत् प्रातर्मरुतः क्रीडिनो यजति, इन्द्रो वै मरुतः क्रीडिनः, तस्मादेनानिन्द्रेणोपसंहितान् यजति। अथ यदग्निं प्रणयन्ति, यमेवामुं वैश्वदेवे मन्थन्ति, तमेव तत् प्रणयन्ति, यन्मथ्यते तस्योक्तं ब्राह्मणम्। अथ यत् सप्तदशसामिधेन्यः, सद्वन्तावाज्यभागौ, विराजौ संयाज्ये, तेषामुक्तं ब्राह्मणम्। अथ यन्नव प्रयाजा नवानुयाजा अष्टौ हवींषि समानानि त्वेव षट् सञ्चराणि हवींषि भवन्त्यैन्द्राग्नान्तानि, तेषामुक्तं ब्राह्मणम्। अथ यन्महेन्द्रमन्ततो यजति, अन्तं वै श्रेष्ठी भजते, तस्मादेनमन्ततो यजति। अथ यद्वैश्वकर्म्मण एककपालः,

---

१ यजन्तीति ख० ।

२ चरतीति ग०, भ० च ।

३ गृहे मेधीयस्येति ख०, ग०, च ।

४ पर्णदर्व्येति ख० ।

असौ वै विश्वकर्म्मा, योऽसौ तपत्येतमेव तेन प्रीणाति। अथ यदृषभङ्गां ददाति, ऐन्द्रो ह यज्ञक्रतुः॥ २३॥

अथ यदपराह्णे पितृयज्ञेन चरन्ति, अपराह्णभाजो वै पितरः, तस्मादपराह्णे पितृयज्ञेन चरन्ति। तदाहुर्यदपरपक्षभाजो वै पितरः, कस्मादेनान्(१) पूर्वपक्षे यजन्तीति। देवा वा एते पितरः, तस्मादेनान् पूर्वपक्षे यजन्तीति। अथ यदेकाꣳसामिधेनीन्त्रिरन्वाह, सकृदु ह वै पितरः, तस्मादेकां सामिधेनीन्त्रिरन्वाह। अथ यद्यजमानस्यार्षेऽन्वाह(२), नेद्यजमानं प्रमृणजानीति। अथ यत् सोमम्पितृमन्तं पितॄन् सोमवतः पितॄन्बर्हिषदः पितॄनग्निष्वात्तानित्यावाहयन्ति, न हैके स्वं महिमानमावाहयन्ति,(३) यजमानस्यैष महिमेति वदत आवाहयेदिति, त्वेव स्थितमग्नेर्ह्येष महिमा भवति; ओं स्वधेत्याश्रावयति, अस्तु स्वधेति प्रत्याश्रावयति, स्वधाकारो हि(४) पितॄणाम्। अथ यत् प्रयाजानुयाजेभ्यो बर्हिरन्तावुद्धरति, प्रजा वै बर्हिः, नेत् प्रजां पितृषु दधानीति। ते वै षट् सम्पद्यन्ते, षड्वा ऋतवः, ऋतवः पितरः, पितॄणामाप्त्यै॥ २४॥

अथ यज्जीवनवन्तावाज्यभागौ भवतः, यजमानमेव तज्जीवयतः। अथ यदेकैकस्य हविषस्तिस्रस्तिस्रो याज्या भवन्ति, क्षयत्येवैनां प्रथमया, द्वितीयया गमयति, प्रैव तृतीयया यच्छति। अथो

१ तस्मादेनानिति घ०।

२ यजमानस्या र्षेयन्वाह इति ख०, ग० च। यजमानस्यारिष्येन्वाहेति घ०।

३ इत्यावाहयति न्वहैके ख० महिमानमावाहयति इति ग०।

४ स्वधाकारो वै इति भ०।

देवयज्ञमेवैनं पितृयज्ञेन व्यावर्त्तयन्ति, अथो दक्षिणासंस्थो वै पितृयज्ञः, तमेवैतदुदक्संस्थं कुर्वन्ति। अथ यदग्निं कव्यवाहनमन्ततो यजति, एतत् स्विष्टकृतो वै पितरः, तस्मादग्निं कव्यवाहनमन्ततो यजति। अथ यदिडामुपहूयावघ्राय न प्राश्नन्ति, पशवो वा इडा, नेत्पशून् प्रमृणजानीति। अथ यत् सूक्तवाके यजमानस्याशिषोन्वाह[१], नेद्यजमानं प्रमृणजानीति। अथ यत् पत्नीश्च संयाजयन्ति, नेत्पत्नीं प्रमृणजानीति। अथ यत् पवित्रवति मार्ज्जयन्ते, शान्तिर्वै भेषजमापः, शान्तिरेवैषां भेषजमन्ततो यज्ञे क्रियते। अथ यदध्वर्युः पितृभ्यो निपृणाति, जीवानेव तत् पितॄननु[२] मनुष्याः पितरोऽनुप्रवहन्ति। अथो देवयज्ञमेवैनं पितृयज्ञेन व्यावर्त्तयन्ति। अथो दक्षिणासंस्थो वै पितृयज्ञः, तमेवैतदुदक्संस्थं कुर्वन्ति। अथ यत् प्राञ्चोऽभ्युत्क्रम्यादित्यमुपतिष्ठन्ते, देवलोको वा आदित्यः, पितृलोकः पितरः, देवलोकमेवैनं पितृलोकादुपसङ्क्रामन्तीति। अथ यद्दक्षिणाञ्चोऽभ्युत्क्रम्याग्नीनुपतिष्ठन्ते, प्रीत्यैव तद्देवेष्वन्ततोऽर्द्धं चरन्ति। अथ यदुदञ्चोऽभ्युत्क्रम्य त्रैयम्बकैर्यजन्ते, रुद्रमेव तत् स्वस्यां दिशि प्रीणन्ति। अथो देवज्ञमेवैनं पितृयज्ञेन व्यावर्त्तयन्ति। अथो दक्षिणासंस्थो वै पितृयज्ञः, तमेवैतदुदक्संस्थं कुर्वन्ति। अथ यदन्तत आदित्येष्ठ्या यजति[३] इयं वा अदितिरस्यामेवैनमन्ततः प्रतिष्ठापयति। अथ

---

(१) यजमानस्यार्षेन्वाहेति ख०, ग०, च। यजमानस्याशि षेन्वाहेति घ०। यजमानस्या शिर्षेन्वाहेति ट०।

(२) पितेननु इति ख०, ट०, च।

(३) यजन्तीति ख०।

यत्परस्तात् पौर्णमासेन यजते, तथाहास्य पूर्वपक्षे साकमेधैरिष्टं भवति ॥ २५ ॥

त्रयोदशं वा एतं मासमाप्नोति, यच्छुनासीर्य्येण यजते, एतावान्वै संवत्सरः, यावानेष त्रयोदशो मासः। अथ यदग्निं प्रणयन्ति, यमेवामुं वैश्वदेवे मन्थन्ति, तमेव तत् प्रणयन्ति, यन्मथ्यते, तस्योक्तं ब्राह्मणं, यद्यु न मथ्यते पौर्णमासमेव तन्त्वं भवति, प्रतिष्ठा वै पौर्णमासं, प्रतिष्ठित्या एव। अथ यद्वायुं यजति, प्राणो वै वायुः, प्राणमेव तेन प्रीणाति। अथ यच्छुनासीरं यजति, संवत्सरो वै सुनासीरः, संवत्सरमेव तेन प्रीणाति। अथ यत्सूर्य्यं यजति, असौ वै सूर्य्यः, योसौ तपति, एतमेव तेन प्रीणाति। अथ यच्छ्वेता दक्षिणा ददाति, एतस्यैव तद्रूपं क्रियते। अथ यत् प्रायश्चित्तप्रतिनिधिं[१] कुर्वन्ति, स्वस्त्ययनमेव तत् कुर्वन्ति, यज्ञस्यैव शान्तिर्यजमानस्य भैषज्याय। तैर्वा एतैश्चातुर्मास्यैर्देवाः सर्वान् कामानाप्नुवन्, सर्वा इष्टीः सर्वममृतत्वं। स वा एष प्रजापतिः चतुर्विंशः, यच्चातुर्मास्यानि, तस्य मुखमेव वैश्वदेवं, बाहू वरुणप्रघासाः प्राणोऽपानो व्यान इत्येतास्तिस्र इष्टयः, आत्मा महाहविः, प्रतिष्ठा शुनासीरं, स वा एष प्रजापतिरेव संवत्सरः, यच्चातुर्मास्यानि, सर्वं वै प्रजापतिः, सर्वं चातुर्मास्यानि, तत्सर्वेणैव सर्वमाप्नोति, य एवं वेद, यश्चैवं विद्वांश्चातुर्मास्यैर्यजते चातुर्मास्यैर्यजते ॥ २६ ॥

इत्यथर्ववेदोत्तरगोपथब्राह्मणस्य प्रथमः प्रपाठकः समाप्तः ॥ १ ॥

---

(१) प्रायश्चित्तं प्रतिनिधिमिति क०। प्रायश्चित्तः प्रतिनिधिमिति ख०, ग०, भा०, ट० च।

## अथ द्वितीयः प्रपाठकः।

ओम्। मांसीयन्ति वा आहिताग्नेरग्नयः, त एनमेवाग्नेऽभिध्यायन्ति यजमानं, य एतमैन्द्राग्नं पशुं षष्ठे षष्ठे मासे(१) आलभते, तेनैवेन्द्राग्निभ्यां ग्रसितमात्मानं निरवदयत। आयुष्काम आलभेत, प्राणापानौ वा इन्द्राग्नी, प्राणापानावेवात्मनि धत्ते, आयुष्मान् भवति। प्रजाकाम आलभेत, प्राणापानौ वा इन्द्राग्नी, प्राणापानौ प्रजा अनुप्रजायन्ते, प्रजावान् भवति। पशुकाम आलभेत, प्राणापानौ वा इन्द्राग्नी, प्राणापानौ पशवोऽनुप्रजायन्ते, पशुमान् भवति। यामं शुक्लं हरितमालभेत शठं वायःकामः(२), एता नाम यः पितृलोके स्यामित्येतेन ह वै यमोऽमुष्मिंल्लोक आर्ध्नोत्, पितृलोक एवार्ध्नोति(३)। त्वाष्ट्रं वडवमालभेत प्रजाकामः, प्रजापतिर्वै प्रजाः ससृजमानः स द्वितीयं मिथुनमन्वाविन्दत्(४), स त्वाष्ट्रं वडवमपश्यत्, त्वष्टा हि रूपाणां प्रजनयिता, तेन प्रजा असृजन, तेन मिथुनमविन्दत्। प्रजावान् मिथुनवान् भवति, य एवं वेद, यश्चैवं विद्वानेतमालभते, योनीन् वा एष काम्यान् पशूनालभते, योनिष्ट्वैन्द्राग्नेन काम्यं पशुमालभन्त(५) इष्टालम्भः समृध्यै॥ १॥

पञ्चधा वै देवा व्युत्क्रामन्, अग्निर्वसुभिः, सोमो रुद्रैः, इन्द्रो

---

(१) षष्ठे मासे इति ख०, ग० च।

(२) नटं वायःकाम इति क०।

(३) एवर्द्धांतीति ख०, भ० च०। एव ऋध्नोतीति ट०।

(४) मिथुनन्वाविन्ददिति च०, भ०, च०। मिथुनं विन्ददिति ढ०।

(५) पशुमालभतेति ट०।

मरुद्भिः, वरुण आदित्यैः, बृहस्पतिर्विश्वैर्देवैः। ते देवा अब्रुवन्, असुरेभ्यो वा इदं भ्रातृव्येभ्यो रध्यामः, यन्मिथो विप्रियास्मः, या न इमाः प्रियास्तन्वस्ताः समवद्यामहा इति। ताः समवाद्यन्त, ताभ्यः सन्निर्ऋच्छात्, यो नः प्रथमोऽन्योन्यस्मै द्रुह्यादिति। यत्तन्वः समवाद्यन्त, तत् तानूनप्त्रस्य तानूनप्त्रत्वं। ततो देवा अभवन् परासुराः। तस्माद्यस्तानूनप्त्रिणां प्रथमो द्रुह्यति, स आर्त्तिमार्च्छति। यत्तानूनप्त्रꣳ समवद्यति, भ्रातृव्याभिभूत्यै भवति, आत्मना परास्याप्रियो भ्रातृव्यो भवति ॥ २ ॥

पञ्चकृत्वोऽवद्यति, पाङ्क्तो यज्ञः, पञ्चधा हि ते ताः समवाद्यन्त। आपतये त्वा गृह्णामीत्याह, प्राणो वा आपतिः, प्राणमेव तेन प्रीणाति। परिपतये त्वेत्याह, मनो वै परिपतिः, मन एव तेन प्रीणाति। तनूनप्त्र इत्याह, तन्वो हि ते ताः समवाद्यन्त। शाक्वरायेत्याह, शक्त्यꣳ(१) हि ते ताः समवाद्यन्त। शक्मन्नोजिष्ठायेत्याह, ओजिष्ठं हि ते तदात्मनः समवाद्यन्त। अनाधृष्टमित्याह, अनाधृष्टं ह्येतत् (२)। अनाधृष्यमित्याह, अनाधृष्यं ह्येतत्(३)। देवानामोज इत्याह, देवानाꣳ ह्येतदोजः। अभिशस्तिपा इत्याह, अभिशस्तिपा ह्येतत्। अनभिशस्तेन्यमित्याह, अनभिशस्तेनꣳ ह्येतदनु मे दीक्षां दीक्षापतिर्मन्यतामनु तपस्तपस्पति। अञ्जसा सत्यमुपगेषꣳ स्विते माधा इत्याह, यथा यजुरेवैतत् ॥ ३ ॥

---

१ शक्तिमिति च०।

२ अनाधृष्टमित्याहानाधृष्टं ह्येतदिति भ०। अनाधृष्टमित्याहानाधृष्टं ह्येतदिति ट०।

३ अनाधृष्यमित्याह, अनाधृष्यं ह्येतदिति भ०।

एतं वै देवा वज्रं कृत्वा सोममघ्नन्(१)। स्रुचौ बाहू, तस्मात् स्रुचौ सौमीमाहुतिं नाश्नाते। अवधीयेत सोमः, तस्मात् स्रुचौ चाज्यं चान्तिकमाहार्षीत्। अन्तिकमिव खलु वा अस्यैतत् प्रचरन्ति, यत्तानूनप्त्रेण प्रचरन्ति। अंशुरंशुष्टे देवसोमाप्यायतामिन्द्रायैकधनविद इत्याह, यदेवास्यापवायते यन्मीयते, तदेवास्यैतेनाप्याययन्ति। आ तुभ्यमिन्द्रः प्यायतामात्वमिन्द्राय प्यायस्वेत्याह, उभावेवेन्द्रञ्च सोमं चाप्याययन्ति। आप्याययास्मान्त्सखीन् सन्या मेधया प्रजया धनेनेत्याह, ऋत्विजो वा एतस्य सखायः, तानेवास्यैतेनाप्याययन्ति। स्वस्ति ते देव सोमसुत्यामुदृचमशीयेत्याह, आशिषमेवैतामाशास्ते, प्र वा एतस्माल्लोकाच्च्यवन्ते, ये सोममाप्याययन्ति। अन्तरिक्षदेवत्यो हि(२) सोमः आप्यायत एष्टा राय एष्टा वामानि प्रेषे भगाय ऋतमृतवादिभ्यो नमो दिवे नमः पृथिव्या इति, द्यावापृथिवीभ्यामेव नमस्कृत्यास्मिंल्लोके प्रतितिष्ठति प्रतितिष्ठति ॥ ४ ॥

मख इत्येतद् यज्ञनामधेयं, छिद्रप्रतिषेधसामर्थ्यात् छिद्रं खमित्युक्तं, तस्य मेति प्रतिषेधः, मा यज्ञं छिद्रं करिष्यतीति। छिद्रो हि यज्ञो भिन्न इवोदधिर्विस्रवति। तद्वै खलु छिद्रं भवति, ऋत्विग्यजमानविमानाद्वापि वैषां व्यपेक्षया मन्त्रकल्पब्राह्मणानामप्रयोगाद् यथोक्तानां वा दक्षिणानामप्रदानाद्धीनाद्वातिरिक्ताद्वोत्पाताद् भूतेषु प्रायश्चित्तव्यतिक्रमादिति। इत्येतद्वै सर्वं ब्रह्मण्यर्पितं।

१ सोममघ्नान्त इति भा०।

२ अन्तरिक्षे दवत्यो हीति च०, क०, ०, ट० ष।

ब्रह्मैव विद्वान् यद् भृग्वङ्गिरोवित्सम्यगधीयानश्चरितब्रह्मचर्य्योऽ-
न्यूनातिरिक्ताङ्गः(१) अप्रमत्तो यज्ञं रक्षति, तस्य प्रमादाद्यदि
वाप्यसान्निध्याद्यथा भिन्ना नौरगाधे महत्युदके सम्प्लवेत्, मत्स्य-
कच्छपशिशुमारनक्रमकरपुण्डरीकजखर(२) जसपिशाचानां भाग-
धेयं भवति, एवमादीनां चान्येषां विनष्टोपजीविनाम्। एवं
खल्वपि यज्ञश्छिन्नभिन्नोऽपध्वस्त उत्पाताद्भुतो बहुलोऽथर्वभिर-
संस्कृतोऽसुरगन्धर्वयक्षराक्षसपिशाचानां भागधेयं भवति, एव-
मादीनां चान्येषां विनष्टोपजीविनां। तदपि श्लोकाः,

छिन्नभिन्नोपध्वस्तो विश्रुतो बहुधा मखः।
इष्टापूर्त्तंद्रविणं गृह्यं यजमानस्यावापतत्॥
ऋत्विजां च विनाशाय राज्ञो जनपदस्य च।
संवत्सरविरिष्टं तद् यत्र यज्ञो विरिष्यते॥
दक्षिणाप्रवणीभूतो यज्ञो दक्षिणतः स्मृतः।
हीनाङ्गो रक्षसाभागो ब्रह्मवेदादसंस्कृतः॥
चतुष्पात् सकलो यज्ञश्चातुर्होत्रविनिर्मितः।
चतुर्विधैः स्थितो मन्त्रैर्ऋत्विग्भिर्वेदपारगैः॥
प्रायश्चित्तैरनुध्यानैरनुज्ञानानुमन्त्रणैः।
होमैश्च यज्ञविभ्रंशं सर्वं ब्रह्मा प्रपूरयेत्॥ इति।

तस्माद् यजमानो भृग्वङ्गिरोविदमेव तत्र ब्रह्माणं वृणीयात्।
स हि यज्ञन्तारयतीति ब्राह्मणम्॥ ५॥

---

१ अन्यूनानतिरिक्ताङ्ग इति च०, भ०, ठ० च। नातिरिक्ताङ्ग इति ग०। न्यूना-
तिरिक्ताङ्ग इति ख०।

२ जखरेति ख०, ग० च।

यज्ञो वै देवेभ्य उदक्रामत्, न वोऽहमन्नं भविष्यामीति। नेति देवा अब्रुवन्, अन्नमेव नो भविष्यसीति। तं देवा विमेथिरे। स एभ्यो विहृतः(१)न प्रबभूव। ते ह्योचुर्देवाः, न वै न इच्छन् विहृतः(२) अलं भविष्यति, हन्तेमꣳ सम्भरामीति। तं सꣳजभ्रुः। तं सम्भृत्योचतुरश्विनौ, इमं भिषज्यतमिति। अश्विनौ वै देवानां भिषजावश्विनावध्वर्यू, तस्मादध्वर्यू घर्मं सम्भरत। तꣳ सम्भृत्योचतुः, ब्रह्मन् घर्मेण प्रचरिष्यामः, होतर्घर्ममभिष्टुहि, उद्गातः सामानि गायेति। प्रचरत घर्ममित्यनुजानाति। ब्रह्मप्रसूता हि प्रचरन्ति, ब्रह्म हेदं प्रसवानामीशे, सवितृप्रसूततायै घर्मं तपामि, ब्रह्म जज्ञानमियमित्त्रा राष्ट्रे त्वग्र इति। घर्मं ताप्यमानमुपासीत, शस्त्रवदर्धर्चश आहावप्रतिगरवर्जं रूपसमृद्धाभिः। एतद्वै यज्ञस्य समृद्धं, यद्रूपसमृद्धं। यत् कर्म क्रियमाणमृग्यजुर्वाभिवदति, स्वस्ति तस्य यज्ञस्य पारमश्नुते। य एवं वेद, वेदमिथुनं वा एतत् यद् घर्मः, तस्मादन्तर्धा हि(३) प्रचरन्त्यन्तर्हिता वै मिथुनं चरन्तीति। तदेतदेव मिथुनमित्याचक्षते, तस्य यो घर्मः, तच्छिश्नं, यौ शफौ, तावाण्डौ, य उपयमनीके, श्रोणिकपाले, यत्पयः, तद्रेतः, तदग्नौ देवयोन्यां रेतो ब्रह्ममयं धत्ते प्रजननाय। सोऽग्निर्देवयोनिर्ऋङ्मयो यजुर्मयः साममयो ब्रह्ममयोऽमृतमय आहुतिमयः सर्वेन्द्रियः सम्पन्नो यजमान ऊर्ध्वः स्वर्गं लोकमेति। तदाहुः, न प्रथमयज्ञे

---

१, २, विरत इति ख०। विह्वृत इति भ०।

३ अन्तर्धायेति छ०।

प्रवर्ग्यं कुर्वीत, अनुपनामका (१) ह वा एनमुत्तरे यज्ञक्रतवो भवन्तीति। कामन्तु योनूचानः(२) श्रोत्रियःस्यात्, तस्य प्रवृञ्ज्यात्, आत्मा वै स यज्ञस्येति विज्ञायते, अपशिरसा ह वा एष यज्ञेन यजते, योऽप्रवर्ग्येण यजते। शिरो ह वा एतद्यज्ञस्य, यत् प्रवर्ग्यः। तस्मात् प्रवर्ग्यवत्यैव (३) याजयेन्नाप्रवर्ग्येण। तदप्येषाभ्यनूक्ता, चत्वारि शृङ्गेति ॥ ६ ॥

देवाश्च ह वा ऋषयश्चासुरैः संयत्ता आसन्। तेषामसुराणामिमाः पुरः प्रत्यभिजिता आसन्, अयस्मयी पृथिवी, रजतान्तरिक्षं, हरिणी द्यौ। ते देवाः सङ्घातं सङ्घातं पराजयन्त। ते विदुः, अनायतना हि वै स्मः, स्मः ? तस्मात् पराजयामहा इति एताः ता पुरः प्रत्यकुर्वत, हविर्धानन्दिव आग्नीध्रमन्तरिक्षात्सदः पृथिव्याः। ते देवा अब्रुवन्, उपसदमुपायाम, उपसदा वै महापुरञ्जयन्तीति। त एभ्यो लोकेभ्यो निरघ्नन्, एकयामुष्माल्लोकादेकयान्तरिक्षादेकया पृथिव्याः। तस्मादाहुः, उपसदा वै महापुरञ्जयन्तीति। त एभ्यो लोकेभ्यो निर्हता ऋतून् प्राविशन्। ते षडुपायन्, तानुपसद्भिरेवर्तुभ्यो निरघ्नन्, द्वाभ्याममुष्माल्लोकाद् द्वाभ्यामन्तरिक्षाद् द्वाभ्यां पृथिव्याः। त ऋतुभ्यो निर्हताः संवत्सरं प्राविशन्। ते द्वादशोपायन्, तानुपसद्भिरेव संवत्सरान्निरघ्नन्, चतसृभिरमुष्माल्लोकाच्चतसृभिरन्तरिक्षाच्चतसृभिः पृथिव्याः। ते संवत्सरा निर्हता अहोरात्रे प्राविशन्, ते यत्साय-

१ कुर्वीतामुपनामका इति भ०, ट० च।

२ कामं रूपोनूचान इति ख०, ग० च।

३ प्रवर्ग्यवतैवेति ग०, भ०, ट० च। प्रवर्ग्यतयैवेति क०।

मुपायन्, तेनैनान् रात्र्या अनुदन्त,[१] यत् प्रातः, तेनाह्नः। तस्माद्गौः सायम्प्रातस्तनमाप्यायते। प्रातःसायन्तनन्तानुपसद्भिरेवैभ्यो लोकेभ्यो नुदमान आयन्। ततो देवा अभवन् परासुराः। सर्वेभ्य एवैभ्यो लोकेभ्यो भ्रातृव्यन्नुदमान एति, य एवं विद्वानुपसदमुपैति॥ ७॥

न द्वादशाग्निष्टोमस्योपसदः स्युः, अशान्ता निर्मृज्येरन्[२]तिस्रोऽहीनस्य, उपरिष्टाद्यज्ञक्रतुर्गरीयानभिषीदेत्, यथागुरुर्भारो ग्रीवा निश्शीर्णीयादार्त्तिमार्च्छेदत्। द्वादशाहीनस्य कुर्यात्, प्रत्यु तथैव[३] सयत्वाय। तिस्रोऽग्निष्टोमस्योपसदः स्युः, शान्ताग्निर्मार्गाय। ते देवा असुर्य्यान्[४] इमांल्लोकानान्ववैतुमाधृष्णुवन्[५]। तानग्निना मुखेनान्ववायन्, यदग्निमनुष्टुपसदां प्रतीकानि भवन्ति। यथा क्षेत्रपतिः क्षेत्रे न्ववनयन्ति एवमेवैतदग्निना मुखेनेमांल्लोकानभिनयन्तो यन्ति। यो ह वै देवान् साध्यान्वेद, सिध्यत्यस्मै। इमे वाव लोकाः, यत्साध्या देवाः। स य एवमेतान् साध्यान्वेद, सिध्यत्यस्मै सिध्यत्यमुष्मै। सिध्यत्यस्माल्लोकात्, य एवं विद्वानुपसदमुपैति॥ ८॥

अथ यत्ताह, अध्वर्युरग्नीद्देवपत्नीर्व्याचक्ष्व, सुब्रह्मण्य सुब्रह्मण्यमाह्वयेति। तदपरेण गार्हपत्यं प्राङ्मुखस्तिष्ठन्ननवानन्नाग्नीध्रो[६]

---

१ आनुदन्तेति च०।

२ निरमृज्येरन्निति भ०, ट० च।

३ प्रत्युत्तथै इति ख०, च०, छ० च। प्रत्यु तथैवा इति ग०।

४ असूर्यानिति छ०।

५ नान्ववैतमाधृष्णुवन्निति भ०। नान्वैतमाधृष्णुवन्निति ट०

६ तिष्ठन्नत्यननन्नाग्नीध्र इति छ०। तिष्ठन्ननवानननाग्नीध इति ग०।

देवपत्नीर्व्याचष्टे, पृथिव्यग्नेः पत्नी, वाग् वातस्य पत्नी, सेनेन्द्रस्य पत्नी, धेना बृहस्पतेः पत्नी, पथ्या पूष्णः पत्नी, गायत्री वसूनां पत्नी, त्रिष्टुप् रुद्राणां पत्नी, जगत्यादित्यानां पत्नी, अनुष्टप् मित्रस्य पत्नी, विराड् वरुणस्य पत्नी, पङ्क्तिर्विष्णोः पत्नी, दीक्षा सोमस्य राज्ञः पत्नीति । अतिभ्रातृव्यानारोहति, नैनं भ्रातृव्या आरोहन्ति, उपरि भ्रातृव्यानारोहति, य एवं विद्वानग्नीध्रो देवपत्नीर्व्याचष्टे ॥ ९ ॥

यथा वै रथ एकैकमरमभिप्रतितिष्ठन् वर्त्तते, एवं यज्ञ एकैकां तन्वमभिप्रतितिष्ठन्नेति । पुरा प्रचरितोराग्नीध्रीये होतव्या एतद्ध वा उवाच वासिष्ठः सात्यहव्यः, अस्कां सोम इत्युक्ता मा सूर्च्चत प्रचरत प्रातर्वावाद्याहं सोमं संस्थापयामीति । नास्य सोम स्कन्दति, य एवं विद्वान्त् सोमं पिवति, स ह स्म वसैहासन्यामासीनः सक्तुभिरुपमथ्य सोमं पिवति, अहं वाव सर्वतो यज्ञं वेद, य एतान्(१) वेद, न मामेष हिंसिष्यतीति । नैनं सोमपीथोनपेयो हिनस्ति, य एवं विद्वान्त् सोमं पिवति । तं ह स्म यदाहुः, कस्मात्त्वमिदमासन्द्यामासीनः सक्तुभिरुपमथ्य सोमं पिवसीति । देवतास्वेव यज्ञं प्रतिष्ठापयामीति अब्रवीद्ब्राह्मणः । यस्यैवं विदुषो यस्यैवं विद्वान् यज्ञार्त्तान् यज्ञे प्रायश्चित्तं(२) जुहोति, देवतास्वेव यज्ञं प्रतिष्ठापयति । यज्ञार्त्तिं प्रतिजुहुयात्, सयोनित्वाय । त्रयस्त्रिंशद्वै यज्ञस्य तन्व इति, एकान्नत्रिंशत्स्तोमभागाः, त्रीणि सवनानि, यज्ञश्चतुर्थः, स्तोमभागैरेवैतत्

१ एमामिति ख०, च०, छ०, च ।

२ प्रायश्चित्तिमिति च०, छ० च ।

स्तोमभागान् प्रति प्रयुङ्क्ते, सवनैः सवनानि, यज्ञेन यज्ञं, सर्वा ह वा अस्य यज्ञस्य तन्वः प्रयुक्ता भवन्ति, सर्वा आप्ताः सर्वा अवरुद्धा देवस्य सवितुः प्रसवे बृहस्पतये स्तुतेति। यद्यद्वै सविता देवेभ्यः प्रासुवत् तेनार्ध्नुवन्, सवितृप्रसूता एव स्तुवन् ऋध्नुवन्, ऋध्यन्ते ह वा अस्य स्तोमाः, यज्ञ ऋध्यते, यजमान ऋध्यते, प्रजाया ऋध्यते, पशुभ्य ऋध्यते, ब्रह्मणे यस्यैवं विद्वान् ब्रह्मा भवति ॥१०॥

देवाश्च ह वा असुराश्चास्पर्धन्त, ते देवाः समावद्देवा यज्ञे कुर्वाणा आसन्, यदेव देवा अकुर्वत, तदसुरा अकुर्वत, तेन व्यावृत्तमगच्छन्(१)। ते देवा अब्रुवन्, नयतेमं यज्ञं तिर उपर्यसुरेभ्यस्तंस्यामहै इति। तमेताभिराच्छायोदक्रामन्ति, यजूंषि यज्ञे समिधः स्वाहेति। तन्तिर उपर्यसुरेभ्यो यज्ञमतन्वत, तमेषां यज्ञमसुराणां न्ववाय, ततोनदेवा अभवन् परासुराः। स य एवं विद्वांस्तिर उपर्यसुरेभ्यो यज्ञं तनुते, भवत्यात्मना परास्याप्रियो भ्रातृव्यो भवति। एतैरेव जुहुयात्स्तुतयज्ञे(२) चतुर्भिश्चतुर्भिरन्वाख्यानं पुरस्तात् प्रातरनुवाकस्य जुहुयात्, एतावान् वै यज्ञः, यावानेष यज्ञस्तं वृङ्क्ते, स यज्ञो भवति, अयज्ञ इतरः। एतैरेव जुहुयात्, पुरस्ताद् द्वादशाहस्य। एष ह वै प्रत्यक्षं द्वादशाहः, तमेव आलभ्य एतैरेव जुहुयात्, पुरस्ताद् दीक्षायाः। एषा ह वै प्रत्यक्षं दीक्षा, तामेवालभ्यैतैरेवातिथ्यमभिमृशेत्, यज्ञेन यज्ञमयजन्त देवा इति ॥११॥

यत्र विजानाति, ब्रह्मन्त्सोमोऽस्कन्निति। तमेतयालभ्याभिम-

---

१ व्यावर्त्तमगच्छन्निति भ०, ट० च।

२ स्तुतयज्ञ इति क०।

न्वयते, अभूद्देवः सविता वन्द्योनूनः(१) इदानीमह्न उपवाच्यो नृभिः, वि यो रत्ना भजति(२) मानवेभ्यः श्रेष्ठन्नो अत्र द्रविणं यथा दधदिति। ये अग्नयो अप्स्वन्तरिति सप्तभिरभिजुहोति। यदेवास्यावस्कन्नं भवति, तदेवास्यैतदग्नौ स्वगाकरोति। अग्निर्हि सुकृतीनां(३) हविषां प्रतिष्ठा। अथ विसृप्य वैप्रुषान् होमान् जुह्वति, द्रप्सश्चस्कन्देति। या एवास्याभिषूयमाणस्य विप्रुषः स्कन्दन्ति, अंशुर्वा ता एवास्यैतदाहवनीये स्वगाकरोति। आहवनीयो ह्याहुतीनां प्रतिष्ठा। यस्ते द्रप्स स्कन्दतीति, स्तोको वै द्रप्सः। यस्ते अंशुर्बाहुच्युतो धिषणाया उपस्थादिति, बाहुभिरभिच्युतोंशुरधिषवणाभ्यामधिस्कन्दन्ति। अध्वर्योर्वा पपर्युः पवित्रात्तन्ते जुहोमि मनसा वषट्कृतमिति, तद्यथा, वषट्कृतं स्वाहाकृतं हुतमेवं भवति॥ १२॥

ऋषयो वा इन्द्रं प्रत्यक्षं नापश्यन्। तं वसिष्ठ एव प्रत्यक्षमपश्यत्। सोऽबिभेत्, इतरेभ्य ऋषिभ्यो मा प्रवोचदिति। सोऽब्रवीत्, ब्राह्मणन्ते वक्ष्यामि, यथा त्वत्पुरोहिताः प्रजाः प्रजनयिष्यन्ते(४), अथेतरेभ्य ऋषिभ्यो मा प्रवोचदिति। तस्मा एतान् स्तोमभागानुवाच। ततो वसिष्ठपुरोहिताः प्रजाः प्रजायन्त। स्तोमो वा एतेषां भागः, तत्स्तोमभागानां स्तोमभा-

---

१ वन्द्योनुन इति ख०, भ०, ड० च।

२ वि यो रत्नाभजतीति ख०. ग०, घ०।

३ सुकृप्तीनामिति ख०, च०, भ० च।

४ प्रजनिष्यन्ते इति भ०।

यज्ञं प्राह। प्रेतिरसि धर्म्मणे त्वेति, धर्मो मनुष्याः, मनुष्येभ्य एव यज्ञं प्राह। अन्वितिरसि सन्धिरसि प्रतिधिरसीति, त्रयो वै लोकाः लोकेष्वेव यज्ञं प्रतिष्ठापयति। विष्टम्भोसीति, वृष्टिमेवावरुन्धे। प्रावोस्यह्नाऽसीति(१), मिथुनमेव करोति। उशिगसि प्रकेतोऽसि सुदितिरसीति, अष्टौ वसव एकादश रुद्रा द्वादशादित्या वाग् द्वात्रिंशी स्वरस्त्रयस्त्रिंशस्त्रयस्त्रिंशद्देवा देवेभ्य एव यज्ञं प्राह। ओजोसि पितृभ्यस्त्वेति, बलमेव तत् पितॄननुसन्तनोति। तन्तुरसि प्रजाभ्यस्त्वेति, प्रजा एव पशू-ननुसन्तनोति। रेवदस्योषधीभ्यस्त्वेति, ओषधीष्वेव यज्ञं प्रति-ष्ठापयति। पृतनाषाडसि पशुभ्यस्त्वेति, प्रजा एव पशूननु-सन्तनोति। अभिजिदसीति, वज्रो वै षोड़शी, व्यावृत्तोसौ वज्रः, तस्मादेषोन्यै व्यावृत्तः। नाभुरसीति, प्रजापतिर्वै सप्त-दशः, प्रजापतिमेवावरुन्धे ॥ १३ ॥

अधिपतिरसि धरुणोसि सꣳसर्पोसि वयोधा असीति(२), प्राणोपानश्चक्षुः श्रोत्रमित्येतानि वै पुरुषमकरन्। प्राणानुपैति, प्रजात्या एव। त्रिवृदसि प्रवृदसि स्ववृदस्यनुवृदसीति, मिथुन-मेव करोति। आरोहोसि प्ररोहोसि(३) संरोहोस्यनुरोहोसीति, प्रजापतिरेव। वसुकोसि वस्यष्टिरसि वेषश्रीरसीति(४), प्रति-गत्वं। रश्मिरसि क्षयाय त्वेति, क्षयो वै देवाः, देवेभ्य एव

१ प्रावोस्यह्नासीति इति ग०।

२ वयोधासीति च०, छ०, च।

३ प्रारोहोसि इति भ०।

४ वृषश्रीरसीति भ०।

ष्ठितिरेव। आक्रमोसि सङ्क्रमोस्युत्क्रमोस्युत्क्रान्तिरसीति, ऋद्धिरेव(१)। यद्ध्वै सविता देवेभ्यः प्रासुवत्, तेनार्भुवत्(२) सवितृप्रसूता एव स्तुवन् न्यृभ्नुवन्ति (३)। बृहस्पतये स्तुतेति, बृहस्पतिर्वा आङ्गिरसो देवानां ब्रह्मा। तदनुमत्यै वों भूर्जनदिति,(४) प्रातःसवन ऋग्भिरेवोभयतोथर्वाङ्गिरोभिर्गुप्ताभिर्गुप्तै स्तुतेत्येव। ओं भुवो जनदिति, माध्यन्दिने सवने यजुर्भिरेवोभयतोथर्वाङ्गिरोभिर्गुप्ताभिर्गुप्तैस्तुतेत्येव। ओं स्वर्जनदिति, तृतीयसवने सामभिरेवोभयतोथर्वाङ्गिरोभिर्गुप्ताभिर्गुप्तै स्तुतेत्येव। अथ यद्यहीन उक्थ्यः षोडशी वाजपेयोतिरात्रोऽप्तोर्यामा वा स्यात्, सर्व्वाभिः सर्वाभिरत ऊर्द्धं व्याहृतिभिरनुजानाति। ओं भूर्भुवः स्वर्जनदृधत् करद्रुहन् महत्तच्छमोमिन्द्रवन्त स्तुतेति, सेन्द्रान्मापगायत सेन्द्राꣳस्तुत इत्येव। इन्द्रियवान् न्यृद्धिमान्(५) वशीयान् भवति, य एवं वेद, यश्चैवं विद्वान् स्तोमभागैर्यजते॥ १४॥

यो ह वा आयताꣳश्च प्रतियताꣳश्च स्तोमभागान् विद्याच्च(६) विष्पर्धमानयोः सह्रतसोमयोः, ब्रह्मास्यास्तुतोषे स्तुतोर्जं स्तुतदेवस्य सवितुः सवे बृहस्पतिं वः प्रजापतिं वो वसून्वो देवान् रुद्रान्वो

---

१ ऋग्भिरेवेति ख०, ग०, च० च।

२ तेनार्धुवन् इति च०।

३ रिध्नुवन्ति इति ख०, ग०, च। यृद्ध्नुवतीति च०।

४ वाभूर्जनदिति इति ख० ग०, च।

५ सेन्द्रियांस्तुतेत्येवेन्द्रियावानृद्धिमान् इति ख०,। सेन्द्रियांस्तथेत्येवेन्द्रियवान् न्यृधिमानिति च०।

६ विन्द्याचेति ख०।

देवानादित्यान्वो देवान् साध्यान्वो देवानाप्त्यान्वो देवान्विश्वान्वो देवान् सर्वान्वो देवान्विश्वतस्परि हवामहे जनेभ्योऽस्माकमस्तु केवल इतः क्रणोतु वीर्य्यम्, इत्येते ह वा आयताश्च प्रतियताश्च स्तोमभागाः, तान्जपन्नुपर्य्युपरि परेषां ब्रह्माणमवेक्षेत(१)। तत एषामधःशिरा ब्रह्मा पतति, ततो यज्ञः, ततो यजमानः। यजमानेऽधःशिरसि पतिति स द्वेष्योऽधःशिराः पतति। यस्मिन्नर्धे यजन्ते देवाश्च ह वा असुराश्च, सहृतसोमो यज्ञावतनुताम्। अथ बृहस्पतिराङ्गिरसो देवानां ब्रह्मा, स आयताꣳश्च प्रतियताꣳश्च स्तोमभागान् जपन्नुपर्य्युपर्यसुराणां ब्रह्माणमवैक्षेत। तत एषामधःशिरा ब्रह्माऽपतत्, ततो यज्ञः, ततोऽसुरा इति ॥ १५ ॥

देवा यज्ञं पराजयन्त, तमाग्नीध्रात्पुनरुपाजयन्त, तदेतद्यज्ञस्यापराजितं, यदाग्नीध्रं यदाग्नीध्राधिष्ण्यान्विहरति। तत एवैनं पुनस्तनुते पराजित्यै। अप खलु वा एते गच्छन्ति, ये बहिष्पवमानं सर्पन्ति। बहिष्पवमाने स्तुत आह अग्नीत्, अग्नीन्विहर, बर्हिः स्तृणीहि, पुरोडाशानलङ्कुर्विति। यज्ञमेवापराजित्य पुनस्तन्वाना आयन्त्यङ्गारैर्द्वे सवने विहरति, शलाकाभिस्तृतीयसवनं सशुक्रत्वाय। अथो सम्भवत्येवमेवैतत्, दक्षिणतो वै देवानां यज्ञं रक्षांस्यजिघांसन्, तान्याग्नीध्रेणापाघ्नत। तस्माद्दक्षिणामुखस्तिष्ठन्नग्नीत् प्रत्याश्रावयति, यज्ञस्याभिजित्यै रक्षसामपहत्यै रक्षसामपहत्यै ॥ १६ ॥

---

१ ब्रह्माणमवेक्षते इति ह० ।

तदाहुः, अथ कस्मात् सौम्य एवाध्वरे प्रवृत्ताहुतीर्जुह्वति, न हविर्यज्ञ इति । अकृत्स्ना वा एषा देवयज्या, यद्धविर्यज्ञः । अथ हैषैव कृत्स्ना एषा देवयज्या, यत् सौम्योध्वरः, तस्मात् सौम्य एवाध्वरे प्रवृत्ताहुतीर्जुह्वति । जुष्टो वाचे भूयासं जुष्टो वाचस्पतये देवि वाग् यद्वाचो मधुमत्तमं, तस्मिन्मा धाः स्वाहा वाचे स्वाहा वाचस्पतये स्वाहा सरस्वत्यै स्वाहा सरस्वत्या इति, पुरस्तात् स्वाहाकारेण जुहोति । तस्माद्वाग् अत ऊर्द्ध्वमुत्सृष्टा यज्ञं वहति । मनसोन्तरा(१), मनसा हि मनः प्रीतम् । तदु हैके सप्ताहुतीर्जुह्वति, सप्त छन्दांसि प्रवृत्तानि प्रतिमन्त्रमिति वदन्तः । यथा मेखला पर्य्यस्यते मेध्यस्य चामेध्यस्य च विहृत्यै, एवं हैवैते न्युप्यन्ते, मेध्यस्य च विहृत्यै यज्ञस्य विहृत्यै । प्राचीनं हि धिष्ण्येभ्यो देवानां लोकाः, प्रतीचीनं मनुष्याणां । तस्मात् सोमं पिवता प्राञ्चो धिष्ण्या नोपसर्प्याः । जनं ह्येतद्देवलोकां ह्यु ध्यारोहन्ति, तेषामेतदायतनं चोद्यनं च, यदाग्नीध्रं च सदश्च । तद्योऽविद्वान् सञ्चरति, आर्त्तिमार्च्छति । अथ यो विद्वान्, सञ्चरति, न स धिष्ण्यीयामार्त्तिमार्च्छति ॥ १७ ॥

प्रजापतिर्वै यज्ञः, तस्मिन् सर्वे कामाः सर्वा इष्टीः सर्वममृतत्वं । तस्य हैते गोप्तारः, यद्धिष्ण्यीयः, तान् सदः प्रसृप्स्यन्(२) नमस्करोति, नमो नम इति । न हि नमस्कारमतिदेवाः, ते ह नमसिताः कर्त्तारमतिसृजन्तीति । तत एतं प्रजापतिं यज्ञं प्रपद्यते, नमो नम

१ मनसोन्तरामिति ख० ।

२ प्रसृप्स्यन्निति ख० ।

इति। न हि नमस्कारमतिदेवाः, स तत्रैव यजमानः सर्वान् कामानाप्नोति सर्वान् कामानाप्नोति ॥ १८ ॥

यो वै सदस्यान् गन्धर्वान्वेद, न सदस्यामर्त्तिमार्च्छति। सदः प्रसर्पन्(१)ब्रूयादुपद्रष्ट्रे नम इति, अग्निर्वै द्रष्टा, तस्मा उएवात्मानं परिदधाति सर्वमायुरेति न पुरा जरसः प्रमीयते। य एवं वेद, सदः प्रसृप्य ब्रूयादुपश्रोत्रे नम इति। वायुर्वाउ उपश्रोता, तस्मा उ एवात्मानं परिदधाति सर्व्वमायुरेति न पुरा जरसः प्रमीयते, य एवं वेद। सदः प्रसर्पन् ब्रूयात्, अनुख्यात्रे नम इति, आदित्यो वा अनुख्याता तस्मा उ एवात्मानं परिदधाति सर्व्वमायुरेति न पुरा जरसः प्रमीयते। य एवं वेद सदः प्रसृप्तो ब्रूयात्, उपद्रष्ट्रे नम इति। ब्राह्मणो वा उपद्रष्टा, तस्मा ऊ एवात्मानं परिदधाति सर्वमायुरेति न पुरा जरसः प्रमीयते। य एवं वेद, एते वै सदस्या गन्धर्वाः, स एवमेतान् सदस्यान् गन्धर्वानविद्वान् सदः प्रसर्पति, स सदस्यामार्त्तिमार्च्छति, अथ यो विद्वान् सञ्चरति, न सदस्यामार्त्तिमार्च्छति। एतेन ह स्म वा आङ्गिरसः सर्व्वं सदः पर्य्याहुः, ते न सदस्यामार्त्तिमार्च्छन्ति। अथ यान् कामयेत न सदस्यामार्त्तिमार्च्छेयुरिति। तेभ्य एतेन सर्वं सदः परिब्रूयात्तेन सदस्यामार्त्तिमार्च्छन्ति। अथ यं कामयेत प्रमीयतेति, तमेतेभ्य आवृश्चेत् प्रमीयते ॥ १९ ॥

तदाहुः, यदैन्द्रो यज्ञोथ कस्मात् वावेव प्रातःसवने प्रस्थितानां प्रत्यक्षादैन्द्रीभ्यां यजतो होता चैव ब्राह्मणाच्छंसी च। इदं ते सोम्यं मध्विति होता यजति। इन्द्र त्वा, वृषभं वयमिति

१ प्रसर्पस्येति ख०। प्रसपृप्सन्निति ङ०।

ब्राह्मणाच्छंसी। नानादेवत्याभिरितरे। कथं तेषामैन्द्रियो भवन्ति(१)। मित्रं वयं हवामह इति, मैत्रावरुणो यजति। वरुणं सोमपीतय इति, यद्वै किञ्च पीतवत्, तदैन्द्रं रूपं, तेनेन्द्रं प्रीणाति। मरुतो यस्य हि क्षय इति, पोता यजति। ससुगोपातमो जन इति, इन्द्रो वै गोपाः, तदैन्द्रं रूपं, तेनेन्द्रं प्रीणाति। अग्ने पत्नीरिहावहेति, नेष्टा यजति। त्वष्टारं सोमपीतय इति, यद्वै किञ्च पीतवत्, तदैन्द्रं रूपं, तेनेन्द्रं प्रीणाति। उक्षान्नाय वशान्नायेत्याग्नीध्रो यजति। सोमपृष्ठाय वेधस इति, इन्द्रो वै वेधाः, तदैन्द्रं रूपं, तेनेन्द्रं प्रीणाति। प्रातर्यावभिरागतं देवेभिर्जन्या(२)वसू, इन्द्राग्नी सोमपीतय इति। स्वयं समृद्धा अच्छावाकस्यैवमु हैता ऐन्द्रियो भवन्ति, यन्नानादेवत्याः, तेनान्या देवताः प्रीणाति। यद्गायत्र्यः, तेनाग्नेय्यः, तस्मादेताभिस्त्रयमवाप्तं भवति॥ २०॥

ते वै खलु सर्व एव माध्यन्दिने प्रस्थितानां प्रत्यक्षादैन्द्रीभिर्यजन्ति, अभिरूपवतीभिरेकेऽपि वा। सोममभि यमुग्रतर्द इति, होता यजति। सईम्पाहि य ऋजीषी तरुत्र इति, मैत्रावरुणः। एवा पाहि प्रत्नथा मन्दतु त्वेति, ब्राह्मणाच्छंसी। आर्वाङेहि सोमकामन्त्वाहुरिति, पोता। तवायं सोमस्त्वमेह्यर्वाङिति, नेष्टा। इन्द्राय सोमाः प्र दिवो विदाना इति, अच्छावाकः आपूर्णो अस्य कलशः स्वाहेति आग्नीध्रः। एवमु हैता अभिरूपवत्यो भवन्ति। इन्द्रो वै प्रातः सवनन्नाभ्यजयत्, स

१ भवन्तीति इति ग०।

२ जेन्या इति ख०, ग०, च। जेन्या इति भ० ट० च।

एताभिर्माध्यन्दिनं सवनमभ्यतृणवत्, तद्यदेताभिर्माध्यन्दिनं सवनमभ्यतृणवत्, तस्मादेता अभितृणवत्यो भवन्ति ॥ २१ ॥

तदाहुः, यदैन्द्रार्भवं तृतीयसवनमथ कस्मादेक एव तृतीयसवने प्रस्थितानां प्रत्यक्षादैन्द्रार्भव्या यजति। इन्द्र ऋभुभिर्वाजवद्भिः(१) समुक्षितमिति होतैव नानादेवत्याभिरितरे कथं तेषा मैन्द्रार्भव्यो भवन्ति। इन्द्रावरुणा सुतपाविमꣳसुतमिति मैत्रावरुणो यजति। युवो रथो अध्वरो देववीतय इति, बहूनि वा ह तदृभूणां रूपम्। इन्द्रश्च सोमं पिबतं बृहस्पत इति ब्राह्मणाच्छंसी यजति। आवां विशन्त्विन्दवः स्वाभुव इति, बहूनि वा ह तदृभूणां रूपं। आ वो वहन्तु सप्तयो रघुष्यद इति पोता यजति। रघुपत्वा नः प्र जिगात बाहुभिरिति, बहूनि वा ह तदृभूणा रूपं। अमेव नः सुहवा आ हि गन्तनेति नेष्टा यजति। गन्तनेति, बहूनि वा ह तदृभूणां रूपम्। इन्द्राविष्णू पिबतं मध्वो अस्येत्यच्छावाको यजति। आ वामन्धांसि मदिराण्यग्मन्निति, बहूनि वा ह तदृभूणां रूपम्। इमꣳस्तोममर्हते जातवेदस इत्याग्नीध्रो यजति रथमिव संमहेमा मनीषयेति, बहूनि वा ह तदृभूणां रूपम्। एवमु हैता ऐन्द्रार्भव्यो भवन्ति, यन्नानादेवत्यास्तेनान्या देवताः प्रीणाति। यदु जगत् प्रासाहै जागतमु वै तृतीयसवनं तृतीयसवनस्य समृद्ध्यै ॥ २२ ॥

विचक्षणवतीं वाचं भाषन्ते(२) च नसितवतीं। विचक्षयन्ति ब्राह्मणं च न सपन्ति, प्राजापत्यं सत्यं वदन्ति। एतद्वै मनुष्येषु सत्यं

१ वाजमभिरिति भ०।

२ भाषते इति ख०।

यच्चक्षुः। तस्मादाहुराचक्षाणमद्रागिति[१]। स यदाहाद्राक्षमिति। तथाहास्य श्रद्दधति, यद्यु वै स्वयं वै दृष्टं[२] भवति, न बहूनां जनानामपि श्रद्दधाति। तस्माद्विचक्षणवतीं वाचं भाषन्ते च न सितवतीं। सत्योत्तरा हैवैषां वागुदिता भवति ॥ २३ ॥

सन्ततयज्ञो वा एषः, यद्दर्शपूर्णमासौ। कस्य वाव देवा यज्ञमागच्छन्ति, कस्य वा न। बहूनां वा एतत् यजमानानां सामान्यमहः। तस्मात् पूर्वेद्युर्देवताः परिगृह्णीयात्। यो ह वै पूर्वेद्युर्देवताः परिगृह्णाति, तस्य श्वोभूते यज्ञमागच्छन्ति। तस्माद्विहव्यस्य चतस्र ऋचो जपेत्। यज्ञविदो हि मन्यन्ते, सोम एव सन्तत इति, यज्ञो यज्ञेन सन्ततः ॥ २४ ॥

इत्यथर्ववेदोत्तरगोपथब्राह्मणस्य द्वितीयः प्रपाठकः समाप्तः ॥२॥

---

## अथ तृतीयप्रपाठकः।

ओम्। देवपात्रं वै वषट्कारः। यद्वषट् करोति, देवपात्रेणैव तद्देवतास्तर्पयति। अथो यदाभितृष्यन्तोरभिसंस्थं[३] तर्पयति, एवमेतद्देवतास्तर्पयति। यदनु वषट् करोति, तद्यथैवादोऽश्वान्वा[४]गा वा पुनरभ्याघारं तर्पयति। एवमेव तद्देवतास्तर्पयति, यदनु

१ श्याचक्षाणमद्रागितीति भा०।

२ रिष्टमिति ट०।

३ तृप्यन्तीभिरभिसंस्थमिति क०।

४ श्वमा वेति ट०।

वषट् करोति। इमानेवाग्नीनुपासत इत्याहुर्धिष्ण्यानथ कस्मात् पूर्वस्मिन्नेवाग्नौ जुह्वति पूर्वस्मिन्वषट् करोति। यदेव सोमस्याग्ने वीहीति अनु वषट् करोति, तेनैव वषट् करोति, धिष्ण्यान् प्रीणाति। अथ संस्थितान् सोमान् भक्षयन्तीत्याहुः। येषां नानु वषट् करोति, तदाहुः, को नु सोमस्य स्विष्टकृद्भाग इति। यदेव सोमस्याग्ने वीहीत्यनु वषट् करोति, तेनैव संस्थितान् सोमान् भक्षयन्तीत्याहुः। स उ एष सोमस्य स्विष्टकृद्भागः, यदनु वषट् करोति ॥ १ ॥

वज्रो वै वषट्कारः। स यं(१), द्विष्यात् तं मनसा ध्यायन् वषट् कुर्यात्। तस्मिंस्तद्वज्रमास्थापयति। षडिति वषट्करोति। षड्वा ऋतवः, ऋतूनामाप्त्यै। वौषडिति वषट् करोति। असौ वाव वौ ऋतवः षट्, एतमेव तदृतुष्वादधाति, ऋतुषु प्रतिष्ठापयति। तदु ह स्माह, वै त एतानिव(२) एतेन षट् प्रतिष्ठापयति। द्यौरन्तरिक्षे प्रतिष्ठाता, अन्तरिक्षं पृथिव्यां, पृथिव्यप्सु, आपः सत्येन, सत्यं ब्रह्मणि, ब्रह्म तपसि। इत्येता एव तद्देवताः प्रतिष्ठान्याः प्रतिष्ठन्तीरिदं सर्वमनुप्रतितिष्ठति। प्रतितिष्ठति प्रजया पशुभिः, य एवं वेद ॥ २ ॥

त्रयो वै वषट्काराः, वज्रो धामच्छदक्तः(३)। स यदेवोच्चैर्बलवषट् करोति, स वज्रस्तन्तं(४) प्रहरति द्विषते भ्रातृव्याय, बधं

१ स्वयमिति ग०, च०, झ० च।

२ एतानि वा इति क०।

३ धामच्छदक्त इति ग०।

४ वज्रस्तन्त्रमिति झ०, ट० च।

योस्य स्तृत्यः, तस्मै स्तरीतवे[१)। तस्मात् स भ्रातृव्यवता[२] वषट् कृत्यः। अथ यः स यः सन्ततो निर्ह्राणच्छ[३] स्वधामच्छत्, तन्तं प्रजाश्च पशवश्चानूपतिष्ठन्ते। तस्मात् स प्रजाकामेन पशुकामेन वषट्कृत्यः। अथ येनैव षट् पराप्नोति,[४] स ऋत्क्वो रित्वयात्मानं[५] रिणक्ति यजमानस्य। पापीयान् वषट्कर्त्ता भवति, पापीयान् यस्मै वषट् करोति। तस्मात्तस्याशान्नेयात्। किंस्वित् स यजमानस्य पापभद्रमाद्रियेतेति ह स्माह, योस्य वषट् कर्ता भवति, अत्रैवैनं यथा कामयेत तथा कुर्य्याद्यं कामयेत यथैवानीजानोभूत्तथैवेजानः स्यादिति। यथैवास्यर्चं ब्रूयात्तथैवास्य वषट्कुर्य्यात्। समानमेवैनं तत् करोति, यङ्कामयेत पापीयान् स्यादिति। उच्चैस्तरामस्यर्चं ब्रूयान्नीचैस्तरावषट्[६] कुर्य्यात्। पापीयाꣳसमेवैनं तत् करोति, यं कामयेत श्रेयान् स्यादिति। नीचैस्तरामस्यर्चं ब्रूयादुच्चै स्तरान्वषट् कुर्य्यात्, श्रेयाꣳसमेवैनं तत् करोति, श्रिय एवैनं तच्छ्रियमादधाति॥ २॥

यस्यै देवतायै हविर्गृहीतं स्यात्, तां मनसा ध्यायन् वषट्

---

१ योस्य स्तृतस्तस्मै स्तरीतस्तवे इति ङ०। योस्य स्तृतस्तस्मै तरीतवे इति ग०, च० च।

२ भ्रातृव्याय इति भ०, ट० च।

३ निर्ह्राणच्छदिति ङ०।

४ येनैव वषट् पराप्नोति इति ट०। येनैव षडपराप्नोतीति ग०, ङ०, भ० च।

५ रिणक्त्यात्मानमिति च०, ट० च।

६ नीचैस्तराम् वषडिति च० भ० ट० च।

कुर्य्यात्। साचादेव तद्देवतां प्रीणाति, प्रत्यचाद्देवतां परि-गृह्णाति। संततमृचा वषट्कृत्यं सन्तत्यै सन्धीयते प्रजया-पशुभिः, य एवं वेद॥ ४॥

वज्रो वै वषट्कारः। स उ एष प्रहृतः(१) शांतोदीदाय। तस्य ह न सर्व एव शान्तिं वेद नो प्रतिष्ठां। तस्माद्धाप्येतर्हि भूयानिव मृत्युः, तस्य हैषैव शान्तिरेषा प्रतिष्ठा, यद्वागिति। वषट्कृत्य वागित्यनुमन्त्रयते, वषट्कार मा मां प्रमृचो माहं त्वां प्रमृचं बृहता मन उपह्वये व्यानेन शरीरं प्रतिष्ठामि, प्रतिष्ठां गच्छन् प्रतिष्ठां मा गमयेदिति। तदु ह स्माह, दीर्घमेवैतत् सदः प्रभोजः। सह ओज इत्यनुमन्त्रयेत, ओजश्च ह वै सहश्च वषट्कारस्य प्रियतमे तन्वौ प्रियाभ्यामेव तत्तनूभ्यां समर्द्धयति। प्रियया तन्वा समृध्यते, य एवं वेद॥ ५॥

वाक् च ह वै प्राणापानौ च वषट्कारः, ते वषट्कृतेवषट्कृते व्युत्क्रामन्ति।ताननुमन्त्रयते, वागोजः सह ओजो मयि प्राणापानाविति। वाचं चैव तत् प्राणापानौ च होता आत्मनि प्रतिष्ठापयति, सर्वमायुरेति, न पुरा जरसः प्रमीयते, य एवं वेद। शन्नो भव हृद आपीत इन्दो पितेव सोमसूनवे सुशेवः। सखेव सख्य उरु शंꣳस धीरः प्र ण आयुर्जीवसे सोम तारीरित्यात्मनं प्रत्यभिमृशति, ईश्वरो वा एषो प्रत्यभिमृष्टो यजमानस्यायुः प्रत्यविहर्त्तुमेनरिहस्माभचयेदिति। तद्यदेतेन प्रत्यभिमृशति, आयुरेवास्मै तत् प्रतिरते। आप्यायस्वसंतेपयांꣳसीति द्वाभ्यां चमसानाप्याययन्त्यभिरूपाभ्यां। यद् यज्ञेभिरूपं, तत् समृद्धं॥ ६॥

---

१ प्राकृत इति क०।

प्राणा वा ऋतुयाजाः, तद्यदृतुयाजैश्चरन्ति, प्राणानेव तद्यजमाने दधति। षड्ऋतुनेति यजन्ति, प्राणमेव तद्यजमाने दधति। चत्वार ऋतुभिर्यजन्ति, अपानमेव तद्यजमाने दधति। द्विर्ऋतुनेति उपरिष्टाद्, व्यानमेव तद्यजमाने दधति। स वा अस्य सम्भृतस्त्रेधाविहृतः[१], प्राणोऽपानो व्यान इति। ततोऽन्यत्र गुणितस्तथाह यजमानः, सर्वमायुरेत्यस्मिंल्लोक आप्नोत्याप्नोत्यमृतत्वमक्षितं स्वर्गे लोके। ते वा एते प्राणा एव, यदृतुयाजाः। तस्मादनवानं[२] ततो यजन्ति[३], प्राणानां सन्तत्यै। सन्तता इव हीमे प्राणाः। अथो ऋतवो वा ऋतुयाजाः। असंस्थानुवषट्कारः। यो त्वानुवषट्[४] कुर्यात्, असंस्थितानृतून् संस्थापयेत्। यस्तं तत्र ब्रूयात्, असंस्थितानृतून् समतिष्ठि। यो दुःखमनुभविष्यतीति[५], प्रभ्वत्तथा स्यात् ॥ ७॥

तदाहुः, यद्धोता यक्षद्धोता यक्षदिति, मैत्रावरुणो होत्रे प्रेष्यति, अथ कस्मादृहोतृभ्यः सद्भ्यो होत्राशंसिभ्यो होता यक्षद्धोता यक्षदिति[६] प्रेष्यतीति। वाग्वै होता, वाक् सर्व ऋत्विजः, वाग् यक्षद्वाग् यक्षदिति। अथो सर्वे वा एते सप्तहोतारोऽपि वा ऋचाभ्युदितं, सप्तहोतार ऋतुथा यजन्तीति। अथ य उपरिष्टाद्

---

१ विहूत इति ग०। विहित इति च०।

२ तस्मादन्वानमिति झ०, ठ० च।

३ यजतीति ग०।

४ योक्त्रानुवषडिति ग०, च०, झ०, ठ० च।

५ दुःखमं भविष्यतीतीति च०, झ०, ठ० च।

६ होत्राशंसिभ्यो होता यक्षदितीति ग०।

संवत्सरः, संवत्सरः प्रजापतिः, प्रजापतिर्यज्ञः। स योऽत्र भक्षयेद्यस्तं तत्र ब्रूयात्, अशान्तो भक्षो नानुवषट्कृत आत्मानमन्तरगान्न जीविष्यतीति। तथा ह्यस्याद्यो(१) वै भक्षयेत्,(२) प्राणो द्वादशर्चं जामितायै, ते वै द्वादश भवन्ति, द्वादश ह वै मासाः, भक्षः प्राण आत्मनमन्तरगादिति। तथैव ह भवति लिप्सेदिति वाव जिघ्रेत्तत्र(३) त द्विदेवत्येषु(४) चेति, तदु तत्र शासनं वेदयन्ते(५) अथ यदमू व्यभिचरतो नानान्योन्यमनुप्रपद्येते अध्वर्यू। तस्मादृतुरृतुर्नानुप्रपद्येते ॥ ८॥

प्रजापतिर्वै यत् प्रजा असृजत, ता वै तान्ता असृजत। ता हिङ्कारेणैवाभ्यजिघ्रत्। ताः प्रजा अमारन्(६), तद्वध्यते वा एतद्यज्ञो यद्धवींषि पच्यन्ते। यत् सोमः सूयते, यत् पशुरालभ्यते, हिङ्कारेण वा एतत् प्रजापतिर्हि तमभिजिघ्रति, यज्ञस्याहतायै (७)यज्ञस्यास्थै यज्ञस्य वीर्यवत्तया इति। तस्मादु हिङ्क्रियते, तस्मादु य एव पिता पुत्राणां सूर्चति, स श्रेष्ठो भवति, प्रजापतिर्हि तमभिजिघ्रति। यच्छकुनिराण्डमध्यास्ते(८) यत्र सूयते,

१ ह स्याद्य इति क०, ट० च।

२ भक्षेदिति भा०।

३ जिघ्रे तच्चेति च०, भा०, ट० च।

४ तद्विदेव तेषु इति म०, भा०, ट०, च। तद्विदेव तेषु इति क०।

५ तदुत्तरशासनं वेदयते इति ग०।

६ अम्रमारन् इति क०। अम्रमारन्निति भा०।

७ यज्ञस्याहततायै इति च०, भा० च।

८ मध्य आस्ते इति भा०।

तद्धि सापि हिङ्कृणोति । अथो खल्वाहुः, महर्षिर्वा(१) एतद्यज्ञस्याग्रे गेयमपश्यत् । तदेतद्यज्ञस्याग्रे गेयं, यद्धिङ्कारः । तं देवाश्च ऋषयश्चाब्रुवन्, वसिष्ठोयमस्तु, यो नो यज्ञस्याग्रे गेयमद्राक्षीदिति(२) । तदेतद्यज्ञस्याग्रे गेयं, यद्धिङ्कारः । ततो वै स देवानां श्रेष्ठोभवत् । यो न वै श्रेष्ठः, तेन वसिष्ठः । तस्मादु यस्मिन्वासिष्ठो ब्राह्मणः स्यात्, तं दक्षिणाया नान्तरीयात् । तथा ह्यस्य प्रीतो हिङ्कारो भवति । अथ देवाश्च ह वा ऋषयश्च यदृक्सामे अपश्यन् । ते ह स्नैने(३) अपश्यन् । ते यत्रैने अपश्यन्, तत एवैनं सर्वं दोहमदुहन् । ते वा एते दुग्धे यातयामे, य ऋक्सामे । ते हिङ्कारेणैवाप्यायेते । हिङ्कारेण वा ऋक्सामे आपीने यजमानाय दोहं दुहाते । तस्मादु हिङ्कृत्याध्वर्य्यवः सोममभिषुण्वन्ति । हिङ्कृत्योद्गातारः साम्ना स्तुवन्ति । हिङ्कृत्योक्थश्च ऋचार्त्विज्यं कुर्वन्ति । हिङ्कृत्याथर्वाणो ब्रह्मत्वं कुर्वन्ति । तस्मादु हिङ्क्रियते । प्रजापतिर्हि तमभिजिघ्रति । अथो खल्वाहुः, एको वै प्रजापतेर्व्रतं बिभर्त्ति गौरेव, तदुभये पशव उपजीवन्ति, ये च ग्राम्या ये चारण्या इति ॥ ८ ॥

देवविशः कल्पयितव्या इत्याहुः, छन्दसि प्रतिष्ठाप्यमिति । शꣳसावोमित्याह्वयते, प्रातःसवने त्र्यक्षरेण । शंसावो दैवेत्यध्वर्य्युः प्रतिगृणाति । पञ्चाक्षरं तत् अष्टाक्षरं सम्पद्यते । अष्टाक्षरा

---

१ मह ऋषिर्वेति च०, ग०, च । मह ऋषेर्वेति भ० ।

२ गेयमस्याद्रागिति क० ।

३ ह स्नैने इति ।

वै गायत्री, गायत्रीमेवैतत्(१)। पुरस्तात् प्रातःसवने चोक्लृपता(१)मुक्थं वाचीत्याह, शस्त्वा चतुरक्षरमोमुक्थशा इत्यध्वर्य्युः प्रतिगृणाति। चतुरक्षरं तत्, अष्टाक्षरं सम्पद्यते। अष्टाक्षरा वै गायत्री, गायत्रीमेवैतत्। उभयः प्रातःसवने चोक्लृपता(३)मध्वर्य्यो शंसावोमित्याह्वयते। माध्यन्दिने षड़क्षरेण शंसावो दैवेत्यध्वर्य्युः प्रतिगृणाति। पञ्चाक्षरं तदेकादशाक्षरं सम्पद्यते। एकादशाक्षरा वै त्रिष्टुप्, त्रिष्टुभमेवैतत्। पुरस्तान् माध्यन्दिने चोक्लृपता(४)मुक्थं वाचीन्द्रायेत्याह, शस्त्वा षड़क्षरमोमुक्थशा यजेत्यध्वर्य्युः प्रतिगृणाति। पञ्चाक्षरं तदेकादशाक्षरं सम्पद्यते। एकादशाक्षरा वै त्रिष्टुप्, त्रिष्टुभमेवैतत्। उभयतो माध्यन्दिने चोक्लृपता(५) मध्वर्यो शंशंसावोमित्याह्वयते। तृतीयसवने सप्ताक्षरेण शंसावोदैवेत्यध्वयः प्रतिगृणाति। पञ्चाक्षरं तद्द्वादशाक्षरं सम्पद्यते। द्वादशाक्षरा वै जगती, जगतीमेवैतत्। पुरस्तात्तृतीयसवने चोक्लृपता(६)मुक्थं वाचीन्द्राय देवेभ्य इत्याह, शस्त्वा नवाक्षरमोमुक्थशा इत्यध्वर्य्युः प्रतिगृणाति। त्र्यक्षरं तद् द्वादशाक्षरं सम्पद्यते। द्वाशाक्षरा वै जगती, जगतीमेवैतत्। उभयतस्तृतीयसवने चोक्लृपता(७) मित्येतद्वै छन्दः, छन्दसि प्रतिष्ठापयति। कल्पयत्येव देवविशः, य एवं वेद। तदप्येषाभ्यनूक्ता, यद्गायत्रे अधिगायत्रमाहितमिति ॥ १० ॥

अथैतन्नानाच्छन्दांस्यन्तरेण गर्त्ता इव। अथैते अविष्ठे बलिष्ठे

---

१ गायत्रमेवैतदिति ख०।

२,३,४,५,६,७, चोक्लृप्तेति भा०। चोक्लिप्तेति ट०।

नान्तरे एव ते ताभ्यां[१]प्रतिपद्यते, तद्गर्त्तस्कन्दं रोहस्वरूपं स्वर्गं तदनु वा न[२] सङ्क्रामेत्। अमृतं वै प्रणवः, अमृतेनैव तत् मृत्युं तरति। तद्यथा मन्त्रेण वा वंशेन वा गर्त्तं सङ्क्रामेत्, एवं तत् प्रणवेनोपसन्तनोति। ब्रह्म ह वै प्रणवः, ब्रह्मणैवास्मै तद्ब्रह्मोपसन्तनोति। शुद्धः प्रणवः स्यात् प्रजाकामानां मकरान्तः। प्रतिष्ठाकामानां मकरान्तः प्रणवः स्यादिति हैक आहुः। शुद्ध इति त्वेव स्थितो मीमांसितः प्रणवः। अथात इह शुद्ध इह पूर्ण इति, शुद्धः प्रणवः स्याच्छस्त्रानुवचनयोर्मध्य इति, ह स्माह कौषीतकिः। तयाःसंहितं भवति मकरान्तोवसानार्थे। प्रतिष्ठा वा अवसानं, प्रतिष्ठित्या एव। अथोभयोः कामयोराप्त्या एतौ वै छन्दःप्रवाहावरं छन्दः परच्छन्दोतिप्रवहतः, तस्यायुर्नहिनस्ति, छन्दसां छन्दोतिप्रोढं स्यात्, यत्रैव यं द्विष्यात्तं मनसा प्रैव विध्ये[३] छन्दसां कन्दते द्रवति वाचं वा प्रोष्यत इति। त्रिः प्रथमां त्रिरुत्तमामन्वाह, यज्ञस्यैव तद्बर्हिसौ नह्यति, स्थेम्ने बलायाविस्रंसाय। यद्यपि छन्दः प्रातःसवने युज्येतार्द्धर्चश एव तस्य शंस्यं[४] गायत्र्या रूपेण। अथो प्रातःसवनरूपेणेति, न त्रिष्टुब्जगत्यावेतस्मिं स्थानेर्धर्चशस्ये यत् किञ्चिच्छन्दः प्रातःसवने युज्येतां[५] पच्छ एवैनयोः शस्यमिति सा स्थितिः॥ ११॥

---

१ वलिष्ठेनान्तरेवत्येताभ्यामिति च०।

२ तदनुवानमिति च०, ख०, भा०, ट० च।

३ वैध्ये इति ट०।

४ शंस्यामिति भा०।

५ युज्यतामिति क०।

अथात एकाहस्य प्रातःसवनं। प्रजापतिं ह वै यज्ञं तन्वानं वहिष्पवमान एव मृत्युं मृत्युपाशेन प्रत्युपाक्रामत। स आग्नेय्या गायत्र्याज्यं प्रत्यपद्यत। मृत्युर्वाव तं पश्यत्(१)। प्रजापतिं पर्य्यक्रामत्। तं सामाज्येष्वसीदत्। स वायव्या प्र उ गं प्रत्यपद्यत। मृत्युर्वाव तं पश्यत्(२)। प्रजापतिं पर्य्यक्रामत्। तं माध्यन्दिने पवमाने सीदत्। स ऐन्द्र्या त्रिष्टुभा मरुत्वतीयं प्रत्यपद्यत। मृत्युंवाव तं पश्यत्(३)। प्रजापतिं पर्य्यक्रामत्(४)। स तेनैव द्रविणे पूर्वां निष्केवल्यस्य स्तोत्रियमासीदत्, तमस्तृणोत्। तस्मादु य एव पूर्वमासीदति, स तत् स्तृणुते। विद्वान् मृत्युरनवकाशमपाद्रवत्, अशश्ंसत्, इतरो निष्केवल्यं। तस्मादेकमेवोक्थं होता मरुत्वतीयेन प्रतिपद्यते। निष्केवल्यमेवात्र हि प्रजापतिं मृत्युर्व्यजहात्॥ १२॥

मित्रावरुणावब्रवीत्, युवं न इमं यज्ञस्याङ्गमनुसमाहरतां, मैत्रावरुणीयां। तथेत्यब्रूतां। तौ सयुजौ सबलौ भूत्वा प्रासहा मृत्युमत्यैतां। तौ ह्यस्यैतद्यज्ञस्याङ्गमनुसमाहरतां मैत्रावरुणीयां(५)। तस्मान् मैत्रावरुणः प्रातःसवने मैत्रावरुणानि शंसति। तौ ह्यस्यैतद्यज्ञस्याङ्गमनुसमाहरतां। यद्देव मैत्रावरुणानि शंसति, प्रति

---

१ मृत्युर्वाषदेतं पश्यन् इति क०। मृत्युर्वावदं पश्यदिति ग०, भ० च।

२, ३, मृत्युर्वावदं पश्यदिति भा०, ट० च। मृत्युर्वाव तं पश्यन्निति क०।

४ ट, चिन्हित-पुस्तके तं मध्यन्दिन इत्यादिः पर्यक्रामदित्यन्तः पाठः पुनरुक्तः।

५ ट, चिन्हितपुस्तके तथेत्यब्रूतामित्यादिर्मैत्रावरुणीयामित्यन्तः पाठः पुनरुक्तः।

वां सूर उदिते विधेम नमोभिर्मित्रावरुणोत हव्यैः । उत वा-
मुषसो बुधि:(१) साकं सूर्य्यस्य रश्मिभिरिति ऋचाभ्यनूक्तं ।
मा नो मित्रावरुणा नो गन्तं रिशादसेति, मैत्रावरुणस्य
स्तोत्रियानुरूपौ । प्र वो मित्राय गायतेति उक्थमुखं । प्र मित्र-
योर्वरुणयोरिति पर्य्यासः । आयातं मित्रावरुणेति यजति । एत
एव तद्देवते यथाभागं प्रीणाति वषट्कृत्यानुवषट्करोति । प्रत्ये-
वाभिमृशन्ते नाप्याययन्ति न ह्यनाराशंसाः सीदन्ति ॥ १३ ॥

इन्द्रमब्रवीत्, त्वं न इमं यज्ञस्याङ्गमनुसमाहरन् ब्राह्मणाच्छं-
सीयां । केन सहेति । सूर्य्येणेति । तथेत्यब्रूताम् । तौ सयुजौ
सबलौ भूत्वा प्रासहा मृत्युमत्यैताम् । तौ ह्यस्यैतद्यज्ञस्याङ्ग-
मनुसमाहरतां ब्राह्मणाच्छंसीयां । तस्माद् ब्राह्मणाच्छंसी
प्रातःसवन ऐन्द्राणि सूर्य्यन्यङ्गानि शंसति । तौ ह्यस्यैतद्यज्ञ-
स्याङ्गमनुसमाहरतां । यद्वेव ऐन्द्राणि सूर्य्यन्यङ्गानि शंसति,
इन्द्र पिब प्रतिकामं सुतस्य प्रातःसावस्तव हि पूर्वपीतिरिति
ऋचाभ्यनूक्तम् । आयाहि सुषुमाहित आ नो याहि सुतावत
इति ब्राह्मणाच्छंसिन स्तोत्रियानुरूपौ । अयमु त्वा विचर्षण
इति उक्थमुखं । उद्देदभिश्रुतामघमिति पर्य्यासः । इन्द्र क्रतुविद-
मिति यजति । एते एव तद्देवते यथाभागं प्रीणाति, वषट्
कृत्यानुवषट् करोति । प्रत्येवाभिमृशन्ते नाप्याययन्ति न ह्यना-
राशंसाः सीदन्ति ॥ १४ ॥

इन्द्राग्नी अब्रवीत्, युवन्न इमं यज्ञस्याङ्गमनुसमाहरताम-

---

१ बुद्धिरिति क० ।

च्छावाकीयां। तथेत्यब्रूताम्। तौ सयुजौ सबलौ भूत्वा प्रासहा मृत्युमत्यैताम्। तौ ह्यस्यैतद्यज्ञस्याङ्गमनुसमाहरता-मच्छावाकीयां। तस्मादच्छावाकः प्रातःसवन ऐन्द्राग्नानि शंसति। तौ ह्यस्यैतद्यज्ञस्याङ्गमनुसमाहरतां। यद्वेवैन्द्राग्नानि शंसति, प्रातर्यावभिरागतन्देवेभिर्जेन्या वसू। इन्द्राग्नी सोम-पीतय इति, ऋचाभ्यनूक्तम्। इन्द्राग्नी आगतन्सोशा हत्रहणा हुव इति, अच्छावाकस्य स्तोत्रियानुरूपौ। इद्राग्नी अपसस्परी-त्युक्थमुखं। इहेन्द्राग्नी उपह्वय इति पर्य्यासः। इन्द्राग्नी आगत-मिति, यजति। एते एव तद्देवते यथाभागं प्रीणाति वषट्-कृत्यानुवषट् करोति। प्रत्येवाभिमृशन्ते नाप्याययन्ति न ह्यना-राशꣳसाः सीदन्ति ॥ १५ ॥

अथ शंसावोमिति, स्तोत्रियायानुरूपायोक्थमुखाय परिधानी-यायै इति, चतुश्चतुराह्वयन्ते(१)। चतस्रो वै दिशः, दिक्षु तत् प्रति-तिष्ठन्ते(२)। अथो चतुष्पादः पशवः, पशूनामाप्त्यै। अथो चतु-ष्पर्वाणो हि प्रातःसवने होत्रकाः। तस्माच्चतुःसर्वे गायत्राणि शंसन्ति। गायत्रं हि प्रातःसवनं सर्वे समवतीभिः परिदधति। तद्यत् समवतीभिः परिदधति, अन्तो वै पर्यासोन्त उदर्कः, अन्ते-नैवान्तं परिदधति। सर्वे मद्वतीभिर्यजन्ति, तद्यत् मद्वतीभिर्य-जन्ति। सर्वे सुतवतीभिः पीतवतीभिरभिरूपाभिर्यजन्ति। यद्य-ज्ञेऽभिरूपं, तत्समृद्धं। सवऽनुवषट् कुर्वन्ति, स्विष्टकृत्त्वा अनु-

---

१ आवह्वयते इति ग०।

२ प्रतितिष्ठन्तीति क०। प्रतितिष्ठते इति ग०।

वषट्कारो नेत् स्विष्टकृतमन्तरयामेति । अयं वै लोकः प्रातः-
सवनं । तस्य पञ्च दिशः पञ्चोक्थानि । प्रातःसवनस्य स एतैः
पञ्चभिरुक्थैरेताः पञ्च दिश आप्नोत्येताः पञ्च दिश आ-
प्नोति ॥ १६ ॥

घ्नन्ति वा एतत्सोमं, यदभिषुण्वन्ति । यज्ञं वा एतद्घ्नन्ति,
यद्दक्षिणा नीयन्ते । यज्ञं वा एताः समन्वक्षियन्ति, तद्दक्षिणानां
दक्षिणात्वं । स्वर्गो वै लोको माध्यन्दिनं सवनं । यन्माध्यन्दिने
सवने दक्षिणा नीयन्ते, स्वर्गस्य लोकस्य समष्ट्यै । बहुदेयं सेतुं वा
एतत् यजमानः संस्कुरुते स्वर्गस्य लोकस्याक्रान्त्यै प्रजाक्रान्त्यै ।
द्वाभ्यां गार्हपत्ये[1] जुहोत्यध्वर्युः, अस्याक्रान्तिनाक्रमयत्याग्नेय्या-
ग्नीध्रीये, अन्तरिक्षं तेन । यन्मध्यन्दिने सवने दक्षिणा नीयन्ते,
स्वर्ग एतेन लोके हिरण्यं हस्ते भवति । अथ नयति, सत्यं वै
हिरण्यं, सत्येनैवैनं तन्नयति अग्रेण गार्हपत्यं जघनेन सदो-
न्तराग्नीध्रीयञ्च सदश्च । ता उदीचीरन्तराग्नीध्रीयञ्च सदश्च
चात्वालञ्चोत्सृजन्ति । एतेन ह स्म वा अङ्गिरसः स्वर्गं लोक-
मायन् । ता वा एताः पन्थानमभिवहन्ति ॥ १७ ॥

अग्नीध्रे[2] अग्रे ददाति । यज्ञमुखं वा अग्नीत्, यज्ञमुखेनैव
तद्यज्ञमुखं समर्धयति । ब्रह्मणे ददाति । प्राजापत्यो वै ब्रह्मा,
प्रजापतिमेव तेन प्रीणाति । ऋत्विग्भ्यो ददाति, होत्रा एव तया
प्रीणाति । सदस्येभ्यो ददाति, सोमपीथस्तया निष्क्रीणीते । न हि
तस्मा अर्हति सोमपीथः, तया निष्क्रीणीयात् । यां शुश्रूषव आर्षे-

---

१ गार्हपत्येनेति भ०, ड०, च ।

२ आग्नीध्र इति छ० च ।

याय ददाति, देवलोके तयार्ध्नोति। यामश्रुश्रूषवेऽनार्षेयाय ददाति, मनुष्यलोके तयार्ध्नोति। यामं प्रस्नुमाय ददाति, वनस्पतयस्तया प्रथन्ते। यां याचमानाय ददाति, भ्रातृव्यन्तया जिन्वीते। यां भीषाचन्न्, तया ब्रह्मातीयात्। यां प्रतिनुदन्ते, सा व्याघ्री दक्षिणा। यस्तां पुनः प्रतिगृह्णीयात्, व्याघ्री ह्येनं भूत्वा प्रवृणीयात्। अन्यया सह प्रतिगृह्णीयात्, अथ हैनन्न प्रवृणाति॥ १८॥

यद्गां ददाति, वैश्वदेवी वै गौः, विश्वेषामेव तद्देवानां तेन प्रियं धामोपैति। यदजं ददाति, आग्नेयो वा अजः, अग्नेरेव तेन प्रियन्धामोपैति। यदविं ददाति, आव्यन्तेनापजयति। यत्क्षताम्नं ददाति, मांसन्तेन निष्क्रीणीते। यदनो वा रथो वा, शरीरन्तेन। यद्वासो ददाति, बृहस्पतिं तेन। यद्धिरण्यं ददाति, आयुस्तेन वर्षीयः कुरुते। यदश्वं ददाति, सौर्यो वा अश्वः, सूर्यस्यैव तेन प्रियन्धामोपैति। अन्ततः प्रतिहर्त्रे देयं। रौद्रो वै प्रतिहर्त्ता, रुद्रमेव तन्निरवजयति। यन्मध्यतः प्रतिहर्त्रे दद्यात्, मध्यतो रुद्रमन्ववयजेत्। स्वर्भानुर्वा आसुरिः सूर्यन्तमसाविध्यत्। तदत्रिरपनुनोद। तदत्रिरन्वपश्यत्। यदात्रेयाय हिरण्यं ददाति, तम एव तेनापहेत। अथो ज्योतिरुपरिष्टाद्धारयति, स्वर्गस्य लोकस्य समष्ट्यै॥ १९॥

अथात एकाहस्यैव माध्यन्दिनम्। ऋक् च वा इदमग्रे साम चास्तां(१), सैव नामर्गासीत्। अमो नाम साम, सा वा ऋक् सामोपावदत्, मिथुनं सम्भवाव प्रजात्या इति(२)। नेत्यब्रवोत्साम, ज्यायान्

१ चास्तामिति ङ०। ग्रस्तार्मिति ट०।

२ प्रजापत्या इति ङ०। प्राजापत्या इति च०, भ०, थ।

वा अती मम महिमेति। ते द्वे भूत्वोपावदताम्। ते न प्रतिवचनं समवदत। तास्तिस्रो भूत्वोपावदन्। यत् तिस्रो भूत्वोपावदन्, तत् तिसृभिः समभवत्। यत् तिसृभिः समभवत्, तस्मात्तिसृभिः स्तुवन्ति, तिसृभिरुद्गायन्ति, तिसृभिर्हि साम सम्मितं भवति। तस्मादेकस्य बह्व्यो जाया भवन्ति, न हैकस्या बहवः सहपतयः। यद्वै तच्चा चामश्च समवदताम्, तत् सामाभवत्। तत् साम्नः सामत्वं। सामं भवति श्रेष्ठतां गच्छति। यो वै भवति, स सामं भवति। असामान्य इति ह निन्दन्ते। ते वै पञ्चान्यद्भूत्वा पञ्चान्यद्भूत्वा कल्पेताम्, आहावश्च हिङ्कारश्च प्रस्तावश्च प्रथमा चोद्गीथश्च मध्यमा च प्रतिहारश्चोत्तमा च निधनञ्च वषट्कारश्च। ते यत् पञ्चान्यद्भूत्वा पञ्चान्यद्भूत्वा कल्पेतां, तस्मादाहुः, पाङ्क्तो यज्ञः पाङ्क्ताः पशव इति। यदु विराजं दशनीमभिसम्पद्येयातां, तस्मादाहुर्विराजो यज्ञो दशन्यां प्रतिष्ठित इति। यदु बृहत्याः प्रतिपद्यते। बार्हतो वा एषः, य एषस्तपति। तदेनं स्वेनरूपेण समर्धयति। द्वे तिस्रः करोति। पुनरादायं प्रजात्यै रूपं द्वाविवाग्रे भवतः। तत उपप्रजायते॥ २०॥

आत्मा वै स्तोत्रियः, प्राजा अनुरूपः, पत्नी धाय्या, पशवः प्रगाथः, ग्रहाः(१) सूक्तं, यदन्तरात्मन्, तन्निवित्, प्रतिष्ठा परिधानीया, अन्नं याज्या। सोऽस्मिंश्च लोके भवत्यमुष्मिंश्च प्रजया च पशुभिश्च गृहेषु भवति, य एवं वेद॥ २१॥

स्तोत्रियं शंसति। आत्मा वै स्तोत्रियः, स मध्यमया वाचा शंस्तव्य आत्मानमेवा अस्य तत् कल्पयति। अनुरूपं शंसति,

१ गृहा इति ग०, छ० च।

प्रजा वा अनुरूपः, तस्मात् प्रतिरूपमनुरूपं कुर्वन्ति। प्रतिरूपो हैवास्य प्र जायामाजायते नाप्रतिरूपः। तस्मात् प्रतिरूपमनुरूपं कुर्वन्ति। स उच्चैस्तरामिव शंस्तव्यः, प्रजामेवास्य तच्छ्रेयसीं करोति। धाय्यां शंसति, पत्नी वै धाय्या, सा नीचैस्तरामिव शंस्तव्या। प्रतिवादिनी हैवास्य गृहेषु पत्नी भवति, यत्नैवं विद्वान् नीचैस्तरान्धाय्यां शंसति। प्रगाथं शंसति, पशवो वै प्रगाथः, स स्वरवत्या वाचा शंस्तव्यः। पशवो वै प्रगाथः, पशवः स्वरः, पशूनामाप्त्यै सूक्तं शंसति। गृहा वै सूक्तं, प्रतिवीतं तत्, प्रतिवीततमया वाचा शंस्तव्यम्। स यद्यपि ह दूरात् पशूं-ल्लभते, गृहानेवैनानाजिगमिषति। गृहा हि पशूनां प्रतिष्ठा। निविदं शंसति, यदन्तरात्मन्, तन्निवित्, तदेवास्य तत् कल्पयति। परिधानीयां शंसति, प्रतिष्ठा वै परिधानीया, प्रतिष्ठाया एवैनमन्ततः प्रतिष्ठापयति। याज्यया यजति, अन्नं वै याज्या, अन्नाद्यमेवास्य तत् कल्पयति। मूलं वा एतद्यज्ञस्य, यद्धाय्याश्च याज्याश्च। तद्यदन्याः अन्या(१) धाय्याश्च याज्याश्च कुर्युं-उन्मूलमेव तद्यज्ञं कुर्युः। तस्मात्ताः सामान्य एव स्युः॥ २२॥

तदाहुः, किन्देवत्यो यज्ञ इति। ऐन्द्र इति ब्रूयात्, ऐन्द्रे वाव यज्ञे सति यथाभागमन्या देवता न्ववायन्। ता प्रातःसवने मरुत्वतीये तृतीयसवने च। अथ हैतत् केवलमेवेन्द्रस्य, यदूर्ध्वं मरुत्वतीयात्। तस्मात् सर्वे निष्केवल्यानि शंसन्ति। यदेव निष्केवल्यानि, तत् स्वर्गस्य लोकस्य (२) रूपं। य इवनिष्केवल्यानि, एकं

१ तद्यन्या अन्य इति क०। तदान्यान्या इति ग०।

२ रूपस्येति क०।

ह वा अग्रे सवनमासीत् प्रातःसवनमेव। अथ हैतं प्रजापतिरिन्द्राय ज्येष्ठाय पुत्रायैतत् सवनं निरमिमत, यन् माध्यन्दिनं सवनं। तस्मान् माध्यन्दिने सवने सर्वे निष्केवल्यानि शंसन्ति। यदेव निष्केवल्यानि, तत् स्वर्गस्य लोकस्य रूपं। यद्देव निष्केवल्यानि, या ह वै देवताः प्रातःसवने होता शंसति, ताः शस्त्वा होत्राशंसिनोनुशंसन्ति। मैत्रावरुणं त्टचं प्र उगे होता शंसति, तदुभयं मैत्रावरुणं। मैत्रावरुणं मैत्रावरुणोनुशंसति। ऐन्द्रं त्टचं प्र उगे होता शंसति, तदुभयमैन्द्रं। ऐन्द्रं ब्राह्मणाच्छंस्यनुशंसति, ऐन्द्राग्नं त्टचं प्र उगे होता शंसति, तदुभयमैन्द्राग्नं। ऐन्द्राग्नमच्छावाकोऽनुशंसति। अथ हैतत् केवलमेवेन्द्रस्य, यदूर्द्ध्वंमरुत्वतीया। तस्मात् सर्वे निष्केवल्यानि शंसन्ति। यदेव निष्केवल्यानि, तत् स्वर्गस्य लोकस्य रूपं। यद्देव निष्केवल्यानि, यदेददेवीरसहिष्ठमाया अथाभवत् केवलः सोमो अस्येति ऋचाभ्यनूक्तं। देवान् ह यज्ञन्तन्वाना असुररक्षांस्यजिघांसन्। तेऽब्रुवन्, वामदेवं त्वं न इमं यज्ञं दक्षिणतो गोपायेति, मध्यतो वसिष्ठं, उत्तरतो भरद्वाजं, सर्वाननु विश्वामित्रं। तस्मान् मैत्रावरुणो वामदेवान्न प्रच्यवते, वसिष्ठाद्ब्राह्मणाच्छंसी, भरद्वाजादच्छावाकः, सर्वे विश्वामित्रात्। एत एवास्मैतदृषयो हरहर्नमगा अप्रमत्ता यज्ञं रक्षन्ति, य एवं वेद य एवं वेद॥ २३॥

इत्यथर्ववेदोत्तरगोपथब्राह्मणस्य तृतीयः प्रपाठकः समाप्तः॥ ३॥

---

## अथ चतुर्थप्रपाठकः।

ओम्। कया नश्चित्र आभुवत् कया त्वं न ऊत्येति मैत्रावरु-

णस्य स्तोत्रियानुरूपौ। कस्तमिन्द्र त्वा वसुमिति बार्हतः प्रगाथः। तस्योपरिष्टाद्ब्राह्मणं। सद्यो ह जातो वृषभः कनीन इति उक्थमुखम्। एवा त्वामिन्द्र वज्रिन्नत्रेति पर्य्यासः। उग्रस्तुषुणः(१) सुमना उपाक इति यजति। एतामेव तद्देवतां यथाभागं प्रीणाति, वषट्कृत्यानुवषट्करोति। प्रत्येवाभिमृशन्ते नाप्याययन्ति, न ह्यनाराशंसाः सीदन्ति॥ १॥

तं वोदस्म मृतीषहं तत्त्वा यामि सुवीर्य्यमिति ब्राह्मणाच्छंसिनः स्तोत्रियानुरूपौ। उदु त्ये मधुमत्तमा गिर इति बार्हतः प्रगाथः। पशवो वै प्रगाथः, पशवः स्वरः, पशूनामाप्त्यै। अतो मध्यं वै सर्वेषां छन्दसां बृहती, मध्यं माध्यन्दिनं सवनानां, तन्मध्येनैव मध्यं समर्द्धयति। इन्द्रः पूर्भिदातिरद्दासमर्कैरित्युक्थमुखं। उदु ब्रह्माण्यैरत श्रवस्येति पर्य्यासः। एवेदिन्द्रं वृषणं वज्रबाहुमिति, परिदधाति। वसिष्ठासो अभ्यर्चन्ति, अर्कैरिति। अन्नं वा अर्कः, अन्नाद्यमेवास्मै तत्परिदधाति। स न स्तुतो वीरवद्धातु गोमदिति, प्रजाश्चैवास्मै तत्पशूंश्चाशास्ते। यूयं पात स्वस्तिभिः सदा न इति, स्वस्तिमतो रूपसमृद्धा। एतद्वै यज्ञस्य समृद्धं, यत् रूपसमृद्धं। यत् कर्म्म क्रियमाणमृग्यजुर्वाभिवदति, स्वस्ति तस्य यज्ञस्य पारमश्नुते। य एवं वेद यश्चैवं विद्वान् ब्राह्मणाच्छंसी एतया परिदधाति। ऋजीषी वज्री वृषभस्तुराषाडिति यजति। एतामेव तद्देवतां यथाभागं प्रीणाति, वषट्कृत्यानुवषट्करोति। प्रत्येवाभिमृशन्ते नाप्याययन्ति, न ह्यनाराशंसाः सीदन्ति॥ २॥

तरोभिर्वो विदद्वसुमन्तरणिरित्सिषासतीति, अच्छावाकस्य स्तो-

---

१ उग्रस्तुषण इति ग०।

त्रियानुरूपौ। उदिन्वस्य रिच्यत इति, बार्हतः प्रगाथः। तस्योक्तं ब्राह्मणं। भूय इद्वावृधे वीर्य्यायेति उक्थमुखम्। इमामूषु प्रभृतिं सातयेधा इति, पर्य्यासः। तस्य दशमोमुद्धरति। घोरस्य वा आङ्गिरसस्यैतदार्षं नेदग्निं निर्दहेत् शस्यमानं पिबा वर्धस्व तव घा सुतास इति यजति। एतामेव तद्देवतां यथाभागं प्रीणाति वषट्कृत्यानुवषट् करोति। प्रत्येवाभिमृशन्ते नाप्यायन्ति, न ह्यनाराशंसाः सीदन्ति ॥ ३ ॥

अथाध्वर्य्यो शंसावोमिति, स्तोत्रियानुरूपाय प्रगाथायो-क्थमुखाय परिधानीयाया इति, पञ्चकृत्व आह्वयन्ते। पञ्चपदा पङ्क्तिः, पाङ्क्तो यज्ञः। सर्वे ऐन्द्राणि त्रैष्टुभानि शंसन्ति। ऐन्द्र हि त्रैष्टुभं माध्यन्दिनं सवनं। सर्वे समवतीभिः परिदधति, तद्यत् समवतीभिः परिदधति। अन्तो वै पर्य्यासोन्त उदर्कः, अन्तेनैवान्तं परिदधति(१)। सर्वे मदतीभिर्यजन्ति, तद्यत् मद-तीभिर्यजन्ति। सर्वे सुतवतीभिः पीतवतीभिरभिरूपाभिर्यजन्ति। यद्यज्ञेभिरूपं, तत् समृद्धं। सर्वेनुवषट् कुर्वन्ति, स्विष्टकृत्त्वा अनु वषट्कारो नेत् स्विष्टकृतमन्तरयामेति। अन्तरिक्षलोको माध्यन्दिनं सवनं। तस्य पञ्च दिशः, पञ्चोक्थानि माध्यन्दिनस्य सवनस्य। स एतैः पञ्चभिरुक्थैरेताः पञ्च दिश आप्नोत्येताः पञ्च दिश आप्नोति ॥ ४ ॥

अथ यदौपासनं तृतीयसवन उपास्यन्ते, पितॄनेव तेन प्रीणा-ति। उपांशु पात्नीवतस्याग्नीध्रो यजति, रेतो वै पात्नीवतः, उपांश्विव वै रेतः सिच्यते, तन्नानुवषट्करोति, नेद्रेतः सिक्तं

१ परिदधातीति ठ०।

संस्थापयामीति। असंस्थितमिव वै रेतः सिक्तं समृद्धं। संस्था वा एषा, यदनुवषट्कारः। तस्मान्नानुवषट् करोति। नेष्टुरुपस्थे धिष्ण्यान्ते वासीनो भक्षयन्ति, पत्नीभाजनं वै नेष्टा, अग्नीत् पत्नीषु रेतो धत्ते, रेतसः सिक्ताः प्रजाः प्रजायन्ते प्रजानां प्रजननाय। प्रजावान् प्रजनयिष्णुर्भवति प्रजात्यै। प्रजायते प्रजया पशुभिः, य एवं वेद ॥ ५ ॥

अथ शाकलां जुह्वति। तद्यथाहिर्जीर्णायास्त्वचो निर्मुच्येत इषीका वा मुञ्जात्, एवं हैवैते सर्वस्मात्पापमनः सम्प्रमुच्यन्ते, ये शाकलां जुव्हति। द्रोणकलशे धाना भवन्ति, तासां हस्तैरा-दधति। पशवो वै धानाः, ता आहवनीयस्य भस्मान्ते निव-पन्ति। योनिर्वै पशूनामाहवनीयः, स्व एवैनंस्तद्गोष्ठे निरपक्रमे निदधति। अथ स व्याहृतोप्सु सोमानाप्याययन्ति, तान् ह अन्त-र्वेद्यां सादयन्ति, तद्धि सोमस्यायतनं। चात्वालादपरेणाध्वर्यु-श्चमसानद्भिः पूरयित्वोदीचः प्रणिधाय हरितानि तृणानि व्यव-दधति। यदा वा आपश्चौषधयश्च सङ्गच्छन्ते, अथ कृत्स्नः सोमः सम्पद्यते। ता वैष्णव्यर्चा निनयन्ति। यज्ञो वै विष्णुः, यज्ञमेवै-नमन्ततः(१) प्रतिष्ठापयति। अथ यज्ञचः प्रतिनिधिं कुर्वन्ति, मानुषेणैवैनं तद्धक्षेण दैवं भक्षमन्तर्दधति ॥ ६ ॥

पूतिर्वा एषोमुष्मिंल्लोकेध्वर्युश्च यजमानश्चाभिवहति, तद्यदेनं दध्नानभिहुत्यावभृथमुपहरेयुः। यथा कुणपं वाति, एवमेवैनं तत् करोति। अथ यदेनं दध्नानभिहुत्यावभृथमुपहरन्ति, सर्वमेवैनं सयोनिं सन्तनुते, समृद्धिं सम्भरन्ति। अभूद्देवः सविता वन्द्यो

१ यज्ञ एवैनमन्तत इति ग०।

नून(१) इति जुहोति, सर्वमेवैनं सपर्वाणं सम्भरन्ति(२)। तिसृभिस्त्रिवृद्भिर्यज्ञो द्रप्सवतीभिरभिजुहोति, सर्वमेवैनं सर्वाङ्गं सम्भरति(३)। सौमीभिरभिजुहोति, सर्वमेवैनं स आत्मानं भरति(४)। पञ्चभिरभिजुहोति, पाङ्क्तो यज्ञः, यज्ञमेवावरुन्धे। पाङ्क्तः पुरुषः, पुरुषमेवाप्नोति। पाङ्क्ताः पशवः, पशुष्वेव प्रतितिष्ठति। प्रतितिष्ठति प्रजया पशुभिः, य एवं वेद ॥ ७ ॥

अग्निर्वाव यम इयं यमी। कुसीदं(५) वा एतद्यमस्य(६) यजमान आदत्ते, यदोषधीभिर्वेदिं स्तृणाति। तां यदनुपोष्य प्रयायात्, यातयेरन्नेनमेऽमुष्मिंल्लोके यमे यत्कुसीदमयमित्यमप्रतीतमिति(७)वेदिमुपोषन्तो(८)हैव सन्यमङ्कुसीदं निरवदाय(९)अनृणो भूत्वा स्वर्गं लोकमेति। विश्वलोपविश्वदावस्य त्वा सं जुहोमीत्याह, होताद्दा यजमानस्यापराभावाय यदु मिश्रमिव चरन्त्यञ्जलिना सक्तून् प्रदाव्ये जुहुयात्। एष ह वा अग्निर्वैश्वानरो यत् प्रदातव्यः, स्वस्यामेवैनं तद्योन्यां सादयति ॥ ८ ॥

अनूहां विधान्यामेकाष्टकायामपूपञ्चतुःशरावं पक्त्वा प्रातरेतेन कक्षमुपोषेत्। यदि दहति पुण्यसमं भवति, यदि न दहति

१ यन्द्गोतुन इति ग०, भ्रा० च।

२ सम्भरति इति ग०, भ्रा०, ट० च।

३,४, सम्भरन्तीति च०।

५ यम इयं पञ्चमो कुसीदसीदमिति ग०। यम इयं यमी यत् कुसीदमिति च०।

६ एतद्यजमानस्येति च०।

७ कुसीदमपमित्यप्रतीतमितीति ट०। कुसीदमपमित्यमप्रतीतमिति च०, भ्रा० च।

८ वेदिमुपोषधीति भ्रा०, ट० च।

९ निर्वदायेति च०, भ्रा०।

पापसमं भवति। एतेन ह स्म वा अङ्गिरसः पुरा विज्ञानेन दीर्घसत्रमुपयन्ति। यो ह वा उपद्रष्टारमुपश्रोतारमनुख्यातारमेव विद्वान्यजते, सममुष्मिंल्लोक इष्टापूर्त्तेन गच्छते। अग्निर्वा उपद्रष्टा, वायुर्वा उपश्रोता, आदित्योवा अनुख्याता, तान्य एवं विद्वान्यजते, सममुष्मिंल्लोक इष्टापूर्त्तेन गच्छते। यन्नो नभसस्पतिरित्याह, अग्निर्वै नभसस्पतिरग्निमेव तदाह। एतन्नो गोपायेति स त्वं नो नभसस्पतिरित्याह, वायुर्वै नभसस्पतिर्वायुमेव तदाह। एतन्नो गोपायेति देव संस्थानेत्याह(१), आदित्यो वै देवसंस्थानः; आदित्यमेव तदाह। एतन्नो गोपायेत्ययं ते योनिरिति, अरण्योरग्निं(२) समारोपयेत्। तदाहुः, यदरण्योः समारूढो नश्येदुदस्याग्निः सीदेत्, पुनराधेयः स्यादिति। या ते अग्नेर्यज्ञिया तनूस्तया मे ह्यारोह तया मे ह्याविशायन्ते योनिरित्यात्मन्नग्नीन् समारोपयेत्। एष ह वा अग्निर्योनिः, स्वस्यामेवैनं तद्योन्यां सादयति ॥ ८ ॥

यो ह वा अग्निष्टोमं सान्हं वेद, अग्निष्टोमस्य सान्हस्य सायुज्यं सलोकतामश्नुते। य एवं वेद, यो ह वा एष तपत्येषोऽग्निष्टोम एष सान्हः, तं सहैवान्हा संस्थापयेयुः, सान्हो वै नामैषः, तेनासन्त्वरमाणाश्चरेयुः(३) यद्व वा इदं पूर्वयोः सवनयोरसन्त्व-

---

१ संस्थानेत्याहेति ग०। सस्थानेत्याहेति ह०।

२ अरण्योरग्नीमिति भ०, ट० च।

३ असत्वरमाणाश्चरेयुरिति ग०, ट० च।

रमाणाश्चरन्ति,(१) तस्मादिद। तं प्राच्यो ग्रामता बहुलाविष्टा। अथ यद्दिदं तृतीयसवने सन्त्वरमाणाश्चरंति,(२) तस्मादिदं प्रत्यञ्चि-दीर्घारण्यानि भवन्ति। यथैव प्रातःसवन एवं माध्यंदिनसवन एवं तृतीयसवने, एवमु ह यजमानो प्रमायुको भवति। तेनासन्त्वर-माणाश्चरेयुः(३)। यदा वा एष प्रातरुदेत्यथ मन्द्रतमं तपति, तस्मान्मन्द्रतमया वाचा प्रातःसवने शंसेत्। अथ यदाभ्येत्यथ बलीयस्तपति, तस्माद्बलीयस्या वाचा माध्यन्दिने सवने शंसेत्। अथो यदाभितरामेत्यथ बलिष्ठतमं तपति, तस्माद्बलिष्ठतमया वाचा तृतीयसवने शंसेत्। एवं शंसेत्, यदि वा त ईशत(४), वाग् हि शस्त्रं, ययानुवाचोत्तरणोत्तरयोत्सहेत्, आसमापनाय-तना प्रतिपद्येत(५)। एतत् सुशस्ततरमिव भवति, स वा एष न कदाचनास्तमयति, नोदयति। तद्यदेनं पश्चादस्तमयतीति मन्यन्ते, अन्ह एव तदन्तं गत्वाथात्मानं विपर्यस्यतेहरेवाधस्तात् कृणुते रात्रीं परस्तात्। स वा एष न कदाचनास्तमयति नोदयति। तद्यदेनं पुरस्तादुदयतीति मन्यन्ते, रात्रेरेव तदन्तं गत्वाथात्मानं विपर्यस्यते रात्रिमेवाधस्तात् कृणुतेऽह्नः पर-स्तात्। स वा एष न कदाचनास्तमयति नोदयति न ह वै

---

१,२. सत्वरमाणाश्चरन्तीति ग०।

३. तेनासत्वरमाणाश्चरेयुरिति ग०।

४ वाच ईशन्तेति ङ०।

५. प्रतिपद्यते इति ग०।

कदाचन निम्लोचति। एतस्यैव सायुज्यं सलोकतामश्नुते, य एवं वेद॥ १०॥

अथात एकाहस्यैव तृतीयसवनं, देवाऽसुरा वा एषु लोकेषु समयतन्त। ते देवा असुरानभ्यजयन्। ते जिता अहोरात्रयोः सन्धिं समभ्यवागुः। स हेन्द्र उवाच, इमे वा असुरा अहोरात्रयोः सन्धिं समभ्यवागुः कश्चाहञ्चेमानसुरानभ्युत्थास्यामहा इति। अहञ्चेत्यग्निरब्रवीत्, अहञ्चेति वरुणः, अहं चेति बृहस्पतिः, अहं चेति विष्णुः। तानभ्युत्थायाहोरात्रयोः सन्धेर्निर्जघ्नुः। यदभ्युत्थाहोरात्रयोः सन्धेर्निर्जघ्नुः, तस्मादुत्था अभ्युत्थाय ह वै द्विषन्तं भ्रातृव्यं निर्हन्ति(१), य एवं वेद। सोऽग्निरश्वो भूत्वा प्रथमः प्रजिगाय। यदग्निरश्वो भूत्वा प्रथमः प्रजिगाय, तस्मादाग्नेयीभिरुक्थानि प्रणयन्ति। यदग्निरश्वो भूत्वा प्रथमः प्रजिगाय, तस्मात्साकमश्वं। यत्पञ्च देवता अभ्युत्तस्थुः(२), तस्मात्पञ्च देवता उक्थे शस्यन्ते। या वाक् सोऽग्निः, यः प्राणः स वरुणः, यन्मनः स इन्द्रः, यच्चक्षुः स बृहस्पतिः, यच्छ्रोत्रं स विष्णुः। एते ह वा एतान् पञ्चभिः प्राणैः समोर्त्थापयन्। तस्मादु ह एवैताः पञ्च देवता उक्थे शस्यन्ते॥ ११॥

प्रजापतिर्ह्येतेभ्यः पञ्चभ्यः प्राणेभ्यो देवान्(३)ससृजे। यदु चेदं किं च पाङ्क्तं तत् सृष्ट्वा व्याज्वलयत्। ते होचुर्देवाः, ग्लानीयं

---

१ निरघ्नीति क०। निदघ्नीति ट०।

२ अभ्यतस्थुरिति क०, ट० च।

३ प्राणेभ्यान्यान्देवानिति क०, ट० च।

पिता मयोभूः, पुनरिमं समीर्योत्थापयामीति(१)। स ह सत्त्वमाख्यायाभ्युपतिष्ठते(२), यदि ह वा अपि निर्ज्ञातस्यैव कुलस्य सम्भुचेण यजते, सत्त्वं हैवाख्यायाभ्युपतिष्ठते। यो वै प्रजापतिः स यज्ञः। स एतैरेव पञ्चभिः प्राणैः समीर्योत्थापितः। ये ह वा एनं पञ्चभिः प्राणैः समीर्योत्थापयंस्ता उ एवैताः पञ्च देवता उक्थे शस्यन्ते॥ १२॥

तदाहुः, यद्द्वयोर्देवतयोस्तुवत इन्द्राग्न्योरिति, अथ कस्माद्भूयिष्ठा देवता उक्थे शस्यन्त(३) इति। अन्तो वा आग्निमारुतमन्तरुक्थान्यन्त आश्विनं कनीयसीषु देवतासु स्तुवते, अन्तेष्विति। अथ कस्माद्भूयिष्ठा देवता उक्थे शस्यन्त(४)इति। द्वे द्वे उक्थमुखे भवतः, तद्यद् द्वे द्वे॥ १३॥

अथ यदैन्द्रावारुणं मैत्रावरुणस्योक्थं भवति। ऐन्द्राबार्हस्पत्यं ब्राह्मणाच्छंसिन उक्थं भवति। ऐन्द्रावैष्णवमच्छावाकस्योक्थं भवति। द्वे संशस्यंस्त ऐन्द्रं च वारुणञ्चैकमैन्द्रावारुणं भवति। द्वे संशस्यंस्त ऐन्द्रं च बार्हस्पत्यञ्चैकमैन्द्राबार्हस्पत्यं भवति। द्वे संशंस्यंस्त (५)ऐन्द्रं च वैष्णवञ्चैकमैन्द्रावैष्णवं भवति। द्वे द्वे उक्थमुखे भवतः, तद्यद् द्वे द्वे॥ १४॥

अथ यदैन्द्रावारुणं मैत्रावरुणस्योक्थं भवति। इन्द्रावरुणा सुतपाविमं सुतं सोमं पिबतं मद्यं धृतव्रतावित्यृचाभ्यनूक्तं।

१ उत्थापयामेतीति च०, ड० च।

२ अभ्युपगम्यते इति क०।

३, ४, शस्यते इति ग०।

५ द्वे शंसस्यंस्त इति भा०। द्वे पंशंसस्यंस्त इति च०।

महद्धि तृतीयसवनम्। एन्यूषु(१) ब्रवाणि ता अग्निरगामि भारत इति मैत्रावरुणस्य स्तोत्रियानुरूपौ। चर्षणी धृतं मघवानमुक्थमित्युक्थमुखं। तस्योपरिष्टाद्ब्राह्मणम्। अस्तभ्नाद्यामसुरो विश्ववेदा इति वारुणं सांशंसिकम्। अहन्वेति वरुणोऽब्रवीद्देवतयोः संशंसायानतिशंसाय। इन्द्रावरुणा युवमध्वराय न इति पर्य्यास ऐन्द्रावारुणे। ऐन्द्रावारुणमस्यैतन्नित्युक्थं(२)। तदेतत् स्वस्मिन्नायतने स्वस्यां प्रतिष्ठायां प्रतिष्ठापयति। द्वन्द्वं वा एता देवता भूत्वा व्यजयन्त विजित्या एव। अथो द्वन्द्वस्यैव मिथुनस्य प्रजात्यै सैकपादिनी(३) भवति। एकपादिन्या होता परिदधाति। यत्र होतुर्होत्रकाणां युञ्जन्ति(४), तत् समृद्धन्तद्वै खल्वावां राजानामध्वरे वर्त्स्यामिति। एवमेव केवलपर्य्यासं कुर्य्यात्। केवलसूक्तं केवलसूक्तमेवोत्तरयोर्भवति। इन्द्रावरुणा मधुमत्तमस्येति यजति। एते एव तद्देवते यथाभागं प्रीणाति, वषट्कृत्यानुवषट्करोति। प्रत्येवाभिमृशन्ते नाप्याययन्ति न ह्यनाराशंसाः सीदन्ति॥१५॥

अथ यदैन्द्राबार्हस्पत्यं ब्राह्मणाच्छंसिन उक्थं भवति, इन्द्रश्च सोमं पिबतं बृहस्पतेऽस्मिन्(५) यज्ञे मन्दसाना वृषण्वसू इत्यृचाभ्यनूक्तं महद्धि तृतीयसवनं। वयमु त्वामपूर्व्य यो न इदमिदं

१ एन्युषु इति ट० च। एन्यूषू इति च०।

२ अस्यैतं नित्यमुक्थमिति च०।

३ सकपादिनीति भ०।

४ युञ्जतीति ग०।

५ बृहस्पते तस्मिन्निति ग०।

पुरेति ब्राह्मणाच्छंसिन स्तोत्रियानुरूपौ। प्र मंहिष्ठाय बृहते बृहद्रय इत्युकथमुखं। ऐन्द्रं जागतं, जागताः पशवः, पशूनामाप्त्यै। जागतमु वै तृतीयसवनं तृतीयसवनस्य रूप। उदप्रुतो (१) न वयो रचमाणा इति बार्हस्पत्यं सांशंसिकं। अहन्नेति बृहस्पतिरब्रवीत्, देवतयोः संशंसायानतिशंसाय(२)। अच्छाम इन्द्रं मतयः स्वर्विद इति पर्य्यास ऐन्द्राबार्हस्पत्ये। ऐन्द्राबार्हस्पत्यमस्यैतं नित्यमुक्थं। तदेतत् स्वस्मिन्नायतने स्वस्यां प्रतिष्ठायां प्रतिष्ठापयति। द्वन्द्वं वा एता देवता भूत्वा व्यजयन्त विजित्या एव, अथो द्वन्द्वस्यैव मिथुनस्य प्रजात्यै। बृहस्पतिर्नः परिपातु पश्चादित्यैन्द्राबार्हस्पत्या परिदधाति। इन्द्राबृहस्पत्योरेव यज्ञं प्रतिष्ठापयति, उतोत्तरस्मादधरादघायोरिन्द्रः पुरस्तादुत मध्यतो नः सखा सखिभ्यो वरिवः कृणोत्विति। सर्वाभ्य एव दिग्भ्य आशिषमाशास्ते, नार्त्तियं कामं कामयते। सोऽस्मै कामः समृध्यते, य एवं वेद। यश्चैवं विद्वान् ब्राह्मणच्छंस्येतया परिदधाति। बृहस्पते युवमिन्द्रश्च वस्व इति यजति। एते एव तद्देवते यथाभागं प्रीणाति वषट्कृत्यानुवषट्करोति। प्रत्येवाभिमृशन्ते नाप्याययन्ति न ह्यनाराशंस्ंसाः सीदन्ति॥ १६॥

अथ यदैन्द्रावैष्णवमच्छावाकस्योक्थं भवति, इन्द्राविष्णू मदपती मदाना मा सोमं यातं द्रविणो दधानेत्यृचा भ्यनूक्तं मदद्धि तृतीयसवनं। अधाहीन्द्र गिर्वण इयन्त इन्द्र गिर्वण इत्यच्छावाकस्य स्तोत्रियानुरूपौ। ऋतुर्जनित्री तस्या अपसस्परीत्युक्थ-

१ उदप्लुत इति ग०।

२ शंसायानतिशंसायेति भा०।

मुखं। तस्योक्तं ब्राह्मणं, नूमर्त्तो दयते स निष्यन्निति वैष्णवं सांश्रंसिकं। अहश्चेति विष्णुरब्रवीत्, देवतयोः संशंसायानतिशंसाय। सं वां कर्मणा समिषा हिनोमीति पर्य्यास ऐन्द्रावैष्णवे। ऐन्द्रावैष्णवमस्यैतं नित्यमुक्थं। तदेतत् स्वस्मिन्नायतने स्वस्यां प्रतिष्ठायां प्रतिष्ठापयति। द्वन्द्वं वा एता देवता भूत्वा व्यजयन्त विजित्या एव। अथो द्वन्द्वस्यैव मिथुनस्य प्रजात्या उभा जिग्यथुर्न पराजयेथे इत्यैन्द्रावैष्णव्यर्चा परिदधाति, इन्द्राविष्णोरेव यज्ञं प्रतिष्ठापयति। इन्द्राविष्णू पिबतं मध्वो अस्येति यजति। एते एव तद्देवते यथाभागं प्रीणाति वषट्कृत्यानुवषट्करोति। प्रत्येवाभिमृशन्ते नाप्याययन्ति न ह्यनाराशंसाः सीदन्ति॥१७॥

अथाध्वर्य्यो शंशंसावोमिति स्तोत्रियायानुरूपायोक्थमुखाय परिदधानीयाया इति चतुश्चतुराह्वयन्ते। चतस्रो वै दिशः, दिक्षु तत् प्रतितिष्ठन्ते। अथो चतुष्पादः पशवः, पशूनामाप्त्यै। अथो चतुष्पर्व्वाणो हि तृतीयसवने होत्रकाः, तस्माच्चतुः सर्वे त्रैष्टुभं जागतानि शंसन्ति। जागतं हि तृतीयसवनं। अथ हैतत् त्रैष्टुभान्यप्रतिभूतमिव हि प्रातःसवने मरुत्वतीये तृतीयसवने च होत्रकाणां शस्त्रं। धीतरसं(१) वा एतत्सवनं, यत्तृतीयसवनं। अथ हैतदधीतरसं शुक्रियं छन्दः, यत् त्रिष्टुभा यातयामसवनस्यैव तत्(२) सरस्वतायै। सर्वे समवतीभिः परिदधति, तद्यत्समवतीभिः परिदधति। अन्तो वै पर्य्यासोऽन्त उदर्कोऽन्तः, सजाया उ ह वा अन्तेनायान्तेनैवान्तं परिदधति। सर्वे मद्वतीभि-

---

१ धीतरसमिति ग०, भा०, ट० च।

२ सवनस्यैतदिति क०।

र्यजन्ति, तद्यन्महतीभिर्यजन्ति । सर्वे सुतवतीभिः पीतवतीभिरभिरूपाभिर्यजन्ति । यद्यज्ञेभिरूपं, तत्समृद्धं । सर्वेनुवषट् कुर्वन्ति, स्विष्टकृत्त्वा अनुवषट्कारी नेत् स्विष्टकृतमन्तरयामीति । असौ वै लोकस्तृतीयसवनं, तस्य पञ्च दिशः, पञ्चोकथानि तृतीयसवनस्य । स एतैः पञ्चभिरुक्थैः एताः पञ्च दिश आप्नोति । तद्यदेषां लोकानां रूपं, या मात्रा । तेन रूपेण तया मात्रयेमांल्लोकानृध्नोतीमांल्लोकानृध्नोतीति ॥ १८ ॥

तदाहुः, किं षोड़शिनः षोडशित्वं, षोडशस्तोत्राणि षोडश शस्त्राणि षोडशभिरक्षरैरादत्ते, ते वा अक्षरे अतिरिच्येते, शोडशिनोनुष्टुभमभिसम्पन्नस्य(१) । वाचो वा एतौ स्तनौ, सत्यानृते वाव ते, अवत्येनं सत्यं, नैनमनृतं हिनस्ति, य एवं वेद ॥ १९ ॥

इत्यथर्ववेदोत्तरगोपथब्राह्मणस्य चतुर्थः प्रपाठकः समाप्तः ॥४॥

---

## अथ पञ्चमप्रपाठकः ।

ओम् । अहर्वै देवा आश्रयन्त रात्रीमसुराः । तेऽसुराः समावद्वीर्या एवासन्, नो व्यावर्त्तन्त । सोऽब्रवीत्, इन्द्रः कश्चाहं चेमानसुरान् रात्रीमन्ववैष्यामहा इति । स देवेषु न प्रत्यविन्दत्, अबिभयू रात्रेस्तमसः । मृत्योस्तम इव हि रात्रिः, मृत्युर्वै तमः, तस्माद्धाप्येतर्हि भूयानिव नक्तं । स यावन्मात्रमिवापक्रम्य बिभेति, तं वै छन्दांस्येवान्ववायन् । तद्यच्छन्दांस्येवान्ववायन्,

१ चतुष्टुभमभिसम्पन्नस्येति क० ।

तस्मादिन्द्रस्य छन्दांसि च रात्रिं वहन्ति, न निविच्छस्यते न पुरोरुग्धाय्या नान्या देवता। इन्द्रस्य ह्येव छन्दांसि च रात्रिं वहन्ति, तान्वै पर्य्यायैः पर्य्यायमनुदन्त। यत् पर्यायैः पर्य्यायमनुदन्त, तस्मात् पर्य्यायाः, तत् पर्य्यायाणां पर्य्यायत्वं। तान्वै प्रथमैरेव पर्य्यायैः पूर्वरात्रादनुदन्त, मध्यमैर्मध्यरात्रादुत्तमैरपररात्रात्। अपिशर्वया अपिस्मसीत्यब्रुवन्। तद्यदपिशर्वया अपिस्मसीत्यब्रुवन्, तदपिशर्वराणामपिशर्वरत्वं। शर्वराणि खलु ह वा अस्यैतानि छन्दांसीति ह स्माह। एतानि ह वा इन्द्रं रात्र्यास्तमसो मृत्योरभिपत्यावारयन्, तदपिशर्वराणामपि शर्वरत्वम्॥ १॥

प्रथमेषु पर्य्यायेषु स्तुवते, प्रथमान्येव पदानि पुनराददते। यदेवैषां मनोरथा आसन्, तदेवैषान्तेनाददते। मध्यमेषु पर्य्यायेषु स्तुवते, मध्यमान्येव पदानि पुनराददते। यदेवैषामश्वा गाव आसन्, तदेवैषां तेनाददते। उत्तमेषु पर्य्यायेषु स्तुवते(१), उत्तमान्येव पदानि पुनराददते। यदेवैषां वासो हिरण्यं मणिरध्यात्ममासीत्, तदेवैषां तेनाददते। आ द्विषतो वसु दत्ते, निरेवैनमेभ्यः सर्वेभ्यो लोकेभ्यो नुदते, य एवं वेद॥ २॥

पवमानवदहरित्याहुः, न रात्रिः पवमानवती, कथमुभ पवमानवती भवतः, केन ते समावद्भाजी भवत इति। यदेवेन्द्राय मद्दने सुतमिदं(२)वसो सुतमन्ध इदं ह्यन्वोजसा सुतमिति स्तुवन्ति

१ स्तुवन्त इति क०।

२ स्तुममिति भ०।

च शंसन्ति (१) च, तेन रात्रिः पवमानवती,(२) तेनोभे पवमानवती भवतः, तेन ते समावद्भाजौ भवतः। पञ्चदशस्तोत्रमहरित्याहुः, न रात्रिः पञ्चदशस्तोत्रा, कथमुभे पञ्चदशस्तोत्रे भवतः, केन ते समावद्भाजौ भवत इति। द्वादशस्तोत्राण्यपिशर्वराणि तिसृभिर्देवताभिः सन्धिना राथन्तरेणाश्विना यः स्तुवते, तेन रात्रिः पञ्चदशस्तोत्रा, तेनोभे पञ्चदशस्तोत्रे भवतः, तेन ते समावद्भाजौ भवतः। परिमितं स्तुवन्त्यपरिमितमनुशंसन्ति, परिमितं भूतमपरिमितं भव्यमपरिमितान्येवावरुन्ध्यादित्यतिशंसन्ति(३)। स्तोममति वै प्रजास्त्वात्मानमतिपशवः(४)। तद्यदेवास्यात्मानन्तदेवास्यैतेनाप्याययन्ति। अथो इयं वा इदं सर्वं स्नेहश्चैव तत्तेजश्च। अथ तदहोरात्राभ्यामाप्तं स्नेहतेजसोराप्त्यै। गायत्रीं स्तोत्रियानुरूपं शंसन्ति, तेजो वै गायत्री, तमः पाप्मा, रात्रिस्तेन तेजसा तमःपाप्मानन्तरन्ति पुनरादायं(५), शंसन्ति। एवं हि सामगाः स्तुवते, यथास्तुतमनुशस्तं भवति। न हि तत् स्तुतं यन्नानुशस्तं। तदाहुः, अथ कस्मादुत्तमात् प्रतीहारादाह्वय साम्ना शस्त्रमुपसन्तन्वन्तीति ॥२॥

पुरुषो वै यज्ञः, तस्यशिर एव हविर्धानं, मुखमाहवनीयः, उदरं सदः, अन्नरक्थानि, बाहू मार्जालीयश्चाग्नीध्रीयश्च, या इमा

१ स्तुवति च शंसतीति ग० ।

२ पवमानवतीतीति ग० ।

३ अतिशंसतीति ग०, भ०, ट० च ।

४ प्रजास्त्वात्मानमितीति ग०, चं० च ।

५ पुनरादायेति ब० ।

देवतास्ति अन्तःसदः, सन्धिष्ठाप्रतिष्ठे(१) गार्हपत्यव्रतश्रवणो इति। अथापरन्तस्य, मन एव ब्रह्मा, प्राण उद्गाता, अपानः प्रस्तोता, व्यानः प्रतिहर्त्ता, वाग्घोता, चक्षुरध्वर्य्युः, प्रजापतिः सदस्यः, अङ्गानि होत्राशंसिनः, आत्मा यजमानः। तद्यदध्वर्य्युस्तोत्रमुपाकारोति सोमः पवत इति, चक्षुरेव तत् प्राणैः सन्दधाति। अथ यत् प्रस्तोता ब्रह्माणमामन्त्रयते, ब्रह्मन् स्तोष्यामः प्रशास्तरिति। मनोग्रणीर्भवति एतेषां प्राणानां, मनसा हि प्रसूताः ,स्तोमेन स्तयामेति, प्राणानेव तत् मनसा सन्दधाति। अथ यद्ब्रह्मा स्तुतेत्युच्चै रनुजानाति, मनो वै ब्रह्मा, मन एव तत् प्राणैः सन्दधाति। अथ यत् प्रस्तोता प्रस्तौति, अपानमेव तत् प्राणैः सन्दधाति। अथ यत् प्रतिहर्त्ता प्रतिहरति, व्यानमेव तदपानैः सन्दधाति। अथ यदुद्गातोद्गायति, समानमेव तत् प्राणैः सन्दधाति। अथ यद्धोता साम्रा ऽशस्त्रमुपसन्तनोति, वाग्वै होता, वाचमेव तत् प्राणैः सन्दधाति। अथ यत् सदस्यो ब्रह्माणमुपासीदति, प्रजापतिर्वै सदस्यः, प्रजापतिमेवाप्नोति। अथ यद्धोत्राशंसिनः सामं सन्तति कुर्वन्ति, अङ्गानि वै होत्राशंसिन, अङ्गान्येवास्य तत् प्राणैः सन्दधाति। अथ यद्यजमानस्तोत्रमुपासीदति, आत्मा वै यजमानः, आत्मानमेवास्य तत् कल्पयति। तस्मान्नैनं बहिर्वेद्यभ्याश्रावयेयुर्नाभ्युदियान्नाभ्यस्तमियान् नाधिष्ण्ये प्रतपेन्नेत् प्राणेभ्य आत्मानमन्तरगादिति॥ ४॥

प्रथमेषु पर्य्यायेषु स्तुवते, प्रथमेषु पदेषु निनर्दयन्ति, प्रथमरात्रादेव तदसुरान्निरघ्नन्ति। मध्यमेषु पर्य्यायेषुस्तुवते, मध्यमेषु पदेषु

१ सन्धिष्ण्याः प्रतिष्ठे इति ग०, घ०, ङ०, च।

निनर्दयन्ति, मध्यमरात्रादेव तदसुरान्निरघ्नन्ति। उत्तमेषु पर्य्यायेषु स्तुवते, उत्तमेषु निनर्दयन्ति, उत्तमरात्रादेव तदसुरान्निरघ्नन्ति। तद्यथाभ्याघारात् पुनः पुनः पाप्मानं निर्हरन्त्येवमेवैतत् स्तोत्रियानुरूपाभ्यामहोरात्राभ्यामेव तदसुरान्निरघ्नन्ति। गायत्रीं शंसन्ति, तेजो वै ब्रह्मवर्चसं गायत्री, तेज एवास्मै तद्ब्रह्मवर्चसं यजमाने दधति। गायत्री शस्त्वा जगतीं शंसन्ति, ब्रह्म ह वै जगती, ब्रह्मणैवास्मै तद् ब्रह्मवर्चसं यजमाने दधति। व्याव्हयन्ते गायत्रीश्च जगतीश्चान्तरेण, छन्दांस्येव तं नानावीर्य्याणि कुर्वन्ति। जगतीः शस्त्वा त्रिष्टुभः शंसन्ति, पशवो वै जगती, पशूनेव तत् त्रिष्टुभः परिदधति। बलं वै वीर्य्यं त्रिष्टुप्, बलमेव तद्वीर्य्यन्ततः(१) प्रतिष्ठापयति। अन्धस्वत्यो मद्वत्यः सुतवत्यः पीतवत्यस्त्रिष्टुभो याज्याः समृद्धाः सुलक्षाः, एतद्वै रात्रीरूपं जाग्रियात्। रात्रिं यावदु ह वै न वा स्तुवते न वा शस्यते, तावदीश्वरा असुररक्षांसि च यज्ञमनुवनयन्ति(२)। तस्मादाहवनीयं समिधमाग्नीध्रीयं गार्हपत्यं धिष्ण्यं समुज्ज्वलयते। अतिभाषयेरन् ज्वलयेरन् प्रकाशमिव वै तस्मादारे भिन्नं सुवीरंस्तान् ह्यातः श्रेष्ठो वा इति पाप्मानाभिह्वक्नोति(३)। ते तमःपाप्मानमपाघ्नते ते तमःपाप्मानमपाघ्नते ॥ ५ ॥

विश्वरूपं वै त्वाष्ट्रमिन्द्रोऽहं स त्वष्टा हतपुत्रोऽभिचरणीयमपेन्द्रं

---

१ तद्वीर्य्यन्तत इति भा०। तद्वीर्य्यं तत इति क०।

२ यज्ञमनु मनयन्तीति भा०। यज्ञमनुमनयतीति ग०।

३ चभिह्नक्नोतीति भा०।

सोममाहरत्(१)। तस्येन्द्रो जज्ञिरे। स संस्कृत्वा(२) प्रासह्य सोममपिवत् स विष्टद्वार्छत्। तस्मात् सोमो नानुपहूतेन(३) न पातव्यः। सोमपीथोऽस्य द्व्यृद्धिको(४) भवति। तस्य मुखात् प्राणेभ्यः श्रीर्यशांस्यूर्ध्वान्युदक्रामत्। तानि पशून् प्राविशन्। तस्मात् पशवो यशोयशो ह भवति, य एवं वेद। ततोऽस्मा एतदश्विनौ च सरस्वती च यज्ञं समभरन्(५), सौत्रामणिं भैषज्याय। तयेन्द्रमभ्यषिञ्चन्। ततो वै स देवानां श्रेष्ठोऽभवत्। श्रेष्ठः स्वानां चान्येषां च भवति, य एवं वेद यश्चैवं विद्वान्त् सौत्रामण्याभिषिच्यते ॥ ६ ॥

अथ साम गायति ब्रह्मा, क्षत्रं वै साम, क्षत्रेणैवैनं तदभिषिञ्चति। अथो साम्राज्यं वै साम, साम्राज्येनैवैनं तत् साम्राज्यं गमयति। अथो सर्वेषां वा एष वेदानां रसः, यत् साम, सर्वेषामेव तद्वेदानां रसेनाभिषिञ्चति। बृहत्यां गायन्ति(६), बृहत्यां वा असावादित्यः श्रियां प्रतिष्ठायां प्रतिष्ठतस्तपति। ऐन्द्र्यां बृहत्यां गायति(७)। ऐन्द्रो वा एष यज्ञक्रतुर्यत् सौत्रामणिः। ऐन्द्रायतन एष एतर्हि यो यजते, स्व एवैनं तदायतने प्रीणाति। अथ कस्मात् संस्थानानि नाम, एतैर्वै सामभिर्देवा

---

१ सोममारदिति च०, भ० च।

२ ससंत्वा इति ग०।

३ नानुपह्वयतेन इति भ०।

४ व्यस्यर्ध्रार्द्धिक इति च०।

५ सम्भरेदिति च०।

६ बृहत्यां गायतीति क०, ख० च। बृहत्या गायतीति ग०।

७ बृहत्या गायतीति ग०।

इन्द्रमिन्द्रियेण वीर्य्येण समभ्यन्(१), तथैवैतद्यजमाना एतैरव सामभिरिन्द्रियेणैव वीर्य्येण समृश्यन्ति। संश्रवसे विश्रवसे सत्यश्रवसे श्रवस इति सामानि भवन्ति। एष्वेवैनं लोकेषु प्रतिष्ठापयति। चतुर्निधनं भवति, चतस्रो वै दिशः, दिक्षु तत् प्रतितिष्ठन्ते। अथो चतुष्पादः पशवः, पशूनामाप्त्यै। तदाहुः, यदेतत् साम गीयते, अथ कैतस्य साम्नमुक्थं, का प्रतिष्ठा। त्रयो देवा एकादशेत्याहुः, एतद्वा एतस्य साम्नमुक्थमेषा प्रतिष्ठा। त्रयस्त्रिंशं ग्रहं गृह्णाति, साम्नः प्रतिष्ठायै प्रतिष्ठायै॥ ७॥

प्रजापतिरकामयत, वाजमाप्नुयात्, स्वर्गं लोकमेति। स एतं वाजपेयमपश्यत्। वाजपेयो वा एषः, य एष तपति, वाजमेतेन यजमानः स्वर्गं लोकमाप्नोति। शुक्रवत्यो ज्योतिष्मत्यः प्रातःसवने भवन्ति, तेजो ब्रह्मवर्चसं ताभिराप्नोति। वाजवत्यो माध्यन्दिने सवने स्वर्गस्य लोकस्य समष्ट्यै। अन्नवत्यो गणवत्यः पशुमत्यस्तृतीयसवने भवन्ति, भूमानं ताभिराप्नोति। सर्वः सप्तदशो भवन्ति(२), प्रजापतिर्वै सप्तदशः, प्रजापतिमेवाप्नोति। हिरण्यस्रज ऋत्विजो भवन्ति, महस एव तद्रूपं क्रियते। एष मेमुष्मिंल्लोके प्रकाशोसदिति, ज्योतिर्वै हिरण्यं, ज्योतिषैवैनमन्तर्दधत्याजिं धावन्ति यजमानमुज्जापयन्ति, नाके रोहति, स महसे रोहति, विश्वमहसे रोहति, सर्वमहसे रोहति, मनुष्यलोकादेवैनमन्तर्दधति। देवस्य सवितुः सवं स्वर्गं लोकं वर्षिष्ठं नाकं रोहेयमिति ब्रह्मा रथचक्रं सर्पति, सवितृप्रसूत एवैनं तत् समर्पयति। अथो

१ समभ्यन् इति च० ।

२ भवतीति ग० ।

प्रजापतिर्वै ब्रह्मा, प्रजापतिमेवैनं वज्रादधिप्रसुवति, नाकस्योज्जित्यै वाजिनां सन्तत्यै। वाजिसामाभिगायति, वाजिमान् भवति। वाजो वै स्वर्गो लोकः, स्वर्गमेव तं लोकं रोहति। विष्णोः शिपिविष्टवतीषु बृहदुत्तमं भवति, स्वर्गमेव तं लोकं रूढ्वा ब्रध्नस्य विष्टपमतिक्रामत्यतिक्रामति ॥ ८ ॥

अथातो अग्नीर्यामाः, प्रजापतिर्वै यत् प्रजा असृजत, ता वै तां ता असृजत। ताः सृष्टाः पराच्य एवासन्नोपावर्तन्त। ता एकेन स्तोमेनोपागृह्णात्। ता अत्यरिच्यन्त, ता द्वाभ्यान्ताः सर्वैः। तस्मात् सर्वस्तोमः, ता एकेन पृष्ठेनोपागृह्णात्। ता अत्यरिच्यन्त, ता द्वाभ्यां ताः सर्वैः, तस्मात् सर्वस्पृष्टः। ता अतिरिक्तोक्थे वारवन्तीयेनावारयन्, तस्मादेषोतिरिक्तोक्थवान् भवति। तस्माद्वारवन्तीयं ता यदाप्ता यच्छत्, अतो वा अग्नीर्यामाः। अथो प्रजावाप्नुरित्याहुः, प्रजानां यमन इतीहैवैतदुक्थम्(१), ता वर्हिः प्रजा आयेरंस्तर्हि हैतेन यजते, स एषोष्टापृष्ठो भवति, तद्यथान्यस्मिन् यज्ञे विश्वजितः पृष्ठमनु सञ्चरं भवति, कथमेतदेवमत्वेति। पितैष यज्ञानां तद्यथा श्रेष्ठिनि संवशेयुरपि विद्विषाणाः, एवमेवैतच्छ्रेष्ठिनो वशीयान्नमन्नस्यानुचर्थ्याय समन्ते ॥ ९ ॥

तद्यथैवादोऽह्न उक्थानामाग्नेयं प्रथमं भवति, एवमेवैतदत्राप्याग्नेयं प्रथमं भवति। ऐन्द्रे वाव तत्रोत्तरे ऐन्द्रे वा एते ऐन्द्रावैष्णवमच्छावाकस्योक्थं भवति। चतुरात्रावान्यतिरिक्तोक्थानि भवन्ति, चतुष्टया वै पशवः, अथो चतुष्पादः पशवः, पशूनामाप्त्यै। त एते स्तोत्रियानुरूपास्तृचा अर्द्धर्चशस्याः। प्रतिष्ठा वा

१ इतिहैवैतदुक्तमिति ट०, भा० च। इती हैवैतदुक्तमिति क०।

अर्धर्चः, प्रतिष्ठित्या एव। अथैतेषामेवाश्विनानां सूक्तानां द्वे द्वे समाहावमेकैकमहरहः शंसति, अश्विनौ वै देवानां भिषजौ, तस्मादाश्विनानि सूक्तानि शꣳसन्ति, तदश्विभ्यां प्रददुरिदं भिषज्यतमिति। चैत्रवत्यः परिधानीया भवन्ति, यत्र हतस्तत् प्रजा अशनायन्तीः पिपासन्तीः संरुद्धा स्थिता आसन्, ता दीना एताभिर्यथाचैत्रं पाययाञ्चकार तर्पयाञ्चकार, अथो इयं वै चैत्रं पृथिवी, अस्यामदीनायामन्ततः प्रतिष्ठास्यामहा इति। त्रिष्टुभो याज्या भवन्ति, यत्र(१) हतस्तत्प्रजा अशनायन्तीः पिपासन्तीः संरुद्धा स्थिता बभूवुः, ता हैवैना एताभिर्यथौकसं व्यवसाययाञ्चकार, तस्मादेता याज्या भवन्ति तस्मादेता याज्या भवन्ति ॥ १०॥

अथातोनैकाहिकं श्वःस्तोत्रियमद्यस्तोत्रियस्यानुरूपं कुर्वन्ति, प्रातःसवनेऽहीनमेव तत्सन्तन्वन्त्यहीनस्य सन्तत्यै। तद्यथा ह वा एकाहस्सुत एवमहीनः सुतः(२), तद्यथैकाहस्य सुतस्य सवनानि सन्तिष्ठमानानि यन्ति, एवमहीनस्य सुतस्याहानि सन्तिष्ठमानानि यन्ति। तद्यच्छ्वःस्तोत्रियमद्यस्तोत्रियस्यानुरूपं कुर्वन्ति, प्रातः सवनेऽहरेव तदह्नो रूपं कुर्वन्ति। अपरेणैव तदन्हापरमहरभ्यारभन्ते(३), तत्तथा न माध्यन्दिने सवने। श्रीर्वै पृष्ठानि तानि तस्मिन्नेवावस्थितानि भवन्ति। एतेनैव विधिना तृतीयसवने न श्वःस्तोत्रियमद्यस्तोत्रियस्यानुरूपं कुर्वन्ति॥ ११॥

---

१ य उ इति ट०।

२ एकाहसुतमहीनः सुत इति च०। एकाहस्सुत एवमहीनसुत इति क०। एकाहसुत एवमहीनसुत इति ग०, ट० च।

३ अभ्यरभ्यन्ते इति ट०।

अथात आरम्भणीया एव, ऋजुनीती नो वरुण इति मैत्रावरुणस्य। मित्रो नयतु विद्वानिति, प्रणेता वा एष होत्रकाणां, यन्मैत्रावरुणः, तस्मादेषा प्रणेतिमती(१) भवति, इन्द्रं वो विश्वतस्परीति ब्राह्मणाच्छंसिनः। हवामहे जनेभ्य इति, इन्द्रमेवैतयाहरहर्निर्ह्वयन्ते, न हैवैषां विह्वेन्य इन्द्रं हवन्ते। यत्रैवं विद्वान् ब्राह्मणाच्छंस्येतामहरहः शंसति। यत् सोम आसतेनर इत्यच्छावाकस्य। इन्द्राग्नी अजोहवुरितीन्द्राग्नी एवैतयाहरहर्निर्ह्वयन्ते, न हैवैषां विह्वेऽन्य इन्द्राग्नी हवन्ते। यत्रैवं विद्वानच्छावाकस्येतामहरहः शंसति, ता वा एताः स्वर्गस्य लोकस्य नावः सन्तारण्यः। स्वर्गमेवैताभिर्लोकमनुसञ्चरन्ति॥ १२॥

अथातः परिधानीया एव, ते स्याम देव वरुणेति, मैत्रावरुणस्य। इषांश्च स्वधीमहीति(२), अयं वै लोक इषमित्यसौ वै लोकः स्वरिति उभावेवैनौ तौ लोकावारभते। व्यन्ततरिक्षमतिरदिति ब्राह्मणाच्छंसिनो विवृत्वं(३)। स्वर्गमेवैताभिर्लोकं विवृणोति। मदे सोमस्य रोचनेन्द्रो यदभिनद्वलमिति, सिषासवो ह वा एते यद्दीक्षिताः, तस्मादेषा बलवती भवति। उद्गा आजदङ्गिरोभ्य आविष्कृण्वन् गुहासतीः। अर्वाञ्चं नुनुदे बलमिति, सनिमेतेभ्य एतयावरुन्धे। इन्द्रेण रोचनादिवो दृढानि दृंहितानि च। स्थिराणि न पराणुद इति, स्वर्गमेवैतयाहरहर्लोकमवरुन्धे। आहं सरस्वतीवतोरित्यच्छावाकस्य। इन्द्राग्न्योरवो वृण इति, एतद्वा इन्द्राग्न्योः प्रियन्धामः,

१ प्रणेयिमतीति क०। प्रणेत्वर्मतीति च०।

२ इषंच स्वधीमहीतीति च०। इषंच स्वधीमहीति क०।

३ व्यविवृत्वमिति च०। विवृत्वमिति क०।

यद्वागिति, प्रियेणैवैनो तद्धाम्ना समर्द्धयति। प्रियेणैव धाम्ना समृध्यते, य एवं वेद॥ १३॥

उभय्यो(१) होत्रकाणां परिधानीया भवन्ति, अहीनपरिधानीयाश्चैकाहिक्यश्च(२), तत एकाहिकीभिरेव मैत्रावरुणः परिदधाति, तेनास्माल्लोकान्न प्रच्यवते। आहिनीकीभिरच्छावाकः स्वर्गस्य लोकस्याप्त्यै, उभयीभिर्ब्राह्मणाच्छंसी। एवमसावुभौ व्यन्वारभमाण एतीमञ्च लोकममुञ्च। अथोऽहीनञ्चैकाहञ्च, अथो संवत्सरञ्चाग्निष्टोमञ्च, अथो मैत्रावरुणञ्चाच्छावाकञ्च, एवमसावुभौ व्यन्वारभमाण एति। अथ तत एकाहिकीभिरेव तृतीयसवने होत्रकाः परिदधाति, तेनास्माल्लोकान्न प्रच्यवते। आहिनीकीभिरच्छावाकः स्वर्गस्य लोकस्य समष्ट्यै। कामं तद्धोता शंसेत्, यद्धोत्रकाः पूर्वेद्युः शंसेयुः। यद्वै होता तद्धोत्रकाः, प्राणो वै होता, अङ्गानि होत्रकाः, समानो वा अयं प्राणोऽङ्गान्यनुसञ्चरन्ति। तस्मात् तत् कामं होता शंसेत्, यद्धोत्रकाः पूर्वेद्युः शंसेयुः। यद्वै होता तद्धोत्रकाः, आत्मा वै होता, अङ्गानि होत्रकाः, समानो वा इमेऽङ्गानामन्ताः, तस्मात् तत् कामं होता शंसेत्। यद्धोत्रकाः पूर्वेद्युः शंसेयुः, यद्वै होता तद्धोत्रकाः, सूक्तान्तैर्होता परिदधाति, अथ समान्य एव होत्रकाणां परिधानीया भवन्ति॥ १४॥

यः श्वःस्तोत्रियमद्यस्तोत्रियस्यानुरूपं कुर्वन्ति, प्रातःसवनेऽहीनमेव तत्सन्तन्वन्ति, अहीनस्य सन्तत्यै। त एते होत्रकाः प्रातःसवने। षडहस्तोत्रियं शस्त्वा माध्यन्दिनेऽहीनसूक्तानि शंस-

१ उभय इति ग०, च०, भ०, ट० च।

२ एकाहिमस्येति छ०।

न्ति,(१) सत्वो यातु मघवां ऋजीषीति। सत्यवान् मैत्रावरुणो अस्मा इदु प्रतवसे तुरायेति ब्राह्मणाच्छंसी। शासद्वह्निर्दुहितुर्नप्त्यंगादित्यच्छावाकः। तदाहुः, कस्मादच्छावाको वह्निवदेतत् सूक्तमुभयत्र शंसति, स पराञ्चु चैवाह सर्वाञ्चु चेति। वीर्य्यवान् वा एष वह्वृचः, यदच्छावाकः। वहति ह वै वह्निर्धुरः, यासु युज्यते। तस्मादच्छावाको वह्निवदेतत् सूक्तमुभयत्र शंसति, स पराञ्चु चैवाह सर्वाञ्चु चेति। तानि पञ्चस्वहःसु शस्यन्ते। चतुर्विंशेऽभिजिति विषुवति विश्वजिति महाव्रते तान्येतान्यहीनसूक्तानीत्याचक्षते। न ह्येषु किञ्चन हीयते, पराञ्चि ह वा एतान्यहान्यभ्यावर्त्तीनि भवन्ति। तस्मादेतान्येतेष्वहःसु शस्यन्ते। यदेतानि शंसन्ति, तत् स्वर्गस्य लोकस्य रूपं। यद्वेवैतानि शंसति, इन्द्रमेवैतैर्निर्ह्वयन्ते, यथ ऋषभं वासितायै ते वैदेवाश्च ऋषयश्चाब्रुवन्, समानेन यज्ञं सन्तन्वामहा इति। तदेतद्यज्ञस्य समानमपश्यत्। समाना प्रगाथा समानी प्रतिपदः समानानि सूक्तानि। ओकःसारी वा इन्द्रो यत्र वा इन्द्रः पूर्वं गच्छति। गच्छत्येव तत्रापरं यज्ञस्यैव सेन्द्रतायै॥ १५॥

इत्यथर्ववेदोत्तरगोपथब्राह्मणस्य पञ्चमः प्रपाठकः समाप्तः॥५॥

---

## अथ षष्ठप्रपाठकः।

ओम्। तान्वा एतान् सम्पातान् विश्वामित्रः प्रथममपश्यत्,

---

(१) शंसतीति ग०, भा० ८० च।

एवा त्वामिन्द्र वज्रिन्नत्र यन्न इन्द्रो जुजुषे यच्च वष्टि कथामहामवृधत् कस्य होतुरिति । तान् विश्वामित्रेण दृष्टान् वामदेवो ऽसृजत । सह रथाश्वक्रे(१) विश्वामित्रो यान् वाहं सम्पातानदर्शं (२), स्तान्वामदेवो ऽसृजत । कानि त्वं हि सूक्तानि सम्पातांस्तत्प्रतिमान् सृजेयमिति । स एतानि सूक्तानि सम्पातांस्तत्प्रतिमाननसृजत, सद्यो ह जातो वृषभः कनीन उदु ब्रह्माण्यैरतश्रवस्याभितष्टे (३) वदीधया मनीषामिति विश्वामित्रः । इन्द्रः पूर्भिदातिरद्दासमर्कैर्य एक इद्धव्यश्चर्षणीनां यस्तिग्मशृङ्गो वृषभो न भीम इति वसिष्ठः । इमामूषुप्रभृतिं सातयेधा इच्छन्ति त्वा सोम्यासः सखायः शासदह्निर्दुहितुर्नप्त्यङ्गादिति(४) भरद्वाजः । एतैर्वै सम्पातैरेत ऋषय इमान् लोकान् समपतन् । तद्यत्समपतन्, तस्मात् सम्पाताः, तत् सम्पातानां सम्पातत्वं । ततो वा एतां स्त्रीन् सम्पातान् मैत्रावरुणो विपर्य्यासमेकैकमहरहः शंसति, एवा त्वामिन्द्र वज्रिन्नत्रेति प्रथमेऽहनि, यन्न इन्द्रो जुजुषे यच्च वष्टीति द्वितीये, कथामहामवृधत् कस्य होतुरिति तृतीये । त्रीनेव सम्पातान् ब्राह्मणाच्छंसी विपर्य्यासमेकैकमहरहः शंसति, इन्द्रः पूर्भिदातिरद्दासमर्कैरिति प्रथमेऽहनि, य एक इद्धव्यश्चर्षणीनामिति द्वितीये, यस्तिग्मशृङ्गो वृषभो न भीम इति तृतीये । त्रीनेव सम्पातानच्छावाको

१ सहेचाश्वक्रे इति ग०, ङ० च ।

२ सम्पातानदृशन्निति च० ।

३ श्रवण्याभितष्टे इति ट० च । श्रवस्याभितष्टे इति ङ० ।

४ नप्त्यङ्गादिति ग०, च०, ङ०, ट० च ।

विपर्यासमेकैकमहरहः शंसति, मामूषुप्रभृतिं सातयेधा इति प्रथमेहनि, इच्छन्ति त्वा सोम्यासः सखाय इति द्वितीये, शास-इह्निर्दुहितुर्नप्त्यङ्गादिति(१) तृतीये। तानि वा एतानि नव त्रीणि चाहरहःशंस्यानि। तानि द्वादश भवन्ति। द्वादश ह वै मासाः संवत्सरः, संवत्सरः प्रजापतिः, प्रजापतिर्यज्ञः, तत् संवत्सरं प्रजापतिं यज्ञमाप्नोति। तस्मिन् संवत्सरे प्रजापतौ यज्ञे अहरहः प्रतितिष्ठन्तो यन्ति, प्रतितिष्ठन्ते। इदं सर्वमनुप्रतितिष्ठति। प्रतितिष्ठति प्रजया पशुभिः, य एवं वेद। तान्यन्तरेणावापमावपेरन्, अन्यूंखा(२)विराजश्चतुर्थेहनि, वैपदीश्च पङ्क्तीः पञ्चमे, पारुच्छेपीं षष्ठेथ यान्यन्यानि महास्तोत्राण्यष्टर्चान्यावपेरन् ॥ १ ॥

को अद्य नर्यो देवकाम इति मैत्रावरुणः। वनेन वा योन्यधायि चाकन्निति ब्राह्मणाच्छंसी। आयाह्यर्वाङुपबन्धुरेष्ट इत्यच्छावाकः। एतानि वा आवपनानि, एतैरेवावपनैर्देवाश्च ऋषयश्च स्वर्गं लोकमायन्। तथैवैतद्यजमाना एतैरेवावपनैः स्वर्गं लोकं यन्ति। सद्यो ह जातो वृषभः कनीन इति मैत्रावरुणः पुरस्तात् सम्पातानामहरहः शंसति। तदेतत् सूक्तं, स्वर्गमेतेन सूक्तेन देवाश्च ऋषयश्च स्वर्गं लोकमायन्। तथैवैतद्यजमाना एतेनैव सूक्तेन स्वर्गं लोकं यन्ति। तदृषभवत् पशुमद्भवति पशूनामाप्त्यै। तत्पाङ्क्तं भवति, अन्नं वै पङ्क्तिः, अन्नाद्यस्यावरुध्यै(३), अरिष्टैर्नः पथिभिः पारयन्त्विति स्वर्गताया एवैतदहरहः

१ नप्त्यङ्गादिति ग०, च०, छ०, ट० च।

२ आवपेरन्नन्यूंखा इति भ०। आवपेरन्यूंखा इति छ०। आवपेरन्नन्यूंषा इति ट०।

३ अवरुध्यै इति छ०।

शंसति। उदु ब्रह्माण्यैरतश्रवस्येति ब्राह्मणाच्छंसी। ब्रह्मण्व देतत् सूक्तं, समृद्धमेतेन सूक्तेन देवाश्च ऋषयश्च स्वर्गं लोकमायन्। तथैवैतद्यजमाना एतेनैव सूक्तेन स्वर्गं लोकं यन्ति। तदु वै षडर्चं, षड् वा ऋतवः, ऋतूनामाप्त्यै। तदुपरिष्टात् सम्पातानामहरहः शंसति। अभितष्टे वदीधया मनीषामित्यच्छावाको अहरहः शंसति। अभिवदति तत्त्यै रूपमभिप्रियाणि मर्मृशत्पराणीति, यान्येव पराण्यहानि, तानि प्रियाणि, तान्येव तदभिमर्मृशन्तो यन्त्यभ्यारभमाणाः। परो वा अस्माल्लोकात्(१) स्वर्गो लोकः, स्वर्गमेव तं लोकमभिमृशन्ति। कवीं ऋच्छामि(२) सन्दृशे सुमेधा इति, ये ह वा अनेन पूर्वे प्रेतास्ते वै कवयः, तान्यमेव तदभ्यभिवदति। यदु वै दशर्चं, दश वै प्राणाः, प्राणानेव तदाप्नोति प्राणानां सन्तत्यै। यदु वै शतर्चं, दश वै पुरुषे प्राणाः, दश स्वर्गा लोकाः, प्राणांश्चैव तत् स्वर्गांश्च लोकानाप्नोति। प्राणेषु चैवैतत् स्वर्गेषु च लोकेषु प्रतितिष्ठन्तो यन्ति। यदु वै दशर्चं, दशाक्षरा विराड्, इयं वै विराड, इयं वै स्वर्गस्य लोकस्य प्रतिष्ठा, तदेतदस्यां प्रतिष्ठायां प्रतिष्ठापयति। सन्नादिन्द्रं निराहते, नेन्द्राद्रूपाश्च प्रच्यवते, तदुपरिष्टात् सम्पातानामहरहः शंसति॥ २॥

कास्तमिन्द्र त्वा वसुं कन्नव्यो अतसीनां कद्रून्वस्यात(३)

---

१ अस्माल्लोका इति क०, भा० च।

२ रिच्छामीति क०। रच्छामीति भा०।

३ कदून्व१स्याचतमिति ग०। कदून्व१स्याकृतमिति भा०, ङ० च। कदून्वा१स्याकृतमिति क०।

इति कद्वन्तः प्रगाथा अहरहः शंसति। एको वै प्रजापतिः, प्रजापतेराप्त्यै। यद्देव कद्वन्तः, तत् स्वर्गस्य लोकस्य रूपं। यद्देव कद्वन्तः, अथो अन्नं वै कं, अथो अन्नस्यावरुध्यै। यद्देव(१)कद्वन्तः, अथो सुखं वै कं, अथो सुखस्यावरुध्यै। यद्देव(२) कद्वन्तः, अथोहरहर्वा एते, श्रान्तान्यहीनसूक्तान्युपयुञ्जाना यन्ति, तानि कद्वद्भिः प्रगाथैः शमयन्ति। तान्येभ्यः शान्तानिकं भवन्ति(३), तान्येताञ् छान्तानि स्वर्गं लोकमभिवहन्ति। त्रिष्टुभः सूक्तः प्रतिपदः शंसेयुः, ता हैके पुरस्तात् प्रगाथानां शंसन्ति, धाय्या इति वदन्तस्तदु तथा न कुर्यात्। क्षत्रं वै होता, विशो होत्राशंसिनः, क्षत्रस्यैव तद्विशं प्रत्युद्यामिनीं कुर्युः। पावमानस्य(४) सन्त्रिष्टुभो मा इमा(५) सूक्तः प्रतिपद इत्येवं विद्यात्, यथा वै समुद्रं प्रस्नरेयुः, एवं हैवैते प्रप्लवयन्ते(६) ये संवत्सरं द्वादशाहं वोपासन्ते, तद्यथा सैरावतीं नावं पारकामाः समारोहेयुः, एवं हैवैतास्त्रिष्टुभः स्वर्गकामाः समारोहन्ति। न ह वा एतच्छन्दो गमयित्वा स्वर्गं लोकमुपावर्त्तन्ते(७)। वीर्य्यवन्तं मंहिताभ्यो नय्याव्हयीत, समानं हि छन्दः, अथोऽन्ये धाय्या

---

१ यद्देवेति च०, छ० च।

२ यद्देवेति च०, ट० च।

३ भवतीति ट०।

४ पावनस्येति च०, भ० च।

५ वा इमा इति क०, ट० च।

६ प्रप्लवंते च०, भ०, ट० च। प्रप्लवते इति ग०।

७ लोकमुपावर्त्तत इति ग०, छ० च।

करवाणीति । यदेनाः शंसन्ति(१), तत् स्वर्गस्य लोकस्य रूपं । यद्वेवैनाः शंसन्ति(२), इन्द्रमेवैतैर्निह्वयन्ते, यथ ऋषभं(३) वासितायै ॥ ३ ॥

अपेन्द्र प्राचो मघवन्नमित्रानिति, मैत्रावरुणः पुरस्तात् सम्पातानामहरहः शंसति । अपापाचो अभिभूते नुदस्वापोदीचो अप शूरा धराच उरौ यथा तव शर्म्मन् मदेमेति, अभयस्य रूपमभयमिव ह्यन्विच्छेति, ब्रह्मणा ते ब्रह्मयुजा युनज्मीति, ब्राह्मणाच्छंसेतामहरहः शंसति । युक्तवतीं युक्त इवाह्यहीनोहीनस्य रूपमुरु नो लोकमनुनेषीति, अच्छावाको अहरहः शंसति । अनुनेषीत्येत इवाह्यहीनोऽहीनस्य रूपं नेषीति सत्रायणरूपं । ओकःसारी हैवैषामिन्द्रो भवति, यथा गौः प्रज्ञातं गोष्ठं, यथा ऋषभं(४) वासितायाः, एवं हैवैषामिन्द्रो यज्ञमागच्छन्ति(५) । न शूनं यथाहीनस्य(६) परिदध्यात् । क्षत्रियो ह राष्ट्राच्च्यवते, यो हैव परो भवति, तमभिव्ह्वयति ॥ ४ ॥

अथातोऽहीनस्य युक्तिश्च विमुक्तिश्च व्यन्तरिक्षमतिरदित्यहीनं युङ्क्ते । एवेदिन्द्रमिति विमुञ्चति । नूनं सा त इत्यहीनं युङ्क्ते । नूष्टत इति विमुञ्चति । एष ह वा अहीनं तन्तुमर्हति, य एनं योक्तुञ्च विमोक्तुञ्च वेद, तस्य हैषैव युक्तिरेषा विमुक्तिः ।

---

१, २, शंसतीति ङ० ।

३ यथाऋषभमिति ग० ।

४ यथऋषभमिति ग०, च०, भ० च ।

५ यज्ञमागच्छतीति ग० ।

न शूनं यथाहीनस्येति ङ० ।

तद्यत् प्रथमेहनि चतुर्विंश एकाह्विकीभिः परिदध्युः, प्रथम एवा-
हनि यज्ञं संस्थापयेयुर्नाहीनकर्म्म कुर्युः। अथ यदहीनः परि-
धानीयाभिः परिदध्युः, तद्यथा युक्तो विमुच्यमाना उत्क्रान्त्येत, एवं
यजमाना उत्क्रान्त्येरन्, नाहीनकर्मं कुर्युः। अथ यदुभयीभिः
परिदध्युः, तद्यथा दीर्घाध्व उपविमोकं यान्याः, तादृक् तत्
समानीभिः परिदध्युः। तदाहुः, एकया द्वाभ्यां वा स्तोम-
मतिशंसेत्, दीर्घारण्यानि भवन्ति, यत्र बह्वीभिः स्तोमोति-
शस्यते, अथो क्षिप्रन्देवेभ्योऽन्नाद्यं सम्प्रयच्छामीति, अपरिमिताभि-
रुत्तरयोः सवनयोः। अपरिमितो वै स्वर्गो लोकः, स्वर्गस्य
लोकस्य समष्ट्यै। तद्यथा अभिहेषते पिपासते क्षिप्रं प्रयच्छेत्,
तादृक् तत् समानीभिः परिदध्युः। सन्ततो हैवैषामारब्धो
विस्रस्तो यज्ञो भवति, सन्ततमृचा वषट् कृत्यं सन्तत्यै सन्धीयते
प्रजया पशुभिः, य एवं वेद ॥ ५ ॥

तदाहुः, कथं द्व्युक्थो होतैकसूक्त एकोक्था होत्रा द्विसूक्ता
इति। असौ वै होता योसौ तपति, स वा एक एव, तस्मादेक-
सूक्तः। स यद्दिध्यातो द्वाविवा भवति, तेज एव मण्डलं भा अपरं
शुक्लमपरं कृष्णं, तस्माद्द्व्युक्थः। रश्मयो वाव होत्राः, ते वा
एकैकं, तस्मादेकोक्थाः। तद्यदेकैकस्य रश्मेर्द्वौ द्वौ वर्णौ भवतः,
तस्माद् द्विसूक्ताः। संवत्सरो वाव होता, स वा एक एव, तस्मा-
देकसूक्तः। तस्य यद् द्वयान्यहानि भवन्ति, शीतान्यन्यान्युष्णान्य-
न्यानि, तस्माद् द्व्युक्थः। ऋतवो वाव होत्राः, ते वा एकैकं, तस्मा-
देकोक्थाः। तद्यदेकैकस्यर्तौ द्वौ द्वौ मासौ भवतः, तस्माद्द्विसूक्ताः।
पुरुषो वाव होता, स वा एक एव, तस्मादेकसूक्तः। स यत्पुरुषो

भवत्यन्यथैव प्रत्यङ् भवत्यन्यथा प्राङ्(१), तस्माद् द्व्युक्थः। अङ्गानि वाव होत्राः, तानि वा एकैकं, तस्मादेकोक्थाः। तं यदेकैकमङ्गं द्युतिर्भवति, तस्माद् द्विसूक्ताः। तदाहुः, यद् द्व्युक्थो होतैकसूक्त एकोक्था होत्रा द्विसूक्ताः, कथं तत् समं भवति, यदेव द्विदेवत्याभिर्यजन्ति, अथो यद् द्विसूक्ता होत्रा इति ब्रूयात्, तदाहुः, यदग्निष्टोम एव सति यज्ञे द्वे होतुरुक्थे अतिरिच्येते, कथं ततो होत्रा न व्यवच्छिद्यन्त इति। यदेव द्विदेवत्याभिर्यजन्ति, अथो यद् द्विसूक्ता होत्रा इति ब्रूयात्, तदाहुः, यदग्निष्टोम एव सति यज्ञे सर्वा देवताः सर्वाणि छन्दांस्याप्याययन्ति, अथ कतमेन छन्दसायातयामान्युक्थानि प्रणयन्ति, कया देवतयेति। गायत्रेण छन्दसाग्निना देवतयेति ब्रूयात्। देवान् ह यज्ञं तन्वाना असुररक्षांस्यभिचेरिरे यज्ञपर्वणि, यज्ञमेषां हनिष्यामस्तृतीयसवनं प्रति तृतीयसवने ह यज्ञस्त्वरिष्टो बलिष्ठः प्रतनुमेषां यज्ञं हनिष्याम इति। ते वरुणं दक्षिणतोऽयोजयन्, मध्यतो बृहस्पतिमुत्तरतो विष्णुं। तेऽब्रुवन्, एकैकाः स्मः, नेदमुत्सहामहेति, स्तुनो द्वितीयो येनेदं सह व्यश्नवामहा इति। तानिन्द्रोऽब्रवीत्, सर्वे मद्द्वितीया स्थेति। ते सर्वे इन्द्रं द्वितीयाः, तस्मादैन्द्रावारुणमैन्द्राबार्हस्पत्यमैन्द्रावैष्णवमनुशस्यते। द्वितीयवन्तो ह वा एतेन स्मा भवन्ति, द्वितीयवन्तो मन्यते, य एवं वेद ॥ ६ ॥

आग्नेयीषु मैत्रावरुणस्योक्थं प्रणयन्ति, वीर्यं वा अग्निः, वीर्येणैवास्मै तत् प्रणयन्ति। ऐन्द्रावारुणमनुशस्यते, वीर्यं वा इन्द्रः, क्षत्रं वरुणः, पशव उक्थानि, वीर्येणैव तत् क्षत्रेण

१ प्राङ् इति ग०, घ०, ट० च।

चोभयतः पशून् परिगृह्णाति स्थित्या अनपक्रान्त्यै। ऐन्द्रीषु ब्राह्मणाच्छंसिन उक्थं प्रणयन्ति, वीर्यं वा इन्द्रः वीर्य्येणैवास्मै तत् प्रणयन्ति। ऐन्द्राबार्हस्पत्यमनुशस्यते, वीर्य्यं वा इन्द्रः, ब्रह्म बृहस्पतिः, पशव उक्थानि, वीर्य्येणैव तद्ब्रह्मणा चोभयतः पशून् परिगृह्णाति स्थित्या अनपक्रान्त्यै। ऐन्द्रीष्वच्छावाकस्योक्थं प्रणयन्ति, वीर्य्यं वा इन्द्रः, वीर्य्येणैवास्मै तत् प्रणयन्ति। ऐन्द्रावैष्णवमनुशस्यते, वीर्य्यं वा इन्द्रः, यज्ञो विष्णुः, पशव उक्थानि, वीर्य्येणैव तद्यज्ञेन चोभयतः पशून् परिगृह्य क्षत्रेन्ततः प्रतिष्ठापयति। तस्मादु क्षत्रियो भूयिष्ठं हि पशूनामीशते अधिष्ठाता प्रदाता, यस्मै प्रत्ता वेदा अवरुद्धाः, तान्येतान्यैन्द्राणि। जागतानि शंसन्ति, अथो एतैरेवसैन्द्रं तृतीयसवनमेतैर्जागतं सवनं, धराणि ह वा अस्यैतान्युक्थानि भवन्ति, यन्नाभानेदिष्टो वालखिल्यो वृषाकपिरेव या मरुत्, तस्मात् तानि सार्द्धमेवोपेयुः, सार्द्धमिदं रेतः सिक्तं समृद्धं, एकधा प्रजनयामीति। ये ह वा एतानि नानूपेयुः, यथा रेतः सिक्तं विलुम्पेत कुमारं वा जातमङ्गशो विभजेत्तादृक् तत्। तस्मात्तानि सार्द्धमेवोपेयुः। सार्धमिदं रेतः सिक्तं समृद्धमेकधा प्रजनयामीति। शिल्पानि शंसति, यदेवशिल्पानि, एतेषां वै शिल्पानामनुकृतिर्हि शिल्पमधिगम्यते। हस्ती कंसो वासो हिरण्यमश्वतरी रथशिल्पं, शिल्पं हास्य(१) समधिगम्यते। य एवं वेद यदेव शिल्पानि शंसति, तत् स्वर्गस्य लोकस्य रूपं। यद्देव शिल्पानि, आत्मसंस्कृतिर्वै शिल्पान्यात्मानमेवास्य तत् संस्कुर्वन्ति ॥ ७ ॥

१ रथशिल्पं हास्येति च०।

नाभानेदिष्टं शंसति, रेतो वै नाभानेदिष्टः । रेत एवास्य तत् कल्पयति । तद्रेतोमिश्रं भवति, छन्दया रेतः सञ्जग्मानो निषिञ्चदिति(१),रेतसः समृध्या एव । तं नाराशंसं संशंसति(२),प्रजा वै नरः, वाक् शंसः, प्रजासु तद्वाचं दधाति । तस्मादिमाः प्रजा अदन्त्यो जायन्ते । तं हैके पुरस्तात् प्रगाथानां शंसन्ति, पुरस्तादायतना वागिति वदन्ते, उपरिष्टादेके । उपरिष्टादायतना वागिति वदन्तो मध्य एव शंसेत्, मध्यायतना वा इयं वाग्, उपरिष्टान्नेदीयसीव तं होता रेतोभूतं शस्त्वा मैत्रावरुणाय सम्प्रयच्छति । एतस्य त्वं प्राणान् कल्पयति, वालखिल्याः शंसन्ति(३), प्राणा वै वालखिल्याः, प्राणानेवास्य तत् कल्पयति । ताविहृताः(४) शंसति, विहृता(५) वै प्राणाः, प्राणेनापानो अपानेन व्यानः । स पच्छः प्रथमे सूक्ते विहरति, अर्धर्चशो द्वितीये, ऋक्शस्तृतीये । स यत् प्रथमे सूक्ते विहरति, वाचं चैव तन्मनश्च विहरति । यद् द्वितीये चक्षुश्चैव, तच्छ्रोत्रं च विहरति । यत्तृतीये प्राणं चैव, तदात्मानं च विहरति । तदुपाप्तो विहरेत्, कामः, अन्ये तु वै प्रगाथाः कल्पयन्तेति(६) मर्शं समेव विहरेत् । तथा वै प्रगाथाः कल्पयन्ते(७) । यदेवातिमर्शं, तत् स्वर्गस्य लोकस्य रूपं । यद्वि-

१ चातिषिञ्चतीति ग० । विषिञ्चदितीति ट० ।

२ नाराशं शंसति इति च०, ट० । नाराशं शंसन्ति भ० ।

३ शंसतीति च०, भ०, ट० च ।

४, ५ विकृता इति ग० । विष्ट्ना इति च० ।

६ नेतुर्वै प्रगाथाः कल्पयन्ते इति ट० । नेतुर्वै प्रगाथाः कल्पन्ते इति भ० ।

७ कल्पन्ते इति च० ।

वातिमर्शं, आत्मा वै बृहती, प्राणाः सतोबृहती, स बृहतीमशंसीत्। स आत्माथ सतोबृहतीं[१], ते प्राणा अथ बृहतीमथ सतोबृहतीं, तदात्मानं प्राणैः परिबृढन्नेति[२]। यद्देवातिमर्शः, आत्मा वै बृहती, प्रजाः सतोबृहती, स बृहतीमशंसीत्। स आत्माथ सतोबृहतीं, ते प्रजा अथ बृहतीमथ सतोबृहतीं, तदात्मानं प्रजया परिबृढन्नेति। यद्देवातिमर्शं[३], आत्मा वै बृहती, पशवः सतोबृहती, स बृहतीमशंसीत्। स आत्माथ सतोबृहतीं, ते पशवोथ बृहतीं, अथ सतोबृहतीं, तदात्मानं पशुभिः परिबृढन्नेति। तस्य मैत्रावरुणः प्राणान् कल्पयित्वा ब्राह्मणाच्छंसिने सम्प्रयच्छति। एतस्य त्वं प्रजनयेति, सुकीर्त्तिं शंसति, देवयोनिर्वै सुकीर्त्तिः, तद्यज्ञियायां देवयोन्यां यजमानं प्रजनयेति। वृषाकपिं शंसति, आत्मा वै वृषाकपिः, आत्मानमेवास्य तत् कल्पयति। तन्यूङ्खं[४] इति, अन्नं वै न्यूङ्खः[५], अन्नाद्यमेवास्मै तत् सम्प्रयच्छति, यथा कुमाराय जाताय स्तनं। स पाङ्क्तो भवति, पाङ्क्तो ह्ययं पुरुषः पञ्चधा विहितः, लोमानि त्वगस्थिमज्जामस्तिष्कं। स यावानेव पुरुषस्तावन्तं यजमानं संस्कृत्याच्छावाकाय सम्प्रयच्छति। एतस्य त्वं प्रतिष्ठां कल्पय, इत्येव या मरुतं शंसति, प्रतिष्ठा वा एव, या मरुत्, प्रतिष्ठाया

---

१ बृहतीति ख०।

२ परिबृहणन्नेतीति ख०।

३ यद्देवाभ्यर्शमेवेति ख०।

४ तन्युङ्खमिति ख०।

५ न्युङ्ख इति ट०।

एवैनमन्ततः प्रतिष्ठापयति । याज्यया यजति, अन्नं वै याज्या, अन्नाद्यमेवास्मै तत् प्रयच्छति ॥ ८ ॥

तानि वा एतानि सहचरणानीत्याचक्षते, यन्नाभानेदिष्ठो बालखिल्यः । वृषाकपिरेव या मरुत्तानि सह वा शंसेत् सह वा न शंसेत् । यदेषामन्तरीयात्(१) तद्यजमानस्यान्तरीयात् । यदि नाभानेदिष्टं रेतोस्यान्तरीयात्,यदि बालखिल्याः प्राणानस्यान्तरीयात्, यदि वृषाकपिमात्मानमस्यान्तरीयात्, यदेव या(२) मरुतं, प्रतिष्ठा वा एव या मरुत्, प्रतिष्ठाया एवैनन्तꣳश्रावयेत् । दैव्याश्च मनुष्याश्च तानि सह वा शंसेत्, सह वा न शंसेत् स ह बुडिल(३) आश्वितरा स्युर्विश्वजितो होता स दीचाञ्चक्रे (४), एतेषां वा एषां शिल्पानां विश्वजिति सांवत्सरिके द्वे होतुरुक्थे माध्यन्दिनमभिप्रचवेते । हन्ताहमिच्छमेव या मरुतं शस्ययानीति, तद्ध तथा शस्ययाञ्चक्रे । तद्ध तथा शस्यमाने गोश्ल आजगाम । स होवाच, होतः कथा ते(५) शस्त्रं विचक्रं प्लवत इति, किं ह्यभूयदित्येव या मरुदयमुत्तरतः शस्यत इति । स होवाच, इन्द्रो वै माध्यन्दिनः, कथेन्द्रं माध्यन्दिनान्नयनीकसीति, नेन्द्रं माध्यन्दिनान्यनीषामिति(६) । स होवाच, छन्दस्विदमु माध्यन्दिनं,

१ य एषामन्तीयादिति ट० ।

२ यद्येव या इति क०, ट० च ।

३ बूडिल इति च० ।

४ सन्दीचाञ्चक्रे इति ग०, च०, भ० च ।

५ स होवाच नमः कथा ते इति क० ।

६ माध्यन्दिनान्यनिषासीतीति भ० । माध्यन्दिनान्यनीकसीतिमितीति क० । माध्यन्दिनान्यनीयामीतीति ट० ।

सातिजागतं वाति, जागतं वा स उ मारुतो मेवं[१] संस्तष्टेति। स होवाच, अस्माच्छावाकेऽन्यथास्मिन्ननुशासनमीषे। स होवाच, इन्द्रमेष विष्णुं न्यङ्गानि[२] शंसति, अथ त्वं होतुरुपरिष्टाद्रौद्रिया धाय्या, या पुरस्तान्मारुतस्य सूक्तस्याप्यस्यधा इति[३]। तथेति। तदप्येतर्हि तथैव शस्यते, यथा षष्ठे पृष्ठ्याहनि[४]। कल्पत एव[५] यज्ञः, कल्पते यजमानस्य प्रजापतिः, कथमत्राशस्त एव नाभानेदिष्टो भवति। अथ बालखिल्याः शंसति, रेतो वा अग्रेथ प्राणा एवं ब्राह्मणाच्छंस्यशस्त एव नाभानेदिष्टो भवति। अथ वृषाकपिं शंसति, रेतो वा अग्रेथात्मा, कथमत्र यजमानस्य प्रजापतिः, कथं प्राणा अवरुद्धा भवन्तीति। यजमानं वा एतेन सर्वेण यज्ञक्रतुना संस्कुर्वन्ति, स यथा गर्भो योन्यामन्तरेवसम्भवच्छेते, न ह वै सकृदेवा[६] अग्रे सर्वं सम्भवति, एकैकं वाङ्गं सम्भवति। सर्वाणि चेत्समानेऽहनि क्रियेरन्, कल्पयत एव यज्ञः, कल्पते यजमानस्य प्रजापतिः। अथ हैव एव या मरुतं होता शंसेत्, तस्यास्य प्रतिष्ठा, तस्या एवैनमन्ततः प्रतिष्ठापयति प्रतिष्ठापयति॥ ९॥

---

१ मारुतो इमेवेति च०। मारुतो मेवामिति ट०।

२ विष्णुन्यङ्गानि इति ड०।

३ सूक्तस्यापिस्यधा इति भ०। सूक्तस्याप्यस्वधा इतीति क०।

४ पृष्ठे पृष्ठ्याह्नीति ग०। षष्ठे षष्ठ्याह्नानि इति क०। षष्ठे पृष्ठ्याहनि इति ट०। षष्ठे पृष्ठ्याह्नानीति च०।

५ कल्पयत एवेति भ०। कल्पयत एव यज्ञः कल्पयते इति ट०।

६ सकृद्देवा इति भ०, ट० च०।

देवक्षेत्रं वै षष्ठमहः। देवक्षेत्रं वा एत आगच्छन्ति, ये षष्ठमहरागच्छन्ति। न वै देवा अन्योन्यस्य गृहे वसन्ति, नर्त्तुं ऋतौ गृहे वसतीत्याहुः,तद्यथायथमृत्विज ऋतुयाजान् यजन्त्यसम्प्रदायम्, तद्यदृतून् कल्पयति, यथायथं जनिता। तदाहुः, नर्त्तुप्रैषौ प्रेष्येयुर्नर्त्तुप्रैषौ वषट् कुर्युः, वाग्वा ऋतुप्रैषा([1]), आप्यायते वै वाक् षष्ठेहनीति। यदृतुप्रैषौ प्रेष्येयुः, यदृतुप्रैषौर्वषट् कुर्य्युः, वाचमेव तदाप्तां श्रान्तामृक्णवतीं वहरावणीमृच्छेयुः, अच्युताद्यज्ञस्य च्यवेरन्, यज्ञान् प्राणान् प्रजायाः पशुभ्यो जिह्मायेयुः, तस्मादृग्मेभ्य एव प्रेषितव्यमृग्मिभ्योधिवषट्कृत्यं। तन्न वाचमाप्तां श्रान्तामृक्णवतीं वहरावणीमृच्छन्ति, नाच्युताद्यज्ञस्य च्यवेरन्, यज्ञान् प्राणान् प्रजायाः, पशुभ्यो जिह्मायन्ति। पारुच्छेपीरुपदधति, द्वयोः सवनयोः पुरस्तात् प्रस्थितयाज्यानां। रोहितं वै नामैतच्छन्दः, यत् पारुच्छेपं। एतेन ह वा इन्द्रः सप्त स्वर्गांल्लोकानारोहत्। आरोहन्ति सप्त स्वर्गांल्लोकान्, य एवं वेद। तदाहुः, यत्पञ्चपद एव पञ्चमस्यान्हो रूपं, षट्पदात् षष्ठस्य, अथ कस्मात् सप्तपदात् षष्ठेहनि शस्यन्त इति। षड्भिरेव पदैः षष्ठमहरहर्वाप्नुवन्ति, विच्छिद्ये वै तदहः, यत् सप्तमं। तदेव सप्तमेन पदेनाभ्यारुह्य वसन्ति, सन्तत्यैस्त्वरहैरव्यवच्छिन्नैर्यन्ति, य एवं विद्वांस उपयन्ति ॥१०॥

देवासुरा वा एषु लोकेषु समयतन्त। ते देवा षष्ठेनान्हा एभ्यो लोकेभ्योऽसुरान् पराणुदन्त। तेषां यान्यन्तर्हस्तानि([2])

---

१ ऋतुं प्रेष आप्यायते इति ख०। ऋतुप्रैष आप्यायते इति ग०।

२ यान्यन्तर्हस्तानीति च०।

वसून्यासन्, तानादायन्(१) समुद्रं प्राप्लवन्त। तेषां वै देवा(२) अनुहायैतेनैव छन्दसा अन्तर्हस्तानि वसून्याददत। तदेवैतत् पदं, पुनःपदं। स वा कुम्प आकुञ्चनायाद्विषतो वसु(३) दत्ते, निरेवैनमेभ्यः सर्वेभ्यो लोकेभ्यो नुदते, य एवं वेद। द्यौर्वै देवताः षष्ठमहर्वहति, त्रयस्त्रिंशस्तोमो रैवतं सामातिच्छन्दश्छन्दो(४) यथादैवतमनेन(५) यथास्तोमं यथासाम यथाछन्दः समृध्नोति, य एवं वेद। यद्वै समानोदर्कं, तत् षष्ठस्यान्हो रूपं। यद्येव प्रथममहः, तदुत्तममहः, तदेवैतत् पदं। पुनर्यत् षष्ठं, यदश्ववद्यद्रथवद्यत् पुनरावृत्तं, यत् पुनर्निवृत्तं, यदन्तरूपं, यदसौ लोकोऽभ्युदितः, यन्नाभानेदिष्टं, यत् प्राकच्छेयं, यन्नाराशंसं, यद् द्वैपदा, यत् सप्तपदा, यत् कृतं, यद्रैवतं, तत्तृतीयस्यान्हो रूपं। एतानि वै षष्ठस्यान्हो रूपाणि छन्दसामु ह षष्ठेनान्हाक्तानां रसो निनेजत्, तं प्रजापतिरुदानए नाराशंस्या गायत्र्या रैभ्या त्रिष्टुभा पारिक्षित्या जगत्या गाथया अनुष्टुभा एतानि वै छन्दांसि षष्ठेऽहनि शस्तानि भवन्ति अयातयामानि, छन्दसामिव तत् सरसतया अयातयामतायै। सरसानि ह्यस्य छन्दांसि षष्ठे ऽहनि शस्तानि भवन्ति, सरसैः छन्दोभिरिष्टं भवति, सरसैः छन्दोभिर्यज्ञं तनुते, य एवं वेद॥ ११॥

---

१ तान्यादायानिति च०।

२ देवाः षष्ठे इति क०।

३ वसू इति भा०।

४ सामानि छन्दश्छन्द इति भा०। सामानि छन्दोतिछन्द इति ट०।

५ यथादैवतमेतेनेति क०।

अथ यद् द्वैपदौ स्तोत्रियानिरूपौ भवतः, इमा नु कं भुवनासीषधामेति । द्विपाद्वै पुरुषः, द्विप्रतिष्ठः(१) पुरुषः, पुरुषो वै यज्ञः, तस्माद् द्वैपदौ स्तोत्रियानुरूपौ भवतः । अथ सुकीर्त्तिं शंसति, अपेन्द्र प्राचो मघवन्नमित्रानिति । देवयोनिर्वै सुकीर्त्तिः, स य एवमेतां देवयोन्यां सुकीर्त्तिं वेदकीर्त्तिं प्रतिष्ठापयति, भूतानां कीर्त्तिमान् स्वर्गे लोके प्रतितिष्ठति । प्रतितिष्ठति प्रजया पशुभिः, य एवं वेद । अथ वृषाकपिं शंसति, विहि सोतोरसृक्षतेति । आदित्योवै वृषाकपिः, तद्यत् कम्पयमानो(२) रेतो वर्षति, तस्माद्वृषाकपिः, तद्वृषाकपेर्वृषाकपित्वं कपिरिववै सर्वेषु लोकेषु भाति, य एवं वेद । तस्य तृतीयेषु पादेष्वाद्यन्तयोर्न्यूंखनिनर्दौ(३) करोति, अन्नं वैन्यूखः, बलं(४) निनर्दः, अन्नाद्यमेवास्मै तद् बले निदधाति । अथ कुन्तापं शंसति, कुयं ह वै नाम कुत्सितं भवति, तद्यत्तपति, तस्मात् कुन्तापाः, तत् कुन्तापानां कुन्तापत्वं । तप्यन्तेस्मै(५) कुयानिति तमकुयः स्वर्गे लोके प्रतितिष्ठति । प्रतितिष्ठति प्रजया पशुभिः, य एवं वेद । तस्य चतुर्द्दशप्रथमा(६) भवन्ति, इदं जना उपश्रुतेति । ताः प्रत्यहं शंसति, यथा वृषाकपिं वार्षरूपं हि वृषाकपेस्तन्न्यायमित्येव । अथ रैभीः शंशति, वच्यस्व रेभ-

---

१ द्विप्रतिष्ठेति भा० ।

२ कम्पायमान इति भा० ।

३ न्यूंखनिनर्दामिति भा० ।

४ न्यूंखपो बलमिति भा० ।

५ तप्यन्ते मस्मै इति भा० ।

६ चतुर्द्दशा प्रथमा इति भा० ।

वच्यस्वेति। रेभन्तो वै देवाश्च ऋषयश्च स्वर्गं लोकमायन्, तथैवैतद्यजमाना रेभन्त एव स्वर्गं लोकं यन्ति, ताः प्रग्राहमित्येव। अथ पारिक्षितीः शंसति, राज्ञो विश्वजनीनस्येति। संवत्सरो वै परिक्षित्, संवत्सरो हीदं सर्वं परिक्षियतीति। अथो खल्वाहुः, अग्निर्वै परिक्षित् अग्निर्हीदं सर्वं परिक्षियतीति। अथो खल्वाहुः, गाथा एवैताः कारव्या राज्ञः परिक्षित इति। स नस्तद्यथा कुर्यात्, यथाकुर्यात्(१), गाथा एवैतास्य शस्ताभवन्ति। यद्यु वै गाथा अग्नेरेव(२) गाथाः संवत्सरस्य वेति ब्रूयात्, यद्यु वै मन्त्रोग्नेरेव मन्त्रः संवत्सरस्य वेति ब्रूयात्, ताः प्रग्राहमित्येव। अथ कारव्याः शंसति, इन्द्रः कारुमबूबुधदिति। यदेव देवाः कल्याणं कर्म कुर्वंस्तत् कारव्याभिरवाप्नुवन्, तथैवैतत् यजमानाः। यदेव देवाः कल्याणं कर्म कुर्वन्ति, तत् कारव्याभिरवाप्नुवन्ति, ताः प्रग्राहमित्येव। अथ दिशां क्लृप्तीः, पूर्वं शस्त्वा यः सभेयो विदथ्य इति। जनकल्पा उत्तराः शंसति, योनाक्ताचो अनभ्यक्त इति, ऋतवो वै दिशः प्रजननः, तद्यद्दिशाङ्क्लृप्तीः पूर्वं शस्त्वा यः सभेयो विदथ्य इति जनकल्पा उत्तराः शंसति, ऋतूनेव तत् कल्पयति, ऋतुषु प्रतिष्ठापयति। प्रतिष्ठन्तीरिदं सर्वमनुप्रतिष्ठति(३)। प्रतितिष्ठति प्रजया पशुभिः, य एवं वेद। ता अर्धर्चशः शंसति, प्रतिष्ठित्या एव। अथैन्द्रगाथाः शंसति,

---

१ सनेद्यत्तद्यथा कुर्यादिति क०।

२ अग्निरेवेति घ०।

३ प्रतितिष्ठन्ति इति क०।

यदिन्द्रोदी दाशराज्ञ इति। इन्द्रगाथाभिर्ह वै देवा असुराना- भ्रायाथैनानन्यायन्, तथैवैतत् यजमाना इन्द्रगाथाभिरेवाप्रियं भ्रातृव्यमागायाथैनमतियन्ति, तामर्द्धर्चशः शंसति, प्रतिष्ठित्या एव॥ १२॥

अथैतशप्रलापं शंसति, एता अश्वा आप्लवन्त इति। ऐतशो ह मुनिर्यज्ञस्यायुर्ददर्श। स ह पुत्रानुवाच, पुत्रका यज्ञस्यायुरभि- दृष्टवांस्तदभिलपिष्यामि मा मा दृप्तं(१) मन्यध्वमिति। तथेति तदभिललाप। तस्य ह इत्यग्निरैतशायनो ज्येष्ठः पुत्रोभिदुद्रुत्य मुखमपि जग्राह, ब्रुवं, दृप्तो नः पितेति। स होवाच, धिक् त्वा जाल्मापरस्य पापिष्ठान्ते प्रजाङ्करिष्यामीति। यो मे मुखं प्राग्र- हीष्यो यदि जाल्म मे मुखं प्राग्रहीष्यः(२),शतायुषं गामकरिष्यं सह- स्रायुषं पुरुषमिति। तस्मादभ्यग्नय ऐतशायना आजानेयाः सन्तः पापिष्ठामन्येषां बलिहृतः(३) पितायच्छं ताः स्वेन प्रजापतिना स्वया देवतया। यदेतशः प्रलापः, तत् स्वर्गस्य लोकस्य रूपं। यद्वेवैतशः प्रलापः, यातयामा वा चितिः, ऐतशैतशः प्रलापो यातयामा मे यज्ञः सदचिति मे यज्ञोसदिति। तं वा ऐतशैतश- प्रलापं शंसति, पदावग्राहन्तासामुत्तमेन पदेन प्रणौति, यथा निविदः। अथ प्रवल्हिकाः पूर्वंशस्त्वा विततौ किरणौ द्वाविति प्रतिराधानुत्तराः शंसति, भुगित्यभिगत इति प्रवल्हिकाभि-

१ दृप्तमिति क०।
२ मुखं न प्राग्रहीष्यो यदि जाल्मे मुखं न प्राग्रहीष्य इति ठ०।
३ बलिलत इति क०। बलिहृत इति ठ०। बलिश्रम इति ग०।

हं वै देवा असुराणां रसान्प्रववृहुः। तद्यथाभिर्हं वै देवा असुराणां रसां प्रववृहुः, तस्मात् प्रवल्हिकाः, तत् प्रवल्हिकानां प्रवल्हिकात्वम्। ता वै प्रतिराधैः प्रत्यराध्नुवन्। तद्यत् प्रतिराधैः प्रत्यराध्नुवन्, तस्मात् प्रतिराधाः, तत् प्रतिराधानां प्रतिराधत्वं। प्रवल्हिकाभिरेव द्विषतां भ्रातृव्याणां रसां प्रवल्हिकास्ता वै प्रतिराधैः प्रतिराध्नुवन्ति, ताः प्रयाहमित्येव। अथाजिज्ञासेन्याः(१) शंसति, दृहेच्छ प्रागपागुदगधरागिति। आजिज्ञासेन्याभिर्हं वै देवा असुरानाज्ञाय अथैनानन्वायन्, तथैवैतद्यजमाना अजिज्ञासेन्याभिरेवाप्रियं भ्रातृव्यमागायाथैनमतियन्ति। ता अर्द्धर्चशः शंसति, प्रतिष्ठित्या एव। अथातिवादं शंसति, वी३मे देवा अक्रंसतेति। श्रीर्वा अतिवादस्तमेकर्चं(२) शंसति, एकस्था वै श्रीस्तां वै विरेभं(३) शंसति, विरेभैः(४) श्रियं पुरुषो वहतीति। तामर्द्धर्चशः शंसति, प्रतिष्ठित्या एव॥ १२॥

अथादित्याश्चाङ्गिरसीश्च शंसति, आदित्याह जरितरङ्गिरोभ्यो दक्षिणामनयन्निति। तद्देवनीथमित्याचक्षते(५)। आदित्याश्च ह वा आङ्गिरसश्च स्वर्गे लोकेऽस्पर्धन्त, वयं पूर्वे स्वरेष्यामो वयं पूर्वे इति। ते हाङ्गिरसः श्वःसुत्यां ददृशुः। ते हाग्निरमूचुः, परेह्यादित्येभ्यः

१ जिन्यासेन्या इति भ०।

२ एकर्चं इति ग०।

३ विरेभमिति च०।

४ विरेभैरिति च०।

५ देवनीत्यमित्याचक्षते इति भ०।

श्वःसुत्यां प्रब्रूहीति। अथादित्या अद्यसुत्यान्ददृशुः, तेहाग्निरमूचुः, अद्यसुत्यास्माकं तेषां नस्त्वं होतासीदुपेमस्त्वामिति। स एत्याग्निरुवाच, अथादित्याः अद्यसुत्यामीचन्ते, कं वो होतारमवोचन्, वाह्वयन्ते,[१] युष्माकं वयमिति। ते[२] हाङ्गिरसश्चक्रुधुः[३], मा त्वं गमो नु वयमिति। नेति हाग्निरुवाच, अनिन्द्या वै माह्वयन्ते किल्बिषं हि तद्योनिन्द्यस्य हवन्न इति। तस्मादतिदूरमत्तल्यमिति, यजमानस्य हवमिया देवाः। किल्बिषं हि तद्योनिन्द्यस्य हवत्वेति। तान् हादित्यानङ्गिरसो याजयाञ्चक्रुः, तेभ्यो हीमां पृथिवीं दक्षिणां निन्युः, तं ह न प्रतिजगृहुः। सा हीयं, निवृत्तोभयतःशीर्ष्णा[४]दक्षिणाः शुचाविद्धाः शोचमाना व्यचरन् कुपिताः, मा नः प्रतिगृहीषुरिति। तस्मा एता निरदीर्यन्ते[५], य एते प्रदरा अधिगम्यन्ते। तस्मान्निवृत्तदक्षिणां नोपाकुर्यात्[६] नैनां प्रमृजेन्निद्दक्षिणां प्रमृणजानीति। तस्माद्य एवास्य समानजन्मा भ्रातृव्यः स्याद्दृणुहयुः, तस्मा एनां दद्यात्। तनः पराची[७] दक्षिणा विवृणक्ति, द्विषति भ्रातृव्येन्ततः शुचं प्रतिष्ठापयति। योऽसौ तपति स वै शंसति, आदित्या ह जरितरङ्गिरोभ्यो दक्षि-

---

१ होतारमवोचन्नाहूयन्ते,ति क०।

२ ते इति च०।

३ चक्रुधुरिति भा०।

४ सायं निवृत्तोभयतःशीर्ष्णा इति च० ट०, च।

५ एतानि निरदीर्यन्त इति च०। एता विनिरदीर्यन्त इति क०।

६ निवृत्तदक्षिणां न्योपाकुर्य्यामिति च०।

७ पराचै इति भा०। प्राची इति च०।

णामनयन् तां ह जरितः प्रत्यायन्निति, न ह्येमां पृथिवीं प्रत्यायंस्तामु ह जरितः प्रत्यायन्निति, प्रतिहितेषु मायंस्तां ह जरितर्नः प्रत्यगृभ्णन्निति, न ह्येमां पृथिवीं प्रत्यगृभ्णंस्तामु ह जरितर्नः प्रत्यगृभ्णन्निति, प्रगृह्यादित्यमगृभ्णम् न ह्यानेतरसन्न विचेतनानीति। एष ह वा अन्हां विचेता, योऽसौ तपति। स वै शंसति, यज्ञानेतरसं न पुरोगवाम इति। एष ह वै यज्ञस्य पुरोगवी, यद्दक्षिणा यथार्हामः स्वस्तमितिरेतदन्तेत्येष एवेश्वर उन्नेता।" उत श्वेत आशुप त्वा उतोपद्याभिर्य्यविष्ठः(१)। उतेमाशुमा नः(२) पिपर्तीत्येष एव श्वेत एष शिशुपत्येष(३) उतोपद्याभिर्यविष्ठः(१) उतेमाशुमानं पिपर्त्तीति, आदित्या रुद्रा वसवस्ते नुतः(४)इदं राधः प्रतिगृभ्णीह्याङ्गिरः। इदं राधो विभुः प्रभुरिदं राधो बृहत्पृथुः। देवा ददत्वासुरन्तद्वो अस्तु सुचेतनं। युष्मांऽ अस्तु दिवे दिवे प्रत्येव गृभायतेति(५)। तद्यदादित्याश्चाङ्गिरसीश्च शंसति, स्वर्गताया एवैतदहरहः शंसति, यथा निविदोथ भूतेच्छन्दः शंसति, त्वमिन्द्र शर्म रिणतीमे(६) वै लोका भूतेच्छन्दोसुरान् ह वै देवा अन्नं सेचिरे। भूतेन भूतेन जिघांसन्तस्तितीर्षमाणास्तानिमे देवाः सर्वेभ्यो भूतेभ्योच्छादयन्।

---

१,४ उतोपद्याभिर्यविष्ठ इति च०।

२ माशुमानमिति च० ट०, च।

३ शिशुपती ति भ०।

४ नुत इति च०।

५ गृभायत्येति च०।

६ शर्म्म रूणोतीति च०।

तद्यदेतानिमे देवाः सर्वेभ्यो भूतेभ्योऽच्छादयन्, तस्माद्भूतेच्छन्दस्त-
द्भूतेच्छन्दां भूतेच्छन्दत्वं। छादयन्ति ह वापरमिमे लोकाः सर्वेभ्यो
भूतेभ्यो निरघ्नन्। सर्वेभ्यो भूतेभ्यच्छन्दते, य एवं वेद ॥ १४ ॥

अथाह नस्याः शंसति, यदस्या अंहु भेद्या इत्याह, न स्याद्दा-
इदं सर्वं प्रजातमाह, न स्याद्दा एतदधिप्रजायतेऽस्यैव सर्वस्यास्यै
प्रजात्यै। ता वै षट् शंसेत्, षड्वा ऋतवः, ऋतवः पितरः, पितरः
प्रजापतिः, प्रजापतिराह, न स्यात् तादृशं शंसेदिति। शाभव्यस्य
वचः, दशाचरा विराड्, वैराजो यज्ञः, तद्गर्भा उपजीवन्ति।
श्रीर्वै विराड्, यशोऽन्नाद्यं, श्रियमेव तद्विराजं यशस्यन्नाद्ये प्रति-
ष्ठापयति। प्रतिष्ठन्तीरिदं सर्वमनु प्रतितिष्ठति। प्रतितिष्ठति
प्रजया पशुभिः, य एवं वेद। तिस्रः शंसेदिति वात्स्यः। चिह्न-
ह्वे रेतः सिक्तं सम्भवत्याण्डमल्पं जरायुस्त्रिवृत् प्रत्ययं, माता
पिता यज्जायते, तत् तृतीयं, अभूतोद्यमेवैतत्, यच्चतुर्थीं शंसेत्।
सर्वा एव षोडश शंसेदिति हैके। कामार्तो वै रेतः(१) सिञ्चति,
रेतसः सिक्ताः प्रजाः प्रजायन्ते, प्रजानां प्रजननाय। प्रजावान्
प्रजनयिष्णुर्भवति, प्रजात्यै प्रजायते प्रजया पशुभिः, य एवं
वेद ॥ १५ ॥

अथ दाधिक्रीं शंसति, दधिक्राव्णो अकारिषमिति(२)। तत-
उत्तराः पावमानीः शंसति, सुतासो मधुमत्तमा इति। अन्नं वै
दधिक्रा, पवित्रं पावमान्यः, तदु हैके पावमानीभिरेव पूर्वं शस्त्वा
तत उत्तरा दाधिक्रीं शंसति। इयं वागन्नाद्या, यः पवत इति

१ विरेत इति भा०।

२ अकार्षमितीति भा० ट०, घ।

वदन्तस्तदु तथा न कुर्य्यात्, उपनश्यति ह वागशनायतो। स दाधिक्रीमेव पूर्वं शस्त्वा तत उत्तराः पावमानीः शंसति। तद्यद्दाधिक्रीं शंसति, इयं वागाह, नस्यां वाचमवादीत्, तद्देवपवित्रेणैव वाचं पुनीते। स वा अनुष्टुप्(१) भवति। वाग्वा अनुष्टुप्, तत् स्वेनैव छन्दसा वाचं पुनीते। तामर्द्धर्चशः(२) शंसति, प्रतिष्ठित्या एव। अथ पावमानीः शंसति, पवित्रं वै पावमान्यः, इयं वागाह नस्यां वाचमवादीत्, तत्पावमानीभिरेव वाचं पुनीते। ताः सर्व्वा अनुष्टुभो भवन्ति, वाग्वा अनुष्टुप्, तत्स्वेनैव छन्दसा वाचं पुनीते। ता अर्द्धर्चशः शंसति, प्रतिष्ठित्या एव अव द्रप्सो अंशुमतीमतिष्ठदिति। एतं तृचमैन्द्राबार्हस्पत्यं सूक्तं शंसति। अथ हैतदुत्सृष्टं, तद्यदेतं तृचमैन्द्राबार्हस्पत्यमन्त्यं तृचमैन्द्राजागतं शंसति, सवनधारणमिदं गुल्माह इति वदन्तस्तदु तथा न कुर्य्यात्। त्रिष्टुभायतना वा इयं वाक् एषां होत्रकाणां, यदैन्द्राबार्हस्पत्या तृतीयसवने। तद्यदेतं तृचमैन्द्राबार्हस्पत्यमन्त्यं तृचमैन्द्राजागतं शंसति, स्व एवैनं तदायतने प्रीणाति, स्वयोर्देवतयोः कामं नित्यमेव परिदध्यात्, कामं तृचस्योत्तमया। तदाहुः, संशंसेत् षष्ठेऽहनि न संशंसेत्, कथमन्येष्वहःसु संशंसति कथमत्र न संशंसतीति। अथो खल्वाहुः, नैव संशंसेत्, स्वर्गो वै लोकाः, षष्ठमहरसमा ये वै स्वर्गा लोकः कश्चिद्वै स्वर्गे लोके शमयतीति। तस्मान्न संशंसति। यदेव न संशंसति, तत् स्वर्गस्य लोकस्य रूपं। यद्देवैनाः संशंसति, यत्राभानेदिष्टे बालखिल्यो

१ सा वा अनुष्टुभ इति च०।

२ ता अर्द्धर्चश इति भा०।

वृषाकपिरेव या मरुत्। एतानि वा अनीक्थानि भवन्ति। तस्मात्र संशंसति। ऐन्द्रो वृषाकपिः सर्वाणि छन्दांस्यैतशःप्रलाप उपाप्तो यदैन्द्रावार्हस्पत्या तृतीयसवने, तद्यदेतं तृचमैन्द्रावार्हस्पत्यं सूक्तं शंसति, ऐन्द्रावार्हस्पत्या परिधानीया विशो अदेवीरभ्याचरन्तीरिति। अपरजना ह वै विशो अदेवीः, न ह्यस्यापरजनं भयं भवति, शान्ताः प्रजाः क्लृप्ताः सहन्ते, यत्रैवंविद्‌ शंसति यत्रैवंविद्‌ शंसतीति ब्राह्मणम्॥ १६॥

इत्यथर्ववेदोत्तरगोपथब्राह्मणस्य षष्ठः प्रपाठकः

समाप्तः॥ ६॥

समाप्तश्चायं ग्रन्थः॥